1997

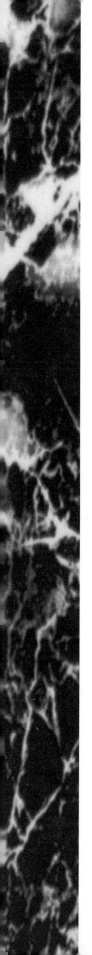

SPORT FACILITY PLANNING AND MANAGEMENT

Peter J. Farmer, Ph.D.
Guilford College

Aaron L. Mulrooney, J.D.
Kent State University

Rob Ammon Jr., Ed.D.
Slippery Rock University

Fitness Information Technology, Inc.
P.O. Box 4425, University Avenue
Morgantown, WV 26504-4425

Photo Credits: By Aaron Mulrooney, courtesy of the CAVS Coliseum Management Company, where appropriate.

Library of Congress Card Catalog Number: 96-84609

ISBN 1-885693-05-2

Cover Design: James M. Williams/Micheal Smyth
Copyeditor: Sandra R. Woods
Printed by: BookCrafters
Production: Pepper Press

Printed in the United States of America
10 9 8 7 6 5 4 3 2 1

Fitness Information Technology, Inc.
P.O. Box 4425, University Avenue
Morgantown, WV 26504 USA
(800) 477-4348
(304) 599-3482 (phone/fax)
E-Mail: FIT@access.mountain.net

Special thanks to our loving families for their support and understanding during this endeavor.

Peter, Aaron and Rob

Sport Management Library

The Sport Management Library is an integrative textbook series targeted toward undergraduate students. The titles included in the Library are reflective of the content areas prescribed by the NASPE/NASSM curriculum standards for undergraduate sport management programs.

Forthcoming Titles in the Sport Management Library

Case Studies in Sport Marketing
Communication in Sport Organizations
Ethics in Sport Management **(Now Available)**
Financing Sport **(Now Available)**
Fundamentals of Sport Marketing **(Now Available)**
Legal Aspects of Sport Entrepreneurship
Management Essentials in Sport Organizations
Sport Governance in the Global Community **(Now Available)**
Sport Management Field Experiences **(Now Available)**

ABOUT THE AUTHORS

Peter J. Farmer, PhD, holds master's degrees in education and business administration, and received his doctoral degree from the University of New Mexico. Currently, he is a member of the faculty and director of the sport management studies program at Guilford College in Greensboro, North Carolina. Previously, he was chair of the Department of Exercise and Sport Sciences and founded the sport management program at Tulane University. Dr. Farmer has published materials in sport policy, facility and event management, and curriculum, and he has given presentations throughout the world. He was a member of the NASPE/NASSM Task Force that developed curriculum standards for sport management programs. Dr. Farmer's professional experience ranges from teaching and coaching at the elementary school level, national coach in track and field, television reporter, and facility manager. Dr. Farmer represented Australia in two Olympic games and was champion of the Commonwealth Games in the hammer throw.

Aaron L. Mulrooney, JD, holds a master of business administration degree in finance and is a licensed attorney in the state of Ohio. He is currently a professor at Kent State University, and he coordinates the graduate program in sport administration at Kent in the School of Exercise, Leisure and Sport. Dr. Mulrooney has published a variety of articles and given numerous presentations on risk management and liability. He has also worked in conjunction with the International Association of Auditorium Managers (IAAM) on presentations, articles, certification, and seminars. Dr. Mulrooney has been involved with the facility management industry for over 15 years and plans on continuing his research endeavors in this discipline and furthering his working relationship with the IAAM. Dr. Mulrooney is a native Ohioan and a former nationally ranked tennis player who competed in many men's national amateur championships and was invited to the 1984 Olympic trials. His current interests include fishing, basketball, riding and training horses, bowling, and golf.

Rob Ammon Jr., EdD, received his undergraduate degree in physical education from the University of Colorado in 1980. After teaching high school for two years he pursued his master's degree in exercise science at Louisiana State University. Dr. Ammon completed his doctorate at the University of Northern Colorado (1993) and was an assistant professor in the Sport Management Division for one year at Bowling Green State University. Presently employed at Slippery Rock University, he teaches graduate and undergraduate courses in sport facility and event management, sport law, sport promotion and fundraising, and management of sport. Dr. Ammon's areas of research include risk management at sports events and facilities, spectator violence, alcohol and sport, crowd management, and legal liabilities involved in sport. In addition, he has been associated with events as a practitioner since 1976, as a consultant and supervisor for a national crowd management company. He has worked various Super Bowls, collegiate athletic events, and hundreds of concerts across the United States. His interests include weight training, running, skiing, and golf.

TABLE OF CONTENTS

ABOUT THE AUTHORS v

PREFACE ix

ACKNOWLEDGMENTS xi

INTRODUCTION 1
  CHAPTER 1
    HISTORY 3

PLANNING, DESIGN, AND CONSTRUCTION 9
  CHAPTER 2
    NEEDS ASSESSMENT AND FACILITY FEASIBILITY 11

  CHAPTER 3
    PLANNING AND DESIGN OF SPORT FACILITIES 21

  CHAPTER 4
    FACILITY DESIGN 41

MANAGEMENT 53
  CHAPTER 5
    MANAGEMENT OVERVIEW 55

  CHAPTER 6
    CONTRACT SERVICES 65

  CHAPTER 7
    RISK MANAGEMENT 77

MARKETING, ADVERTISING, AND PUBLIC RELATIONS 91
  CHAPTER 8
    MARKETING 93

  CHAPTER 9
    ADVERTISING 99

  CHAPTER 10
    MEDIA AND PUBLIC RELATIONS 107

  CHAPTER 11
    FACILITY IMAGE 115

EVENT OPERATIONS 125

CHAPTER 12
OPERATIONAL STRUCTURE 127

CHAPTER 13
CROWD AND ALCOHOL MANAGEMENT 137

CHAPTER 14
HOUSEKEEPING AND MAINTENANCE 149

CHAPTER 15
BOOKING AND SCHEDULING 155

CHAPTER 16
BUSINESS OPERATIONS 165

CHAPTER 17
BOX OFFICE MANAGEMENT 183

CHAPTER 18
CONCESSIONS AND MERCHANDISE 191

CHAPTER 19
EVENT PLANNING AND PRODUCTION 203

APPENDICES

APPENDIX A
THE AMERICANS WITH DISABILITIES ACT 221

APPENDIX B
PLANNING AND DEVELOPING A MULTIPURPOSE SPORT FACILITY 227

APPENDIX C
DESIGN AND CONSTRUCTION OF A PHYSICAL EDUCATION FACILITY 229

APPENDIX D
SWIMMING POOL CONSTRUCTION 231

CASE STUDIES
CUSHING COLISEUM 237
THE VANITY HEALTH and FITNESS CENTER 248
STATE UNIVERSITY FIELD HOUSE 263
YAHOO STADIUM 275
DESERT DOWNS 303

INDEX 329

PREFACE

The sport facility industry offers a wide variety of challenges and career choices for the sport management student. The sport management student will need an expanse of knowledge in order to be adequately prepared to plan and manage sport facilities. This text has been designed to assist in meeting this challenge through a two-pronged approach.

The first section of the text is devoted to the theory behind planning and managing a facility. The text will cover topics ranging from the early history of sport facilities through to the managing of an event within a modern sport facility. Through the mix of practical examples and recognized theory, the student will gain a degree of understanding as to the complexity involved in planning, constructing, promoting, and managing sport facilities.

The second section of the text is devoted completely to case studies. A wide variety of facilities, from fitness centers to race tracks to major stadiums, are used to allow the student to apply the theory that was presented in the first section of the text. The student is asked to critically analyze the cases, correcting any mistakes that may have been made, and to produce a new facility plan and management scheme that improves upon the plans presented in the case studies. After the completion of this exercise, the student should have an excellent foundation in sport facility planning and management.

ACKNOWLEDGMENTS

Management of sport, fitness, and public assembly facilities is a relatively new area of study. Even though this industry has experienced substantial growth in recent years, there is little information or published materials available in the marketplace.

Before the authors could address this complex topic in written form, they had to determine what were the applicable areas of this complex topic known as sport and public assembly facility management. It was finally decided that the focus of this publication should be large sport and public assembly facilities. It was apparent that if an individual understood facility construction and management of a large facility, then it would be a relatively easy transition to a smaller, less complex venue. All topics presented try to address all relevant areas, but, the authors limit their consideration of physical education and fitness facilities, as these topics have been sufficiently addressed already in the marketplace.

The materials responsible for this text have been gathered and adapted from a variety of sources. The authors would especially like to thank for their assistance in developing this publication:

International Association of Auditorium Managers

Thanks to the following individuals for their invaluable assistance and support during the preparation of this text.

Bill Mulrooney, Will Peneguy, Roy Jones, Bob Johnson, Bill Canning, Angelo Chetta, Bill Racek, Bob Rummel, George Lewis, Captain Bill Lewis, Don Hancock, Janet Parks, Sandy Cross, BIll Thomas, Tim Hunyada, Tom Brown, Brad Smith, Ernie Moore, Adam Brinker, Mike Warwick, Mike Sansone, Damon DeMarco, Scott Abel, Alan Werther, Steve Sanderman, Kenny Gray, Carl Schraibman, Ella Taylor, Dean Gogolewski, the undergraduate sport management students at Tulane University, and Slippery Rock University, and the graduate sport administration students at Kent State University.

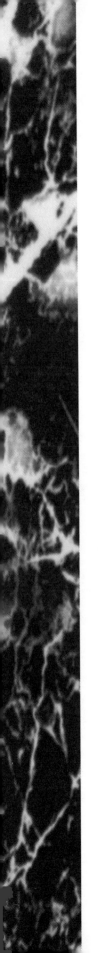

INTRODUCTION

CHAPTER 1

HISTORY

To understand present facility management an understanding of the history of sport and fitness facilities must occur. The focus in this section, as throughout the entire text, dwells on large public assembly sport facilities. Although there will be frequent references and examples of smaller recreational and sport facilities, such as golf courses and fitness centers, the philosophy of the authors and other experts in the field maintains that if readers understand the planning and management elements of large facilities, then these elements will also apply to smaller facilities.

Sport facilities, including the Los Angeles Coliseum, the New Orleans Superdome, and London's Wembly Stadium, are not new concepts. In fact, 2,500 years ago civilizations developed and utilized sport facilities for the health and well-being their people (Van Dalen & Bennett, 1971). Although the primary purpose was to maintain military readiness and entertain the nobility, these facilities were the forerunner of today's large sport structures and complexes. To examine this evolution, ancient Egypt, China, Greece and Rome must be investigated. After this brief visit, today's and tomorrow's facility development will be presented.

Egypt

The Egyptians, from around 1500 BC, promoted sport and physical activities primarily for the military and nobility. Activities with limited facility development included swimming, chariot racing, hunting, fishing, and dancing. However, gymnastics and professional wrestling required the construction of appropriate venues (Labinski, 1989).

China

Eleven hundred years before the birth of Christ, the Chinese had developed activities involving physical conditioning, sport, and entertainment. Examples included archery, fencing, wrestling, dancing, weight lifting, track and field type endeavors, cockfighting, boxing, football, swimming, hunting, and polo. During this period, the Chinese became the first people to construct all-purpose and lighted facilities. The Chinese also developed the all-purpose field with the placement of an oiled cloth, to protect the playing surface from adverse conditions.

Greece

The Greeks became the first civilization to develop facilities specifically designed for sports and entertainment activities. In 776 BC, Olympia was chosen to host the first Olympic Games. This significant religious and athletic event involved all the pageantry and spectacle of today's "mega" events. More significantly, however, this celebration prompted the Greeks to pioneer the construction of numerous sports-related and entertainment facilities throughout Greece.

The equivalent of today's modern stadium included structures such as the Stadia. The Stadia was an extended U-shape structure, with one end open and the other semicircular, built by hollowing out a hillside to facilitate seat placement. Events, such as foot races and other athletic contests, were conducted on the interior track. A modern example is the Olympic Stadium of Athens. First constructed in 331 BC and reconstructed in 160 AD, it held 50,000 spectators. In 1906 this ancient structure hosted the Olympic Games. Another Greek structure using the same hill-excavation technique, became known as the Hippodrome. Although varying in size, primary use was horse and chariot racing.

The Greeks also developed the Theater. The Theaters used types of hill-hollowing construction techniques similar to those employed in the Stadia and the Hippodrome. These theaters consisted of a circular arc around a central stage and

SOLDIER FIELD IN CHICAGO SHOWS THE CLASSIC COLUMNS THAT WERE
PRESENT IN MANY ANCIENT FACILITIES.

were found throughout Greece in any sizable township and city-state.

Rome

After the Greeks, the Romans developed and created some of the most impressive and functional sport, recreational and spectator facilities of the ancient world. The first of these Roman structures was the Circus. It was patterned after the Hippodrome, which also hosted horse and chariot racing. Another facility that appeared throughout the Roman world was the amphitheater. These facilities, used for public rites and plays, were built into the slopes of hills, and similar in design to the Grecian theaters. However, free-standing theater structures were later constructed by the Romans utilizing modern architectural features.

The Romans were also the first to construct stadiums using concrete and vault techniques. The largest, Circus Maximus (46 BC), was constructed in several stages and accommodated up to 200,000 spectators. The Thermae, a smaller stadium, was part of an entertainment complex that consisted of pools, gymnasiums, baths, apartments, and gardens. These ancient Roman facilities were similar to the golf course, recreation center, and combined housing developments of today. The last significant sport-type structure was developed primarily to accommodate displays of mortal combat and local spectacles. These types of facilities were built across the Roman Empire, with the most famous being the Coliseum of Rome. These structures accommodated over 50,000 spectators.

After the downfall of Rome (476 AD), construction of large sport and entertainment stadiums ceased. The only large structures built throughout Europe for hundreds of years were fortress-type buildings, often called castles, and churches or cathedrals. However, some arenas were constructed in Spain and Mexico to host their traditional bullfighting events.

It was not until the 19th century, with the advent of mass participant and spectator sports, such as football, soccer, baseball, and cricket that large facilities once again developed. These structures were initially temporary because they involved rudimentary seating, usually adjacent to the playing field. Other facilities during this period, though smaller in scale, were built to house the emerging military and turnverein movements. These facilities included gymnasiums, pools, and other fitness or sports areas (Labinski, 1989).

Modern Structures of the World

As sports grew in size and importance, facilities correspondingly improved. By the beginning of the 20th century many major sports facilities were already in existence. Some of these structures included Wembly Stadium (Great Britain); the stadiums of Florence and Turin (Italy); Soldier Field (USA); Yankee Stadium (USA); the Los Angeles Coliseum (USA); and the world's largest stadium, Municipal Stadium (Brazil). The development of modern major facilities has also been increased by the reintroduction of the modern Olympic Games in Athens in 1896. Every 4 years, since 1896, with the exception of World War I (1914-1918) and World War II (1939-1945), host countries have developed modern sports stadiums and associated structures to host this major sport enterprise.

JACOB'S FIELD IN CLEVELAND EXHIBITS THE OPENNESS THAT
MANY NEWER FACILITIES ARE MOVING TOWARD.

Summary

1. Sport facilities have existed for more than 2500 years.

2. The Egyptians promoted various sport activities but had few sport-specific venues.

3. The Chinese built all-purpose and lighted facilities before the birth of Christ.

4. The Greeks were the first civilization to construct facilities specifically for sports.

5. The ancient Greeks hollowed out hills for some of their facilities such as the Stadia and Hippodrome.

6. The Romans built their amphitheaters into the slopes of hills similar to the construction methods of the Greeks.

7. The Romans, however, were the first to use concrete and vault construction techniques.

8. Very few sport facilities were constructed between the fall of Rome and the 19th century, with the exception of bullfighting arenas.

9. The Olympics have been responsible for much of the international sport-facility construction since the beginning of the 20th century.

Questions

1. List the various civilizations and facility types that were involved in the development of sport facilities.

2. Contrast and compare the facilities of ancient Greece and Rome.

3. Respond to following statement: "Modern sport facilities are an extension of those created in ancient civilizations."

References

Labinski, R. (1989). History and facility types: sports stadia. *Encyclopedia of architecture: Design, engineering and construction, American Institute of Architects* (Vol. 4). Somerset, NJ: John Wiley & Sons, Inc.

Van Dalen, D., & Bennett, B. (1971). *A world history of physical education: Cultural, philosophical, & comparative.* Englewood Cliffs, NJ: Prentice Hall.

PLANNING, DESIGN, AND CONSTRUCTION

CHAPTER 2

NEEDS ASSESSMENT AND FACILITY FEASIBILITY

This chapter will provide a rudimentary understanding of needs assessment, feasibility studies, and financing and budgeting considerations surrounding the development of a sport and fitness facility.

Determining Need

The demand for new facilities in the local community is driven primarily by increases in the number, type, average size, and attendance at sports and entertainment events. Another reason involves the relocation of major and minor professional sport franchises to communities, where there appear to be opportunities for larger audiences, more attractive rental or income opportunities, and potential growth of new sports. The need for a new or expanded sport facility is often determined by a community's physical suitability, anticipated usage characteristics, and ability to capture the desired market share.

Unless a facility is privately owned, the feasibility of sport and public assembly facilities is rarely measured by their return on investments or operating profits (Kelsey & Gray, 1986). Normally, entertainment and sporting event demands are a direct function of the size of the population within the market area. A small facility, such as an 8,000-seat arena easily may have met the community needs in the 1960's, but if there was a dramatic population growth and demand for sports and entertainment events grew correspondingly, the current facility would be undersized. If the development of a larger structure is not realized, then events would go to another, sometimes smaller, city in the same region with a larger capacity (e.g., 15,000 seat).

The primary motive for developing a new facility may be to attract development, to provide additional visitor activity in a downtown region, or to capture a professional sports franchise. However, favorable publicity and a positive image as a result of a community's having a professional sports team may justify the development of a single-purpose facility used for a limited number of sports activities. This exposure could affect new business development and economic activities related to the sport enterprise. This demand and the potential for additional community benefits should be part of the planning activity when a new sport facility is considered.

Forecasting Growth and Demand

Sport facility attendance levels and event variety are determined by the population (potential users) residing within the market area and by current supply of product. The market area for sport facilities is usually defined by the area covered by the local media: television, radio, and newspapers. Broadcast media refer to this market as the area of dominant influence, or ADI. The ADI indicates how many people can be effectively reached through major local broadcast outlets.

Demand and facility size will be determined by (a) the local population residing in the market area (b) competitive facilities within the market area and region, and (c) the amount of product (i.e., sports and entertainment events) available for the potential users. New construction is justified by growth in demand and functional obsolescence of older facilities. The tools for forecasting growth and demand include surveys of event promoters, review of sports- attendance figures and trends, and evaluations of the event mixes and attendance at competitive facilities in the same area. Sport facilities achieve revenue from a variety of sources, yet the most important is that derived from attendance at the various events held in the facility.

Today, forecasts utilizing computer models and statistical analyses can predict event range, numbers, and attendance. This information is invaluable in determining the type and size of the facility needed in a specific community.

Feasibility Study

A feasibility study is a document that provides a comprehensive analysis of a potential sports facility project from the legal ramifications, usage, design, site, financial, and administrative feasibility of the project:

> A competent and meaningful feasibility study should identify both short-term and long-term costs; estimated economic benefits to the owner; financing mechanism and overall cost, plus any possible economic or cultural losses to the community if the project is not undertaken. (Jewel, 1992, p.4).

Although one or more elements demonstrate the appropriateness and viability of the community project, all elements examined need to be positive, if the project is to proceed to the planning stage.

The purpose of the feasibility study is to provide research information about the community, special interest groups, and its use as a decision-making tool by the community. The feasibility study can be prepared by an individual associated with the proposing organization, but will be more objective if prepared by contracted outside consultants. This process is complicated and may take from 20 days to one year to complete depending upon problems encountered and available financing. The cost of such a single-project study is approximately $6,000. This estimate is based on a community of 75,000 persons, at $0.08 cost per resident (Kelsey & Gray, 1986, p.7).

Feasibility studies, according to Kelsey and Gray (1986), recommend a focus on such elements as

- legal feasibility (deed history and recorded survey, determination of liens, easements, and right-of-ways),

- site feasibility (surface or subsurface analysis or both, vegetation analysis, meteorological analysis, wildlife analysis, utility analysis, and concept-use analysis),

- user-usage feasibility (population analysis, activity usage analysis, standards analysis, and facility availability usage).,

- design feasibility (concept design scenarios and general plans),

- financial feasibility (development costs, construction costs, maintenance costs, equipment costs, operation costs, projected costs, projected revenue, revenue-expenditure charts, and financial options),

- administrative feasibility (development of a policy and management plan).

Economic Impact

Before finishing the topic of feasibility, it is important to realize that sport facilities have a definite economic impact on the local or regional community. The level of this impact depends upon a variety of factors, such as facility size, function, and purpose. The proposed facility, if involved with high profile sports participation (i.e., professional sports events) and other types of entertainment activities (i.e., concerts), is a conduit for the importation of new money into the local economy. Income generated by the facility is spent and passed along to successive recipients both inside and outside the local economy, generating jobs and taxes in the process. Although development of an economic impact study is not primary to this discussion, awareness of the process and potential outcome is important.

Before conducting an economic analysis, specific economic impacts on the local area must be identified. These impacts may be a result of nonresident money from network television or out-of-town spectators for a football game, spending on transportation, food, entertainment, and lodging. Most indigenous sport facilities, such as stadiums and arenas, are built primarily for local consumption and secondarily as a source to attract visitors to the local community. The economic impact in a community could potentially be reduced by local residents spending their dollars elsewhere, potentially in another community, if the proposed sport facility did not exist.

\<Organization\>
\<Address\>
\<City, State Zip\>

Cash Flow Statement
For the [Period (Quarter, Month, etc.)] Ended [Date When Period Ends]

Inflows:
    Cash Receipts   0.00
                                                   0.00
                                                   0.00
                                                   0.00
        Total inflows $ 0.00

Outflows:
    Advertising   0.00
    Employee salaries   0.00
    Legal services   0.00
    Materials   0.00
    This entry has a note[1]   0.00
    Press the "Endnote" button to create your own notes   0.00
                                                  0.00
                                                  0.00
                                                  0.00
                                                   0.00
        Total outflows $ 0.00

Overall Total: $ 0.00

Notes:

1. Sample note.

FIGURE 2-1 - SAMPLE CASH FLOW STATEMENT

Multiplier Effect

The multiplier effect is a calculation that is based on the number of times estimated income is re-spent. This income is derived as a result of events taking place in the proposed local community facility. The money generated by events at sport facilities is re-spent in the local economy. The local economy will then secure 100 % of the spending. This example represents two successive spending rounds. However, with each successive spending round, a portion of money generated will go to non local sources. More populated and diverse communities have higher estimated multipliers than do smaller communities, as a larger portion of each spending cycle would remain in the local area. A city like Cleveland, might have a multiplier of three. This number indicates that the total impact, or sum of all expenditures, is three times the initial expenditure. This impact is expressed in terms of business income, household income, taxes, and jobs (Laventhol & Horwath, 1989).

Community Impact

From the outset and as a direct result of the construction of a new sport facility, new business will be generated in the development of exposition services, catering, security services, and restaurants.   These elements are known as *mixed-use developments.* Here the sports facility is a central component with various hotel, food, and entertainment elements constructed in the same area. (e.g., Madison Square Garden complex in New York City, New York). These auxiliary facilities are developed to attract additional revenue to further stimulate the local economy.

Financing Development Costs

Traditionally, the majority of major sports facilities were sponsored, either wholly or in combination, by local, state, or federal funding sources. However, with the advent of private development of sport facilities, other options have become apparent. Some of these financing options include the sale of revenue bonds, sale or lease of a sport facility by a private corporation, advertising, box suite rentals, joint development efforts with hotels/business ventures, general obligation bonds, tax allocation bonds, state/federal grants, and educational funding. Funding is normally conducted through financing specialists, in conjunction with legal experts.

The primary traditional method of financing development costs has been through municipal bond financing. However, in recent years,

> More innovative financing techniques have been used to minimize the burden on taxpayers for debt repayment...For example, Meadowlands Stadium (New York Giants) in New Jersey and Byrn Arena were financed with pari-mutuel tax revenues from the on-site race track... Texas Stadium (Dallas Cowboys) in Irving, Texas, and Joe Robbie Stadium (Dolphins) in Miami were financed primarily through revenues from the sale of box suites. (Laventhol & Horwath, 1989, p.45).

Laventhol and Horwath (1989) stated that there are a variety of imaginative facility financing methods in use today:

1. The sport facility name may be sold to a private corporation. This method can raise a significant amount of capital. For example, the Carrier Dome in Syracuse, New York received $2,750,000 from the Carrier Corporation; Rich Stadium in Buffalo, New York, received $1.5 million from the Rich Corporation.

2. Advertising scoreboard messages during events are often sold or leased to derive an annual source of revenue. Capital costs of installation and operating expenses for computer scoreboards are often traded for all or part of the advertising generated. For example at Baltimore's Memorial Stadium, the management installed the scoreboard systems at no cost, whereas the facility generated $360,000 per year from the advertising revenue.

3. Seat preference bonds are generated through individuals or

corporations, allowing them to purchase season tickets in prime viewing locations within the facility. For instance, Texas Stadium, home of the Dallas Cowboys, sold $19 million of seat preference bonds to finance its construction costs.

4. Joint ventures between real estate developers, such as hotel and office developments, adjacent to a sport facility, generate funds that can pay for the debt service.

5. General obligation bonds are the traditional form of community financing that assume that the facility is at least a quasi-government entity. These bonds pay interest and principal to the investors through the taxing power of the municipality. Communities finance sport facilities through the community's general fund, and the excess revenue resulting from operations is paid into the general fund thereby paying off the debt.

6. Revenue bonds are secured through revenue generated by facility operations, but they are usually supported by community tax sources (e.g., hotel room tax, food and beverage tax, or sales tax). Tax increment bonds are secured by net increases in property taxes. State and federal grants can be utilized to help fund construction of sport facilities. These are typically matched by private investments.

7. Other methods include joint agreements between the city and regional government entities to fund a portion of facility development; educational institutions that provide funding assistance for the construction of sport facilities on their own property, as well as those located on public lands where student fees pay for the debt service; and public subscriptions through individual donations or a foundation to fund the construction, for example, the Student Activities Center, in Chapel Hill, North Carolina.

Budgeting Overview

Budgeting for the construction of a new facility is a somewhat complex process. Probably the most important questions are how much can be afforded and how much is required to conduct the projected program? When developing a comprehensive budget, the process actually involves four interrelated budgets:

Budget 1. The Project Budget (includes site costs, design, construction, furniture, fixtures, equipment and finance costs)

Budget 2. Pre-opening or start-up or marketing budget

Budget 3. First-Year Operating Budget

Budget 4. Revenue Projections

Operating Budget

Nearly all sports facilities are community-oriented and consequently operate at break-even or sometimes at a loss. This loss is usually supplemented by the community or local government. Currently, 8 to 10 cities are willing to construct new baseball stadiums, whereas 6 to 8 cities are ready to entice NFL teams. Although the rents are unfavorable to bring major league franchises to their cities, potential future earnings and community goodwill are critical factors in these decisions.

Financial planning does not always provide adequate renovation or remodeling. If not planned for, these repairs can result in costly shutdowns of operations, violation of lease agreements with tenants, and negative public relations. The facility must have adequate reserves to pay for unforeseen breakdowns as well as for periodic remodeling and face-lifts.

The variety of taxes used to finance sport facility operations is as diverse as are the types of taxes. Most important is the need for a dedicated source of income or revenue stream. If the facility's net operating cost becomes a line item in the local government's annual budget, the facility is doomed to compete for funds each year with other, more vital community services and departments. Further annual fund allocations will be heavily influenced by the all too frequent budgetary crises, a decline in certain tax revenues, and municipal contract increases.

Building Services

Sport facilities generate income from box office services, tenant rental equipment, concessions, and parking. Event income from food, beverage and merchandise sales are usually more than income received from rent (Jewel, 1992).

Profit margins from parking depend upon the availability and affordability of public transit, nearby competing parking facilities, and the type of parking operation. Large surface parking lots for sports facility events can yield profit margins of 30 to 40 % due to low maintenance and minimal cost of collecting entrance fees. Multipurpose parking structures are more costly to maintain and operate because of increasing labor and operational costs, as a result most facility parking facilities have a difficult supporting themselves. For example, a 70,000-seat stadium, where 95 percent of the patrons arrive by automobile, and 5 % by bus may require more than 200 acres for parking alone. This acreage is calculated as follows: 66,000 seats divided by 3 persons per car equals 22,000 parking spaces; and 22,000 divided by 100 spaces per acre equals 220 acres (International Association of Auditorium Managers [IAAM], 1990).

Site Selection and Acquisition

Site selection will be dictated by locations that will provide patrons with the greatest opportunity to spend money. The most important factors in selecting a site for a sport facility are those directly related to the sport, clientele, marketability, attendance, and occupancy. When planning a stadium, issues of accessibility, parking, and proximity to support elements, such as public transportation should be considered. A site near the center of the city would require less travel time for area residents, thus tending to maximize attendance. Entry to a facility via a local street-grid system is considered more efficient than is access off a major thoroughfare or highway (Kelsey & Gray, 1986).

The potential results of the development of a new community facility would be newly created jobs, commercial developments, and increased tax revenues from out-of-town visitors. Nearly all development budgets are limited and site costs minimized through imaginative developer's proposals, sale of air rights, and careful evaluation of on-site and off-site land development and infrastructure costs.

Summary

1. The relocation of pro franchises as well as increases in the number, type and attendance at sport and entertainment events creates demand for new facilities.

2. The Area of Dominant Influence (ADI) will define the market area for a sport or entertainment facility. ADI is defined as the area covered by local print and electronic media.

3. A feasibility study will be able to provide information regarding the effect of a new facility on a community in a number of ways including legal, user-usage, design, financial, and site studies.

4. Economic impact studies will determine the amount of income generated in the local community due to the construction of a new sport or entertainment facility. These studies are usually measured by the use of multipliers.

5. Various options are used to finance new sport and entertainment facilities. These methods include suite rentals, revenue bonds, business ventures, seat preference bonds, and grants.

6. Sources of income from sport/entertainment facilities include ticket sales, facility rental, concessions, and parking. The majority of income is derived from food and beverage concessions and merchandise sales.

Questions

1. Identify how the need of a facility is determined.

2. List the steps involved in a needs assessment for a sport facility.

3. What is meant by economic impact?

4. Define facility capability and site selection and acquisition.

5. Discuss the implications for financing and budgeting a new facility.

6. List the steps in the development of a feasibility study.

References

International Association of Auditorium Managers (IAAM). (1990). Course materials from the unpublished proceedings of the School for Public Assembly Facility Management, Ogelbay, VA.

Jewel, D. (1992). *Public assembly facilities*. Malabar, FL: Krieger Publishing

Company.

Kelsey, C., & Gray H. (1986). *Feasibility study process for parks and recreation.* Champaign, IL: Sagmore Publishing Co.

Laventhol, & Horwath (1989).   *Conventions, stadiums, and arenas.* Washington, DC: Urban Land Institute.

CHAPTER 3

PLANNING AND DESIGN OF SPORT FACILITIES

This chapter will focus on the various aspects of planning and designing sport facilities. Types of facilities, the planning process and major concerns in the early stages of facility development are addressed. Finally, the various components of facility operations and their associated facility areas will be discussed.

Facility Types

To plan and design a sport facility effectively, it is important to understand the various sport and public assembly facility structures located throughout the world.

Stadium: A stadium is a single or multi-purpose facility hosting a minimum of 40,000 spectators. It is considered an outside structure. Examples are the Los Angeles Coliseum, New Orleans Superdome, Chicago's Soldier Field, and Denver's Mile High Stadium (Laventhol & Horwath, 1989).

Arena: An arena is a flat floor indoor facility with seating for 10,000 to 25,000 spectators on either one or three levels. The sight lines in this facility are usually designed for sports such as basketball, hockey, indoor soccer, and ice events. Examples are the Richfield Coliseum, The Spectrum, Chicago Stadium, The Great Western Forum, Boston Garden, and Madison Square Garden (Laventhol & Horwath, 1989).

Theater: A theater is an indoor structure that accommodates from 300 to 3,000 people. Features include sloping floor, fixed seats, permanent stage, fly loft (specifically designed for opera), acoustical shells, multi-sets, orchestra pit, and dance overlay. Examples are Pantages Theater (Toronto, Ontario), State Theater (Cleveland, Ohio), and Radio City Music Hall, New York (Laventhol & Horwath, 1989).

SOLDIER FIELD'S SEATING ARRANGEMENT IS THE CLASSIC BOWL SHAPE WITH
TWO LEVELS OF SEATING THAT MANY STADIUMS HAVE

THE RICHFIELD COLISEUM EXHIBITS THE TWO-TIERED BOWL SHAPE
THAT MANY ARENAS HAVE.

Auditorium: An auditorium is a horseshoe-shaped structure, relatively small
(between 20,000 and 30,000 sq. ft.), multipurpose, with movable seating. Popular
in the 1930's and 1940's, the auditorium has been replaced by the exhibition hall.
An example is the E. J. Thomas Performing Arts Hall (Akron, Ohio) (Laventhol &

Horwath, 1989).

Exhibition Hall: An exhibition hall is a modern enclosed structure that ranges from 60,000 to 700,000 square feet, with 25-foot to 30-foot ceilings, and able to host relatively small conventions and functions. An example is the Canton Civic Center (Canton, Ohio) (Laventhol & Horwath, 1989).

Convention Center: A convention center is an indoor structure occupying up to one million feet of exhibition and meeting space. These facilities host a broad range of activities from sports award banquets and dances to large conventions. An example is the IX Center (Cleveland, Ohio) (Laventhol & Horwath, 1989).

Planning

Initial Planning and Design

Flynn (1993) stated that before initiating the planning and design of any sports facility, it is essential to understand basic goals and objectives. Additionally, capacity, type, and design of any sport facility will be influenced by its location, development budget, potential and projected usage, and revenues. The initial planning phase will decide issues such as size and capacity, shape and seating configurations, and issues of site planning, urban design relationships, parking, and transportation. Also, at this stage compromises involving facility objectives and cost savings are discussed. An example could be the exchanging of expensive extras, such as roof covering or movable seats, for the inclusion of a larger seating capacity. If these compromises are not made, construction of the facility will not proceed. The planning brief document addresses these various issues and concerns.

Planning Brief

This document is a checklist of issues and concerns that the architect discusses with the client at the outset of the project. Laventhol and Horwath (1989) state that

> The major factors (in preparing a plan) are time, roles, costs and decision points. It is important to identify what must be done, who will do it, what period of time it will take, and when reviews and decisions will be made (p.18).

It is an excellent starting point in the planning process to determine the needs and requirements within the facility confines. A planning brief document is divided into three general areas: building volume, building services, and detailed design.

Building volume. involves collecting general data about the proposed facility. It can include, but may not be limited to, the facility mission, project feasibility, graphic representations, financial information and constraints that may limit the project size and scope, as well as have an impact on the timetable. After the mission and constraints are developed, objectives need to be established. These objectives should focus on the perceived need for the facility, community type, characteristics, and population. Additional considerations should identify competitive facility structures, program needs, and the philosophy and style of the proposed management team. Other elements could include site considerations, building scale, access, exits, and control issues, primary and secondary activity program areas.

Building Services. is primarily concerned with the actual building operation. Components include HVAC (heating, ventilation, and air conditioning), storage, fire requirements, utilities, lighting, acoustics, plumbing, and even vending needs.

Detailed Design. is concerned with the detail and finish of all interior sports venues, change rooms, spectator seating, management, and staff accommodations. This element is also concerned with meeting the needs of the disabled.

Planning Concerns

Multipurpose facility versus single use facility. Today, the trend is to develop multipurpose rather than single-purpose facilities. These multipurpose facilities are cost-effective as they can be utilized for a variety of activities, provide for greater building efficiency (i.e., the facility can be used for activities that have greater range than just football or basketball), and utilized for instructional or special events. Other reasons include increased building efficiency, potential increase in revenue generation, and the greatest use of available space. Disadvantages of multipurpose facilities are design compromise, reduced single functionality, poor traffic control, poor spectator viewing (i.e., improper sight lines), greater maintenance, and shared space with other activities.

Renovation versus Building 'New Facilities' To determine whether an existing facility should be remodeled or a new building constructed, a facility audit should be conducted. Renovation is considered because it is less expensive, recreates the use of existing space, and extends the building life of existing facilities (Miller, 1991). However, during renovation, the facility is unusable. New buildings, on the other hand, provide the opportunity to develop an ideal facility and still maintain the function of the old facility without losing revenue.

The Planning Process

When undertaking the initial planning phase, it is important to identify future needs and issues, as well as immediate demands of the facility. Elements to be addressed during this process include

- planning committee elements and concerns
- the number and types of desired programs
- multiple facility usage
- populations affected and accessibility of all user groups
- facility location influenced by the master plan for the community
- needs of the groups to be served

- cooperation of all planning elements, such as education, planning, architecture, and administration units

- maximum usage

- reduced operational and maintenance costs

- design flexibility

- maximum safety

- adherence to local, state, and federal laws and policies

- effect on adjacent structures, services, and programs

- facility attractiveness

- economic considerations associated with material selection, lay-out, and installation

- provision of effective supervision

- validity provided through needs assessment, legal requirements, building codes, and sports rules (Meagher, 1990).

Planning Committee

This committee is composed of representatives of various factions interested in the construction of the facility project. These groups are inherently different in composition and are dependent upon the enterprise and facility type to be developed. The major function of this committee is to develop a shared vision or consensus, that will enable the facility to be approved by all parties, thereby removing most objections.

The initial step after organizing the committee should be to determine the committee members, individual and coordinated concerns, as well as those of the community. This shared vision can best be achieved through a needs-assessment instrument that will highlight these collective concerns. This information is useful not only for the planning committee in performing their planning, and managing authority but also for the architect in preparing working plans and cost estimates. Other elements include the investigation of funding sources, comparisons of similar facilities, materials, and costs, selection of the project consultant (the go-between for architect and the planning committee), and selection of the architectural firm.

Planning Facilities Checklist

The following are a series of questions that need to be posed, and answers developed, by those individuals responsible for planning new facilities:

- Has need been determined?

- Has the personnel operating the proposed facility been involved in the planning phase?

- Have operating and maintenance costs been determined and allotted?

- Have all legal implications been explored, especially those involved with bond issues?

- Has a time schedule for planning and construction been developed?
- Have the lay and professional planning committees been established to aid in the specifications and requirements?
- Has compliance occurred with all building codes, laws, and state regulations?
- Is the proposed site adequate for present and future needs?
- Is the facility part of the community development master plan?
- Are the bidding contractors qualified for the job?
- Have resource materials been provided for individuals and groups to study to assist in arrival at desirable specifications?
- Will the planning group visit similar facilities?
- Has the proposed facility program been considered, in order to establish facility design and size?
- Have possible social changes or population growth been considered?
- Has an individual been designated to check the construction with plans and specifications?
- Has the expected life of the facility been determined?
- Have equipment needs been included in the cost estimates?
- Has policy been established to ensure effective working relationships between builders, surveyors, advisory groups, inspectors, etc.?
- Have the services of professional advisory groups at local, state and federal levels been sought (i.e.; state departments, fire marshals, safety engineers)?
- Have procedures been developed to handle "change orders" to prevent hasty changes?
- Has installation of fixed equipment (e.g., basketball backboards, machinery) been made part of the contractor's responsibility?
- Has community interest been placed above personal and political interest in the selection of sites, awarding of contracts, and general planning of the facility? (Meagher, 1990)

Design and Development

Common Errors in Facility Design and Development

Today, although there are many more sport and fitness facilities being constructed, problems still exist due to the absence or ignorance of facility standards. Other reasons are the failure of designers and sports program experts to work as a team in the facility development and avoid the mistakes evident in other facilities. Additional concerns that require focus in the planning phase beyond the site development and orientation are elements that deal with spectator facilities, playing fields, team facilities, media and communication facilities, administration, operations, and maintenance, lighting, acoustics and sound systems, and construction materials (Meagher, 1990).

Parking Availability

Site development includes not only the sport structure, but also parking areas, and systems to provide for vehicular and pedestrian movement (Gimple, 1992). In an urban site, where available land is scarce, there will be little potential for extensive facility parking. These sites normally provide on-site parking, but will depend on adjacent available parking facilities and access to public transportation. To determine appropriate parking needs, whether suburban or urban, a parking consultant should be retained to study these elements. Special parking areas should also be provided for the media, those with disabilities, VIPs, sports teams, and operations.

Orientation

The orientation or direction of facility placement should consider the time of day and period of the year that the sport will be played. Analysis of sun locations at the beginning, middle, and end of the day will indicate the facility's ideal orientation. For example, a facility hosting football should situate the field approximately 45 degrees off the north-south axis, whereas baseball should have home plate to third base facing approximately due north or due east (United States Baseball Federation [USBF], 1987).

Capacity

Seating capacity is determined by the type of sports program, size of the market area, sponsors' goals, owners, and public institutions supporting the development. The basic shape of the stadium affects the roof type, quality of view from the seats, and appearance. Sight lines and spectator distance are primary determinants of design, but movable seating sections have been able to increase capacities at sporting events. Other considerations should be concession areas and luxury suites or lounge facilities, which can positively affect the income or bottom line.

External Traffic Flow

The provision of a site that provides adequate access to both pedestrian and vehicular traffic is extremely important. To coordinate circulation patterns appropriate signage, control devices, and equipment designed to provide optional vehicular and pedestrian flow will need to be developed (Jewel, 1992). Pedestrian

MANAGING EXTERNAL TRAFFIC FLOW IN AN EFFICIENT MANNER WILL HELP
TO ENHANCE PATRON SATISFACTION.

COLISEUM TRAFFIC CONTROL STAFFING SHEET

DAY	MON	TUE	WED	THUR	FRI	SAT	SUN		MON	TUE	WED	THUR	FRI	SAT	SUN
DATE															
OHIO STATE PATROL															
SHERIFF'S OFFICE															
RICHFIELD VILLAGE															
RICHFIELD TOWNSHIP															
PENINSULA															
BOSTON															

FIGURE2 3-1 - SAMPLE TRAFFIC STAFFING SHEET

access to the facility should provide freedom of choice and flexibility to the patron,
with the maximum distance from any parked vehicle not to exceed more than one
mile (IAAM, 1990).

Internal Traffic Flow

Internal traffic flow is provided through horizontal and vertical aisles.   The number and width of aisles, concourses, stairways, ramps, and exits depend upon local and national standards, cost, and anticipated usage. Horizontal circulation or concourses are the locations of concessions, toilets, and other spectator and operations facilities. Ramps, stairs, escalators, and elevators, termed vertical circulation, are used to ferry spectators, service, and maintenance personnel. From a risk-management perspective and efficiency, ramps are the most desirable method of moving very large numbers of people vertically, as well as of moving vehicles for service maintenance and concession operations. Escalators should be used as a convenience in cases where travel distances are substantial, as well as, by seniors or the disabled. Elevators should also provide passenger service to VIP, food service, freight, and media personnel (IAAM, 1990).

Seating

Large sporting facilities, such as stadiums, are usually constructed with two to three levels of seating. Each of these levels will partially extrude over the level below, reducing the sight-line distance for the spectators at the higher levels On each seating level, concession stands, toilets, and other necessary facilities should be available for patron usage. In facilities seating up to 40,000 people, a single-level stadium is possible but not usual. All seating should be designed to provide optimal sight lines and unobstructed viewing at all levels (Jewel, 1992).

Type of seating and seat spacing are a function of cost, budget, and usage level with industry standards set at a minimum of 18 inches wide and 30 inches deep. Seating can range from a simple bench to the currently accepted standard of self-rising armchair seats for the majority of seating areas. In the higher paying seating areas wider chairs and more frequent aisle spacing are recommended, whereas bench seating can be used in the lower priced ticket areas.

In all seating areas handrails and guardrails must be provided. Aisles have to comply with safety and building codes and must not obstruct sight lines. Provisions for those with disabilities should be in accordance with national and local laws. This facet of stadium construction is extremely important in order to comply with the Americans with Disabilities Act of 1990 (ADA). (See Appendix A)

Movable seating sections should be utilized to provide assorted arrangements that satisfy the various scheduled facility sports and events. The type of event will dictate the seating configuration. Through movable seating, spectators will be able to achieve acceptable quality viewing for both football and baseball. Movable systems can range from stands mounted on tracks or wheels, to those that utilize an air or water cushion to lift and slide the seating structure.

Luxury or Club Level-Seating

The luxury box area is designed to provide an exclusive seating area that can range from 5,000 to 12,000 seats, based on the results of the feasibility study. Part of this club level may be provided through private suites, with 10 to 40 seats in each area. Private suites usually include amenities such as a fully finished and carpeted lounge area with sink, under counter refrigerator, lounge seating, and

A NEWER INNOVATION IN SEATING IS THE FOLD AWAY SEATING
WHICH ALLOWS FOR BOTH HANDICAPPED AND NONHANDICAPPED SEATING IN
THE SAME LOCATION.

numerous television monitors (Jewel, 1992). Additional amenities may include bar and grill service. Club-level seating is used as a primary vehicle for generating initial facility funding. For example Joe Robbie Stadium in Miami, Florida, sold 10,000 club-level seats as part of the facility financing package.

Public Toilets

Public toilets for men and women should be provided on every concourse level. These public facilities should be constructed with general lighting, exhaust, cold-

LARGE BOGIES ARE USED TO MOVE LARGE SECTIONS OF SEATS IN ORDER TO
CHANGE THE SEATING ARRANGEMENT IN A FACILITY.

water service, and have an available attendant closet with sink and storage.
Appropriate facilities should also be made available for the disabled. The number
and spacing of toilet fixtures should be based on the sum total of seats and

LOGES PROVIDE MANY OF THE SAME ACCOMMODATIONS
AS AN APARTMENT.

expected utilization.   The number of women's and men's facilities should be developed in a ratio of 3:2, as women take 2.5 minutes, compared to 1 minute for men. Another factor is that men are capable of using trough-type facilities whereas women are not (IAAM, 1990).

Concession Areas

Concession areas should be located conveniently on each concourse level. They should be attractive and designed specifically to sell or vend food, beverage, and novelties. It is important that these areas be able to serve large numbers of spectators in a quick but efficient manner. In addition, concession operations

FACILITIES FOR THE HANDICAPPED AND BABY CHANGING
STATIONS ARE COMMONPLACE IN ALL FACILITIES.

require a central office, commissary, and other suitable enclosed spaces for food handling, preparation, and storage (Jewel, 1992). These stands are either operated by in-house personnel or contracted to outside vendors.

Signage

Environmental and directional signs must be planned for the entire facility and site. These include
- identification of site entrances and parking areas
- direction of traffic to and from the facility
- identification of pedestrian gates

- directions to concourse levels, seating sections, aisles, rows
- identification of rest rooms, first aid, exits, concession stands
- specially designated areas for the disabled. (See Appendix A.)

Safety and Security

First-aid facilities for emergency medical treatment should be provided within the stadium. This facility should contain office space for a physician or nurse, cot room, waiting room, storage rooms, and toilet areas.

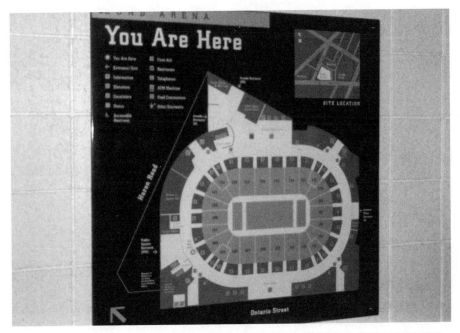

DIRECTIONAL SIGNS HELP PATRONS LOCATE ACCOMMODATIONS AND THEIR SEATS IF THEY ARE UNFAMILIAR WITH THE BUILDING.

Security areas should include a command post for game-day security personnel as well as a detention room. In accordance with applicable building and safety codes, fire protection equipment, sprinklers, and standpipes should be accessible. Fencing, walls, gates, and doors should be in place to secure against illegal entry or improper access to areas within the facility (Jewel, 1992).

The Playing Field

Facility athletic events require substantial space for the development of playing fields and surrounding surface areas. Space requirements for football include 90,000 square feet, and 150,000 square feet is needed for baseball. Today, both natural and synthetic turf systems are utilized for playing fields depending upon facility requirements. Synthetic materials have become popular as they substantially improve playability, drainage, and longevity. A variety of synthetic

FIRST AID FACILITIES SHOULD BE
CONVENIENTLY LOCATED
THROUGHTOUT THE FACILITY.

materials have been developed that include nylon and polypropylene for the turf and underlying pad. Irrigation and drainage systems have also been devised that provide for the construction of a level playing surface, thereby eliminating a drainage "crown" in natural fields (McGraw, 1991).

Natural turf fields have also been developed utilizing "pop-up" irrigation sprinklers or spray units at the edge of the field. However, new systems allow irrigation from beneath the surface with nutrients, weed and pest control. Athletes and sport management personnel appear to prefer natural turf, due to lower injury rates. However, with synthetic turf, facility managers have the ability to stage multiple events, regardless of facility type.

Team Facilities

Sport facilities must be able to serve the needs of various activities and their teams. During the initial planning they should be designed with locker rooms, media facilities, scoreboard and public address systems, administration, lighting, operations and maintenance areas included.

There are usually two locker-room complexes that accommodate the home team and their opponents. Each locker room should include showers, toilets, drying areas, locker rooms, training rooms, coaches' offices, dressing rooms, and team equipment storage. Additional elements may include laundry, weight and exercise rooms, player lounges, hydrotherapy room, rehabilitation room, trainers' and doctors' offices, and meeting rooms. Team facilities should be directly accessible to the playing field. A media interview room, with appropriate electronic media requirements, should be located adjacent to team facilities. Officials must also have their own facilities (IAAM, 1990).

Media Facilities

All modern sport facilities should be designed to support print and electronic media. Media facilities should include a working press and media coverage area,

internal communications, scoreboard and public-address systems.   Press box
facilities should be sufficient to provide working space for all media personnel.   This

LOCKER ROOMS AND WEIGHT ROOMS ARE A NECESSARY COMPONENT
OF ANY SPORT FACILITY.

area should contain writers' stations, broadcasting booths, and support facilities, positioned to provide excellent field-viewing conditions, and television monitors wired for closed-circuit viewing (Jewel, 1992). Media support operations should also include workroom space for statisticians, document reproduction, and fax equipment, equipment repair, darkroom, and a press club room serving the media personnel.

Television camera platforms should be positioned at key locations adjacent to the field surface. Media consultants and network personnel should be consulted in the development of these media facilities.

Scoreboard and Public Address

Today, sport facilities require a scoreboard that is illuminated and electrically operated by remote control. An innovation popular with the patrons is a system with instant-replay capabilities. The complete scoreboard system includes the

PRESS ROW MUST PROVIDE POWER OUTLETS, PHONE SERVICE AND OTHER ACCOMMODATIONS SO THAT THE MEDIA CAN DO THEIR JOB.

scoreboard, supporting structure, and remote control equipment. A working space should be provided for scoreboard operators in the press box area, equipped with controls and a built-in writing counter.

The public-address system should include the announcer's equipment and controls, amplification, and loudspeaker equipment. The announcer's booth, located in the press box area, should be soundproof and able to control the entire public address system.

Administration, Operations, and Maintenance

Space requirements for administrative offices vary depending on the nature and functions of the proposed facilities management team. Provisions for personnel, lockers, maintenance, storage, transportation of equipment, and supplies should be included. Maintenance operations usually require an office, enclosed shop area, and adequate storage for materials and equipment. Hose connections for

A TASTE OF THE OLD (SOLDIER FIELD) AND THE NEW (SKYDOME) LOOK IN SCOREBOARDS PROVIDES AN INTERESTING CONTRAST IN TECHNOLOGY.

maintenance and cleaning should be located throughout the facility. On-the-field maintenance and storage space for sport equipment are required. Refuse-removal facilities should also be included in the design.

Summary

1. Sport and public assembly facilities include various types such as stadiums, arena, theaters, auditoriums, exhibition halls, and convention centers.

2. A planning brief including data about the proposed facility, building services and detailed design must be discussed by the architect and facility management during the initial planning stages.

3. In addition to immediate needs, future demands must also be identified during the planning stage.

4. A planning committee made-up of diverse individuals sharing a common vision should be developed.

5. This committee needs to reach a consensus regarding issues such as parking availability, external and internal traffic flow, seating, and concessions areas.

6. Ease of circulation, safety, comfort, and entertainment, especially during relatively compressed time periods, provide spectators with a satisfactory experience. To maximize patrons' expectations they should have an unobstructed view of the fields of play, adequate numbers of toilets, and concessions.

7. Team facilities need to be large enough to accommodate the various events and teams utilizing the facility.

8. Media facilities should include space and equipment to handle both print and electronic media.

9. Scoreboards must be well lit and provide visual information for the hearing impaired.

10. The lighting will depend on the type of events and athletic teams utilizing the sport and public assembly facility.

Questions

1. Identify the planning elements of a sport facility.

2. List the major factors in planning.

3. Develop a planning committee to participate in the planning of a facility.

4. Recognize the members and functions of the design team.

5. Define the role and function of the facility consultant.

References

Flynn, R. B. (1993). *Facility planning for physical education, recreation and athletics.* Reston, VA: AAHPERD

Gimple, J. (1992, September). Laying the foundation. *Athletic Business*, 32-39.

International Association of Auditorium Managers (IAAM). (1990). Course materials from the unpublished proceedings of the School for Public Assembly Facility Management, Ogelbay, VA.

Jewel, D. (1992). *Public assembly facilities*. Malabar, FL: Krieger Publishing Company.

Laventhol & Horwath (1989). *Conventions, stadiums, and arenas*. Washington, DC: Urban Land Institute.

McGraw, M. (1991, September). Point/Counterpoint: Synthetic turf. *Athletic Business*, 54-60.

Meagher, J. (1990, August). 43 steps to a successful facility. *Athletic Business*, 41-43.

Miller, D. (1991, August). New life for old buildings. *Athletic Business*, 55-57.

United States Baseball Federation (1987). *A baseball facility: It's construction and care*. (Vol. 3).

CHAPTER 4

FACILITY DESIGN

This chapter will provide an introduction to the ideas and issues involved with the design of a sport and fitness facility. Elements such as the design process, the design team, design or building options or both, and design issues will be addressed.

Architect Selection

The design process begins soon after the project has been approved, and budget parameters established. The next stage of development is the selection of a fully qualified design team, which involves selection of the architect or architectural firm. The architect is probably the single most important element in the development of a sport facility. The architectural firm is a comprehensive organization that can provide internal sub specialists, including structural, electrical, and civil engineers and special area consultants.

Selection of the architectural company should not be based on local residence, friendships, or any other subjective factors; it should be based solely on the reputation and experience of the company. To determine experience level an understanding of type and size of recently completed projects, their estimated and budgeted cost and actual costs, and current facility management organization must be elicited. This information should be requested from architect candidates when they submit their resumes and design ideas.

When submitting requested materials and information, candidates should include elaborate brochures and audiovisual presentations. Design competitions are an excellent tool, especially in the case of public projects. However, in the case of sport facilities competitions are not necessarily appropriate as they do not convey pertinent information about the candidate's experience, creativity, and expertise, vital in the development of a sports facility. Normally, an architect candidate with little or no experience would be excluded from the selection process, yet if creativity, a willingness to learn, and cooperation can be demonstrated then consideration is possible. However, in the case of any documented professional misconduct, it is likely that this candidate would be eliminated immediately from any further consideration.

After the candidate field has been narrowed to three or four finalists, these individuals or firms should be interviewed and asked to demonstrate their competence and philosophy in the following areas:

- client's role in the design process,
- number and type of consultants required,
- design or build versus conventional design process,
- extent of engineering services,
- construction supervision,
- numbers of sets of plans and specifications to be provided,
- construction costs,
- factors that may influence construction,
- time schedule and target dates for completion,
- and development of a budget.

At the conclusion of this process, the architect or firm or both is selected, and contracts would be prepared and executed. The architectural fee is dependent on the extent of services to be provided, but usually ranges between 7 to 10% percent of the total cost of the facility project (Laventhol & Horwath, 1989).

Design Team

In addition to the architect or firm as the core of the design team, other members might include food service or equipment advisers, landscape architects, facility managers, user group(s) representatives, acoustical consultants, turf management specialists, and sport facility consultants. These individuals or groups should be selected to ensure that all elements are developed with state-of-the-art layout, equipment, and technology. The creation of a balanced development team can limit domination of the decision making process by a single discipline and make the facility responsive to its intended purpose and audience (Oommen & Maynard, 1989). To enhance the functionality of a facility, various potential user groups, such as sports teams, should provide input during the design phase. Management representing these groups generally is interested in critiquing the design and in assisting the building owner's in selection of interior finishes and specifications. This cooperative approach will make the facility more appropriate to future adaptation and change.

Sport Facility Consultant

The professional consultant can provide numerous services. This experienced individual should serve as a liaison between the managing authority (i.e., planning committee) and the architect. Because 95% of all architects are designing their first sport facility, it is important to have the services of an objective consultant to ensure the architect is aware of the subtleties involved in the development of this facility type. As an expert in the field, the consultant has experience in layout and should be aware of innovations, trends, and needs within the field (Oommen & Maynard, 1989). Additionally, this individual should have had extensive experience in the field and can usually be of assistance in the selection of an appropriate architect or firm.

Design Elements

There are seven elements that need to be considered when designing a sport or entertainment facility:

1. Site Development: This involves the development of the entire construction site, not just the facility building alone. It can include parking, establishing traffic flow, and other associated elements.

2. Site Orientation: The positioning of the facility that should take advantage of the time of day, period of the year and natural lighting factors.

3. Patron Facilities: This involves issues such as security, safety, internal traffic flow, seating type and configuration, toilet facilities and concessions.

4. Playing Surface: This considers appropriate type of field surface for the specific sporting activity. Today, due to the high cost of staging events, it is important to develop facilities that are multipurpose and are multi-usage in design. With this fact in mind it is appropriate to install an artificial surface in most sport venues. Other elements in this issue include the adequacy of drainage and storage concerns.

5. Media Requirements: All modern facilities should have appropriate and adequate public-address, lighting, scoreboard, broadcast and media preparation areas. This is especially vital if a facility is planning a large event.

6. Sport/Team Facilities: This indicates the necessity that a facility make available adequate change and toilet facilities for sports teams, with direct access to the playing field. Auxiliary concerns include meeting and training rooms, as well as adequate medical and first aid stations.

7. Facility Operations: This refers to administrative and tenant considerations. Every facility has administrative, maintenance and operational personnel and requires adequate and appropriate space to maintain their operations (Laventhol & Horwath, 1989).

The Design Process

The designer should be involved from the initial concept stage to better evaluate program requirements, costs, and site needs. Regardless of the design and bid process or design and build process, the architect's work is characterized by the various stages of completion: conceptual, schematic, design or development, and final construction. Each stage in the design evolution influences estimates of development costs, as well as the designer's fee payment schedule.

At the initial or concept stage, an experienced architect can advise the client on budgetary requirements, comparative costs of recently completed facilities, and the development of sketches to help project sponsors and community leaders visualize how the proposed facility will look and relate to surrounding structures. These preliminary design services are important to the initial planning phase, especially when considering the political viewpoint.

Laventhol and Horwath (1989) stated that the conceptual stage involves "initial sketches and drawings which generally illustrate the development scale and spatial relationships" (p.28). General space and functional areas should be considered, and cost estimates should be expressed in broad terms based on comparable, recent developments within the industry (Laventhol & Horwath, 1989).

Schematic Stage. Sketches consisting of multiple drawings and other documents typify this stage. Project components are scaled in sufficient detail to define functional areas and facilitate probable estimates of construction cost based on area and other unit costs (Laventhol & Horwath, 1989). According to Kaiser (1989), "small, uncomplicated projects to be completed in a short period of time may have a simplified set of bid documents. This may consist of several sheets of drawings with specifications written on the drawings" (p. 65).

Design or development stage. At this stage, drawings and documents describing the entire project, from the architectural, structural, mechanical, and electrical systems, to the availability of materials and equipment, potential scheduling, energy conservation, user safety, and maintenance elements, are required. Specifications should be detailed and include construction costs, the guaranteed maximum price, and be able to detail the exterior appearance of the facility, its interior finish, and its function, based on performance specifications (Laventhol & Horwath, 1989).

Final Construction Documents Stage. Laventhol and Horwath (1989) determined that "construction documents form the basis for bidding and should be viewed when they are 50 to 60 percent of the completed level to ascertain if they correspond with the design/development goals and specifications" (p.28). These documents should be consistent with the previous documents and drawings. Construction documents should reflect applicable local codes, schedule changes, or any other special requirements likely to affect the guaranteed maximum price.

Final documents should include all drawings and information documents detailing:

- architectural, structural, mechanical, and electrical systems;

- acoustics;

- landscaping;

- energy conservation;

- communication system,

- user safety, and

- all necessary bid information.

These documents are often organized into bid packages to solicit a price for major portions of the construction with a time frame attended (Laventhol & Horwath, 1989).

Construction options

When all documents are complete, a choice must be made as to whether the project construction will be accomplished by in-house construction personnel or outside contractors.   The availability of staff or preference to use a contractor depends on schedules, project scope, and special trade requirements.

In selecting a building contractor, the owner or managing authority must decide if the primary criterion for selection will be a general contractor based upon the lowest price bid for the project; a construction manager, based upon qualifications, experience, and professional skills of the builder; or a Design and Build option where the architect and contractor both work for the same firm (Laventhol & Horwath, 1989).

Lump sum contract. This is the traditional process. A general contractor is hired for an agree-upon sum, as a result of the lowest bid. This process takes place only after the building has been designed through working drawings, and the architect has prepared the plans, specifications, and bid documents.

A bonded general contractor is hired, as a result of the bid process, to complete a job for a previously agreed-upon sum. The contractor must complete the job according to the contract plans and specifications. Issues such as profit and loss, cost of materials, subcontractors and subsequent payment are the sole responsibility of the contractor. This type of contractual arrangement is not advisable in rehabilitation projects and in periods of high inflation (Laventhol & Horwath, 1989).

Construction Manager. This individual is hired for a fee to recommend the most appropriate sequencing of the work and the most cost-effective means of packaging various components, and to oversee the progress of the construction through all phases.

Responsibilities of a full-time construction manager are to supervise the day-to-day progress of the plan; identify and rank the specialists for approval by the managing authority; prepare the agenda for management meetings; prepare press releases; brief various community groups on the progress of the project; work as a liaison to the various project groups; and complete all tasks required to keep the project on track (Laventhol & Horwath, 1989).

Design and Build Option. The design-and-build option places responsibility for the completion of the facility on the architect and builder who work for the same company. This option emphasizes a fixed price and encourages interaction, as well as eliminates additional costs arising from change in design orders. Example: The owner alters plans to change the planned HVAC to a more efficient unit. This change is negotiated with the design and build team to make the change and consequently minimizes cost (Laventhol & Horwath, 1989).

Construction Process

The conventional construction process is initiated when the owner contracts with a general contractor to build the facility for a designated price. At this juncture, the facility has reached the working drawing stage, and bid documents (plans and specifications) are made available for interested general contractors to review. A public announcement is then released to the media for the submission of bids, while bid procedures, documents, plans and specifications are prepared by the architect. After selection is made and the contract awarded, the architect adopts a supervisory role over the general contractor to ensure the project is built according to original design.

It is usually true that the construction contract is given to the lowest bidder, but this is not always the case, as quality and previous track record are significant influences in the award process. After the awarding of the contract, the architect serves as the owner's representative, overseeing the general contractor's progress and construction schedule.

An alternative to the traditional approach is one in which a general contractor is hired for a fee to make recommendations to the owner as to the most appropriate work and cost-effective sequence for the project. In addition, the contractor is able to recommend a construction manager to oversee the project. The construction-manager process provides the owner with an opportunity to obtain a lower construction price by avoiding the general contractor's built-in profit margin. Under the construction management process contingencies are minimized because the construction manager can bid the work in segments or pieces within a specified time and price frame. This method is increasingly more attractive to the owner, especially if the project is an enormous one (Laventhol & Horwath, 1989).

Fast-track Design Option. As soon as the design and development phase has been completed, the owner's representative will provide authorization to proceed on a fast-rack approach. The fast-track design option, "requires working drawings to be let out for bid to construct while other elements are still being designed" (Laventhol & Horwath, 1989, p.31). This method tends to reduce construction time, minimize interest costs, reduce the risk of cost escalation, and possibly accelerate project completion. Although this fast-track approach has a number of positive attributes, public agencies may be precluded from employing this system due to local or state regulations.

The combining of various methods, such as the design and build fast-track process with a guaranteed maximum price, will create an attractive possibility for some facility managers. Though a joint-venture of a qualified architect or engineering firm and a general contractor (acting as a construction manager), the owner could then purchase design and construction management services. This joint-venture option provides for the assumption of risk for cost overruns that may occur during the design and build period. This option provides the owner with quality, flexibility, and potential lower costs (Laventhol & Horwath, 1989).

Costs

The major costs of a facility project are the purchase price of the land, site preparation, construction labor, building design, climactic conditions, landscaping, and any miscellaneous expenses. In the preliminary stages, site acquisition and development, legal, architectural (i.e., working plans, construction supervision, and engineering requirements) and consultant fees, and promotion and publicity costs are incurred. The costs for construction are developed from the contract and subcontracts, construction permits, and overall project supervision. After construction is complete, both indoor and outdoor equipment and furniture are purchased for up to 15% of the budget. Insurance and contingencies (up to 10% of the total cost) round out the facility construction costs.

Unions

Unions may affect the time and costs involved in the construction of a facility. When dealing with unions, particular attention must be paid to working conditions and job responsibilities, as union workers will not usually perform any tasks outside the scope of their agreement. Wages are typically higher for union workers as opposed to non-union workers, and this disparity may cause budget problems if insufficient funds are allocated for labor.

Strikes are also a possibility, especially if working conditions or some other factor is unsatisfactory to union workers. Unions can also be responsible for construction delay and cost overruns, even if overtime is paid to bring the project back on schedule.

Construction Phase

The construction of a facility is a developmental process. After the selection of the appropriate building site and consideration of the preparation elements, a construction schedule needs to be developed. This schedule evolves from the initial preparatory phases, such as soil preparation and foundation, through the structural phase, to the finishing stage. Although each project has similarities, every construction project has unique facets and problems. To understand more about the process, it is an excellent idea to consult with a local contractor.

Evaluation Process

An evaluation process is an important tool both during the construction phase, and after the project has been completed. During the initial or development phase, each aspect of the project must be critically examined to determine if all specifications and conditions have been satisfied. During this construction period, the facility consultant or an owner's representative must have inspected all stages of the work. If a problem exists, a qualified decision would be made as to the appropriate action to correct the situation. For example, a recreational facility was being constructed in a dry climate. A wooden basketball floor was recommended and ordered. The thickness of the floor was supposed to be 5/8", and the floor was to be made of pine. The floor arrived and was stored, on the construction site. When it came time to place the gymnasium floor, a problem was noted by the facility consultant. This problem originated as a result of 'shrinkage' of the pine, due to a faulty curing process. The contractors complained, but it was in the contract that until the construction was completed, all problems were the responsibility of the contractor.

The next evaluation element should occur at the end of the construction phase. At this juncture, the owners take temporary possession of the completed facility, and a checklist of apparent problems, structural defects, and unsatisfactory workmanship is noted. These construction defects are the responsibility of the contractor and must be corrected before possession is transferred permanently from the contractor to the new owner. This process is known as the facility guarantee and usually is in effect for a one-year period against problems of workmanship or installation of faulty equipment.

At the end of this guarantee period, a final evaluation and inspection is conducted by the owners and contractor. When satisfaction is apparent, the facility is finally handed over to the owners at the end of this probationary period. It should be noted that even after the one-year guarantee period has elapsed, if any major problems are detected, legal action can be initiated to correct the situation.

Structural Materials

Major sport structures are constructed of either steel or reinforced concrete. The majority of these facilities are constructed utilizing partially submerged foundations that provide structural soundness and substantial savings in construction costs. Other factors that influence the choice of materials are

- soil conditions
- facility weight
- costs of construction
- location
- longevity
- climate
- thermal expansion

- maintenance

- protection from deterioration.

Foundations

Foundations are the base support for any building construction. The extent of the foundation depends upon the type of soil. Soil can be classified into three types: (a) coarse-grained, non-cohesive soil that consists of sand and gravel; (b) fine grained cohesive soil that includes silts and clays, which when they become moist, create a stronger bond; and (c) organic fibrous soil, which includes peat and loam (i.e., a mixture of sand and clay).

There are three problems with foundations that should be considered before designing the facility structure:

1. Moisture: The amount of water in the soil at any time can affect the strength of the holding capacity of the soil. This also includes the shrinkage and expansion of the soil.

2. Frost: This is a problem in cold climates.

3. Shifting: The movement of the earth causes movement, sinkage, or sliding of the foundation.

THE FOUNDATION OF A LARGE SPORT FACILITY IS A MASSIVE
CONSTRUCTION PROJECT.

Building Envelope and Walls

Public traffic areas of the facility may be either partially or wholly enclosed, depending upon weather and climate. The design of these areas depends upon the structural system employed, as well as budget and cost considerations.

Wall surface areas of the exterior envelope, concourses, ramps, public areas, and enclosures such as offices are visible to the public and subject to high usage and traffic levels. Many of these surfaces are exposed to weather and must be maintained and able to be adequately cleaned. The facility must also project a positive visual image, which requires maintenance and repair. To limit recurring material and labor costs, concrete is the most common construction agent used in these areas.

Framing

The basic structure of any framing system compromises four components: the roof, floor, beams, and girders. The horizontal elements are supported by the vertical members (i.e., the walls and columns). The entire frame is supported by the foundation.

Windows

Windows shield the internal environment from external conditions. Windows and curtains must be able to prohibit the wind, temperature fluctuations (heat and cold), and external noise. Window frames are constructed from various materials ranging from wood to aluminum, with glass pane centers.

Elevators and Escalators

In every modern facility today, spectators expect to be conveyed to and from the facility viewing areas using either elevators or escalators.

Elevators: Elevators today are either electric or hydraulic. Hydraulic elevators are primarily used in smaller buildings and move at slower speeds (i.e., 3 meters to 45 meters (100 to 150 ft) per minute). Larger and taller buildings utilize the electric type. Elevator size is determined by the type of building. Capacities of 700 to 1,000 kilograms (1,500 to 2,500 pounds) are common in apartment type buildings, whereas, in sport and recreation structures, capacities range between 1500 to 1800 kilograms (3,500 and 4,000 pounds). Elevators can carry up to 2,400 people per hour, depending on the elevator type and size.

Elevator inspections should be completed annually to eliminate any possible hazardous situations from developing. Inspections

- should include all parts to conform to city and state code requirements
- should be completed after any new installations within the structure
- should have results reported to the appropriate building and public authorities.

Any and all recommended repairs should be promptly completed.

Escalators: Escalators, known as "moving stairways", are another common form of vertical transportation. Escalators have an advantage of being in constant motion, carrying up to 5,000 passengers per hour, depending upon the escalator speed and size. They are less expensive and require less operational space than do elevators, but are only successful in facilities less than 3 to 4 stories in height.

Government Agency Involvement

In all construction of new, or renovation of existing, facilities, public concerns will become a part of the proposed project. These concerns are in the form of laws or edicts that have been issued by federal, state, and local authorities. At the federal level, there are a number of elements that must be identified and incorporated into the construction process, for example equal opportunity, access for employment, and the Americans with Disabilities Act.

Risks and Risk Management

Laventhol and Horwath (1989) state that

> Risks of project delays, project cost overruns, the builder's financial stability, or structural failure are increased by the complexity of the project and inversely related to the experience and track record of the builder and designer....high risks and multiple risks are to be expected in projects that take 18 to 30 months to build, require long structural roof spans, and involve simultaneous development of adjacent but separate structures with different owner (p.31)

It is clear that owners accept certain risks, as part of the cost of doing business. Yet, to limit these potential litigious situations, risk management and risk aversion (see chapter 7: Risk Management) procedures have been established at the outset of the project development process. These procedures can be initiated by an agreement with the primary insurer that provides rigorous project cost controls, quality inspection procedures, and an assertive role for the owner's representative. Other risk aversion direction can be construction options, such as guaranteed price and issuance of performance bonds.

Summary

1. The architect is the most important person on the design team for a sport or entertainment facility and the selection of this person should be given the utmost attention.

2. Other members of the design team should include representatives of the user groups, teachers, administrators, consultants, and specialists.

3. Seven elements should be considered when designing a sport or entertainment facility: (a) site development, (b) site orientation, (c) patron facilities, playing surface, (e) media requirements, (f) sport and team facilities, and facility operations.

4. The design phase is divided into several stages: schematic, design and

development, and final construction document. Each stage has specific elements that build upon the previous stage.

5. Three different types of contractors are available. Lump sum is the traditional type, which utilizes a general contractor. Construction management uses a full-time manager to oversee the progress of the construction. The design and build option uses an architect and contractor who both work for the same company. Each of these options has its own strengths and weaknesses.

6. The construction of a building is a developmental process. Once the design phase is complete a contractor is selected, and construction begins. Once the building is complete an evaluation or guarantee phase begins, which usually lasts around one year. During this time the owners examine the building for any deficiencies, which the contractor immediately repairs.

Questions

1. Describe the design process of a sport facility.
2. Discuss the ramifications of the process of selecting the architect.
3. List the members of the design team.
4. Why should a sport facility consultant be part of the design team?
5. Discuss the risks and risk management aspects of a facility design.
6. List the construction options.
7. Describe the roles of the construction manager and the project manager.
8. Describe the differences between design-build, fast-track, and conventional construction techniques.

References

Kaiser, H. (1989). *The facilities manager's reference book*. Kingston, MA: R. S. Means Company.

Laventhol, & Horwath (1989).   *Conventions, stadiums, and arenas*. Washington, DC: Urban Land Institute.

Oommen, G., & Maynard, L. (August, 1989). How to select the right architect. *Athletic Business*, 41-46.

MANAGEMENT

CHAPTER 5

MANAGEMENT OVERVIEW

Management is the determining factor in the success or failure of any sport and public-assembly facility. Management's philosophy can determine the number and type of staff and extent of services (in-house and contract), influence the supply of events, and satisfy the patron through an enjoyable experience (Mulrooney & Farmer, 1995). The quality of management for sport facilities can determine the ability of the facility to attract and retain tenants. Profitability and income for the facility owner, staffing and payroll requirements, and building condition and service levels, such as patron comfort, are also affected by management (Mulrooney & Farmer, 1995). It is important to remember that the main income of the facility is generated from food and beverage sales and is far greater than its net income from any rental lease.

Organization and Management Structure

Laventhol and Horwath (1989) state that operational efficiency and profitability are determined by the building purpose, the relationship between the owner and management, and the type of management. They mention that the financial and economic success of the facility usually depends upon

- rental policy and rate,
- usage scheduling,
- concession and service contracts,
- on-site parking,
- tenant lease terms,
- staff selections and training,
- maintenance levels and expenditures,

- utility costs.

Responsibilities of facility management include

- serving tenants' needs,
- providing a clean, comfortable environment for patrons,
- ensuring that food, beverages and novelties are available,
- providing security,
- providing cleanup and maintenance,
- overseeing facility marketing, advertising and PR,
- and selecting an appropriate management staff.

Other responsibilities in the area of policy and financial control are:

- establishing event scheduling priorities,
- negotiating lease and facility rental,
- negotiating concession and service contracts,
- planning and budgeting capital improvements,
- special event promotions,
- controlling operating deficits or debt service (p. 34-35)

Facility Ownership

Community and State

Initially, most facilities were built by communities to assist with the redevelopment of an under used city center. These redevelopment efforts were funded through a variety of methods, such as charitable donations, federal grants, general assistance bonds, and tax assessments. These public developments initiated a public or community type of administrative effort to govern these new facilities. A typical governance structure consisted of an appointed governing board or commission, with the facility manager being a department head within the city administration. Operation of the facility was usually subsidized by the community from local hotel, motel and amusement sales taxes.

Although this typical governance structure previously described is attributable to a community or city, this model can be used in both county or parish and state operations. The state model would differ only in that it would be a state entity, with limited contact with the local political scene. Additionally, revenue to maintain the operation would probably result from a combination of local and state funding efforts, such as combining income generated from local sales and hotel tax with moneys from state bonds, racing, gambling, and amusement taxes (IAAM, 1990).

Higher Education

Higher education (i.e., colleges and universities) has developed major on-campus facilities used for a variety of purposes, such as the performing arts, entertainment, and sport facilities. Funding for these facilities is based primarily on the assumptions of continued student growth, alumni gifts, event income and institutional subsidization. Management of these facility entities is primarily left to university departments, rather than adopting a community or private facility-governance model. Higher education institutions heavily subsidize these operational entities and will most likely continue to do so in the near future (IAAM, 1990).

Private Enterprise

These facility types involve a variety of groups, which range from private, non profit groups that have developed local performing arts centers and arenas to sport facilities that are leased by a non profit organization. These relatively common scenarios involve the non profit management organization leasing the facility for an annual nominal fee. For example, the Sun Bowl Stadium, El Paso, Texas, is leased to the University of Texas at El Paso, from the city of El Paso, for the sum of $1.00 per year. In this example all liabilities, operational expenses and obligations are the responsibility of the lessor. This type of strategy enables the non profit organization to operate a substantial program without having the initial financial investment.

Private Facilities

Constructed through private financing, sport facilities are usually located in populated urban areas, for the sole purpose of generating profits from events. Community and, in some cases, state agencies have assisted in the development of these facilities by providing financial incentives, such as tax abatements and tax financing programs. Management of the facility is the sole responsibility of the private ownership group.

The quality of management influences the financial performance of the facility more than any other factor. In fact, this vital ingredient can influence the ability of the facility to attract and retain professional tenants; profitability, attainment of strategic goals and objectives, staffing and payroll, facility condition and patron services (Laventhol & Horwath, 1989).

According to the IAAM (1990) management's impact on the financial future of the facility is dependent on

- rental policy and rate schedule,
- scheduling and usage,
- concession and service contracts,
- on-site parking and rates,
- tenant-lease terms,

- staffing and training considerations,

- maintenance levels and expenditures,

- utility costs.

Facility Governance

Management of sport and public assembly facilities today involves a number of management alternatives. These range from facilities operated by their owners, by primary or anchor tenants, by not-for-profit organizations, or by the private management companies.

Owner

The owner management alternative can be applicable to both public or private settings. If the facility is owned and operated by government, a plethora of regulations and procedures is in place that result in a restrictive operational environment. Areas usually involved are purchasing; contract development and approval (especially involving any legislative procedure); personnel hiring, promotion, and dismissal; finance and accounting procedures; and support for other government policies (Mulrooney & Farmer, 1995). Additionally, the area of political patronage inhibits the operational performance of the facility. Increasingly, independent or contract authorities, not-for-profit groups, and private management organizations have been utilized to manage government-owned facilities (Laventhol & Horwath, 1989).

Not-for-Profit

Not-for-profit management organizations usually operate under the auspices of a commission or a board of directors that acts as an instrument of the local government. This board is usually exempted from various government policies and procedures, and at least initially, this provides an efficient operational climate (Mulrooney & Farmer, 1995). However, with the advent of political favoring, it is conceivable that the board and a quality operation will probably decline (Laventhol & Horwath, 1989).

Private Management

The private-management alternative operates solely on a profit motive. All contracts contain some form of incentive bonus or risk arrangement designed to increase revenues and reduce risks. Private management has the flexibility to negotiate labor agreements to designate the type and number of events, and to establish more favorable relationships with event organizers.

"Although sport facilities have traditionally been owned and governed by public authorities, the situation appears to be changing. Sport facilities were originally developed to economically impact the local community" (Mulrooney & Farmer, 1995, p. 224). However, today, many facilities have become a drain on the community resources and the taxpayer.

If a facility has significant problems or the inability to realize expectations, additional management alternatives, other than an internal operation, should be considered. Today, this alternative is the private management organization. It allows the governmental or institutional entity to maintain control over the facility, but with the opportunity to

- decrease financial operating deficit

- provide patrons better service

- allow private management companies to risk their own capital when dealing with different events

- acquire top professionals in the field of facility management

- increase the number and caliber of the events scheduled

- increase the number of contacts within the facility industry

- facilitate improved operational flexibility concerning policies and operational structure (Mulrooney & Farmer, 1995).

The private facility management alternative has experienced dramatic growth, with a number of different types of management groups (i.e., hotels, food service, specialty facility management companies) entering this competitive arena. "Each of these management groups evaluates a facility's needs based on their current financial picture; staffing requirements; marketing needs and event scheduling; and the political situation" (Mulrooney & Farmer, 1995, p. 224). Regardless of the outcome, management groups tend to seek facilities that complement their specific areas of expertise. However, these groups undertake facility management assignments intending on operating at a profit rather than on a community relations basis (IAAM, 1990).

Private Management Options. Although some of these private alternatives have been discussed previously, the IAAM (1990) stated that there are four options currently in use:

1. Not-for-profit organization (discussed previously)

2. Public facility or private contracted management: The community pays a specific fee for all operational aspects. In addition, if all goals are reached, a bonus or incentive is paid to the management group. In the areas of personnel, rules, and policy, the management organization is independent of the community guidelines.

3. Facility Leasing: The management company leases the facility, on a long term basis, from the community. The specifications of each lease agreement are different, but usually there are specified limits of control, as well as a percentage of all ticket sales. Depending upon the lease terms, it is common for profits from other services to be the property of the lessee.

4. Service Contracts: Even though the facility may remain under control of the community, specific services can be contracted to recognized experts in the field. These contracted service areas are

    *   **Concessions** involve not only food and beverage but also novelties and souvenirs. The selected contractor is responsible for all management, labor, and merchandise, and may be responsible for providing an investment in equipment, thereby reducing facility overhead and liability.

    *   **Ticket services** provide a variety of additional ticket outlets that service a significant portion of the public. Although most facilities have their own box office operation, it would be extremely expensive and prohibitive to provide the number of outlets required. The solution may be to contract with a specialty organization for ticket sales, where the cost of the arrangement is a commission off the ticket price and the service is charged to the consumer.

    *   **Advertising and marketing** are necessary to promote the various relatively expensive and specialized events. Although many facilities maintain their own in-house operation, many of the contracted events have their own advertising and marketing services available. If contracting with an outside agency appears to be a reasonable alternative, the facility will pay a commission for these services and in the process limit expenses in the area of labor and operations.

    *   **Housekeeping, Security, and Parking** are usually contracted out, which limits the liability, overhead, and administration, and is cost-effective when compared with in-house alternatives. The advantages of this type of contractual operation are that it provides the facility operation with quality service in the contracted areas, while reducing community and in-house personnel and consequently operational expenses. Outside contractors rather than in-house personnel are utilized, for various reasons:

        a. The selected service may involve a specialty area that management may not feel competent in servicing.

        b. Provision of a service that may require substantial investment, especially in required equipment and accessories.

        c. The service may be able to be provided at a cheaper rate due to increased volume and limited overhead.

        d. There maybe problems with labor, especially in a union or civil service environment.

Whether it is these identified reasons or others, if a private management team is the chosen alternative, the bidding group must be aware of the problems and be active participants in developing appropriate solutions. In addition, the facility's philosophy should be understood by this contracted agency and be the primary concern when developing its mission, goals, objectives, and required planning strategies. As a result of these issues, the process of selecting a management alternative will be substantially easier.

Private Management Selection Process. After the decision is made to pursue private management, the question then becomes how does the facility procures the service of an appropriate contract organization. The first step in this process is the issuance of a *Request for Proposal (RFP)*. This formal document provides potential applicants with information as to expectations from the facility management. Information and materials should also be included that will provide an overall picture of current conditions, including long, and short-term plans and projections, budget and actual income and projections, annual reports, and prevailing contracts (Mulrooney & Farmer, 1995).

The second step is conveying the information to every potential management group for consideration, as well as distributing this information for publication in all appropriate trade and professional magazines. It is important to provide a bid-response period from 30 to 90 days, depending upon the situation. The RFP should also indicate whether the bid will be a public or private process, and if bid proposals will be made available to all competitors (Mulrooney & Farmer, 1995).

Thirdly, all appropriate and interested bid participants will be provided with a facility tour and opportunity to examine all RFP documents (Mulrooney & Farmer, 1995). If any problems or questions arise not included in the prepared materials or as a result of the interaction between potential bidders and the facility governing body, an addendum will be prepared and distributed.

Fourth, all proposals received by the deadline will be reviewed by a specific group whose sole purpose is to select the finalists. All bidders will then be notified as to the outcome of the bid process. All finalists will be provided with an opportunity to make a formal presentation to the review body. It is at this stage that the bidding competitors can be revealed. It is important that flexibility be part of the process, as bidders may desire to change their proposals as information becomes available (Mulrooney & Farmer, 1995).

Fifth, as a result of this personal presentation, the successful bidder will move to the negotiation stage. This negotiation phase involves not only representatives from both groups, but legal assistance as well. It is initiated with a written document based on the RFP and the proposal. An agreement is apparent when there is resolution of the differences between these two documents (Mulrooney & Farmer, 1995).

The approval phase is the last stage in the process. This occurs at the conclusion of all negotiations when the final authority, such as the local community council or state legislature, actually approves the contract document (IAAM, 1990).

Contract Terms. All contractual agreements should be facility specific and able to address the facility mission and objectives. Various contractual scenarios are possible:

1. A contract management group assumes all operational and financial liabilities for a standard fee.

2. Operational and financial risks remain with the facility owners; however, contract management receives a percentage of the amount of money saved from standard operational costs. Incentives are not limited to finance, but can include attendance, number of events, and quality of service.

These various arrangements are common and not the only contractual agreements possible. Regardless of the agreement type, all contract elements should be facility specific and contain adequate incentives or compensation to encourage greater achievement levels from contract management.

Private Facility Management Trends. Today there are four leading private management companies that operate approximately 76+ facilities internationally for a management fee or lease (Sauer, 1993). These companies are Ogden Allied, Centre Management, Leisure Management International, and Spectacor Management Group (SMG). According to the IAAM (1990), the advantages of private management companies are that they are

• able to negotiate labor agreements more efficiently than are government-oriented operations

• flexible; and

• able to increase the number of events through the development of more favorable relationships with concert promoters and event organizers.

Service Contracts

Today most facilities, regardless of management element, contract with companies for security, maintenance, mechanical equipment, and concessions. Also, many facility-event services are contracted in the areas of cleanup, setup, breakdown, ushering, ticket taking, box office, and event security. Unless a facility is booked for more than 200 days per year, it is not cost-effective to hire full-time event labor.

Food and beverage concessions usually provide a net income to the facility between 35 and 55 % of gross sales. This level of profit margin is subject to such factors as facility size, occupancy, event type, and the concessionaires' capital investment in equipment (IAAM, 1990).

Marketing, Advertising and Public Relations

Marketing, advertising, and PR are primarily the function of the building's staff, event promoters, and tenants, although most facilities will have an individual assigned to these efforts. Negotiations by staff members for event promoters to obtain appropriate media coverage costs are usually borne by the event producer. Marketing plans should be developed for all of the facility's prospective activities. This includes a detailed budget and strategy with time line.

Summary

1. The type of management a facility uses will directly impact a variety of issues including   scheduling, leases, financial negotiations, concessions, service controls, and overall environment.

2. Sport facilities may be owned by a state or local governments, non profit organizations, or private individuals or corporations. The sources of funding to construct and manage these facilities will be affected depending on type of ownership.

3. The facility's governance, or operation, also may be accomplished through public, non profit, or private methods.

4. Private management is a trend in the facility management industry that is growing each year. Many publicly owned and managed sport facilities have been losing money and private management is one answer to assist these facilities to become profit centers.

5. Private management companies such as Ogden Allied, SMG, Centre Management, and Leisure Management International usually are contracted to provide services for the entire facility.

6. Specific services, such as crowd management, maintenance, concessions and equipment, usually have separate contractual agreements.

Questions

1. What changes are taking place in today's sport facility management industry?

2. Identify and describe the various management structures available in sport facilities today.

3. Identify the advantages of a private management company in the operation of a sport facility.

4. Identify and describe the various facility departments and responsibilities that are considered the purview of management.

References

International Association of Auditorium Managers (IAAM). (1990). Course materials from the unpublished proceedings of the School for Public Assembly Facility Management, Ogelbay, VA.

Laventhol, & Horwath. (1989). *Convention centers, stadiums and arenas.*

Washington, DC: Urban Land Institute.

Mulrooney, A., & Farmer, P. (1995). Managing the facility. In B. Parkhouse (Ed.), *The management of sport: Its foundation and application* (2nd ed.) (pp. 223-248). St. Louis, MO: Mosby-Year Book.

Sauer, M. F. (1993, Summer). Going private. *Panstadia International*, 23.

CHAPTER 6

CONTRACT SERVICES

Each sport facility has been developed with specific functions and purposes. Contract services can be used as a management tool by the facility manager, regardless of the facility type.

Contract services have been available for many years in the areas of service, equipment and products. However, they have become increasingly popular due to efforts to control cost, responsibilities, and liabilities involved in operating a facility. Contract services can range from decorator companies to full management services responsible for the operations of the entire facility.

Facilities have increasingly begun to look at private management at various levels, from salary-specific operational problems to the running of the entire management operation. Many municipally owned facilities have utilized contract services as a vehicle for developing cost savings or shifting some liability to the private contractor.

Contracts

Legally, a promissory agreement between two or more parties to establish, change, or rescind a legal relationship is known as a contract. Essentials of this document are:

1. There must be a valid offer and acceptance.

2. The contracting parties must possess the legal rights and capacity to make the contract.

3. Proper consideration for services or provisions must be received for all parties involved with the agreement.

4. Adequate time and form of services for all parties must be attained.

Contract Services and the Sports Facility

There are three basic areas of contracted services available to the facility manager: service, equipment, and supplies. Contracts may be executed in one or all three of these areas.

Services. According to the IAAM (1990), contracts for services can include consulting services for legal advice, engineering, architecture, advertising and promotion, planning, development, crowd management (with ticket takers, ushers, directors, door guards, uniformed security, police officers, and peer group security), janitorial, conversions, light maintenance for payroll services, maintenance service (construction, HVAC, groundskeeping), event labor services (with stagehands, spotlights, rigging, audiovisual equipment, decorator, concessions, catering, and novelties), and complete facility management services.

EVENT STAFF, SUCH AS USHERS, ARE JUST ONE OF THE
SERVICES THAT CAN BE CONTRACTED FOR.

Equipment. Contracts for equipment can include staging, barricades, spotlights, rigging cable, electrical cable and supplies, drapery, carpeting, tables, chairs, ropes and stanchions, fork lifts, scissor lifts, trucks, scoreboards, video screens, message boards, audiovisual equipment, and satellite up-link or down-link.

Supplies. Most facilities contract for supplies and have written policies supporting this practice. Contract supply areas include paper products, cleaning solutions and chemicals, first aid supplies, uniforms, linen, and food products.

Projecting Contract Service Needs

Every manager has the option to manage every segment of the facility with an in-house operation. However, this option is predicated on the availability of skilled and semiskilled employees, capable of operating these areas. Contracting all or part of these services is an option, depending upon the circumstances.

To determine whether an in-house or contract situation is appropriate, it is important to identify and gather data about all necessary facility services. Services should be defined with performance standards being determined, monitoring requirements, and an appropriate list of possible contractors to perform the proposed contracted service. Due to the complexity of today's facilities, the need for contracted services must be determined for each facility (Day, 1990).

There are many reasons for using contractors. Some of them include

1. One major determining factor may be overhead ratios or the bottom line or both. Costs incurred by the facility in operating a specific area must be analyzed and compared to the costs and revenues generated by a private contract. Why can an outside contractor offer a service at a lower rate than an in-house operation can? It may be because that there are fewer regulations, flexibility due to lack of organizational constraints, lower personnel costs due to flexibility in pay rates, and economies of scale as contractors can spread capital costs over several jobs. Another factor is payroll expenses involving licensing, training, bonding, memberships, insurance, benefit packages, hiring, and administrative costs.

2. Large-scale items such as scoreboards or decorator equipment involve capital investment. Many times the agreement may include the transfer of property to the facility at the end of the contract period. As a facility matures, repair and maintenance of specific items will become a concern. Contractors may be able to use their own equipment for more than one contract, cutting overhead expenses and saving the facility money in the form of purchasing, storage, and inventory.

3. A private contractor is usually more responsive to personnel management because the policies the contractor is regulated by are not as restrictive as the municipal manager's policies. This element, coupled with eliminating day-to-day routine operations, may ease responsibilities and free the contractor to work on more important or pressing items of concern.

4. Government policies, laws, and ordinances restrict many facility managers in their ability to manage effectively. Personnel matters such as hiring, firing, and disciplinary actions as well as purchasing or contracting can become ineffective in many circumstances under the operation of the municipally owned facility.

5. Protection from litigation may also be a valid reason for a municipally

owned facility wanting to contract services. In some cases, the liability may be shifted to the contractor for the service rendered by the contractor, through "indemnification" of "hold harmless" clauses.

6. The facility manager may need control over certain required contractors whose expenses are passed on to the event promoter. Allowing the facility manager to maintain control while making the event promoter responsible for payment is additional reason for administrators to contract certain services.

7. Other circumstances such as difficult labor (union) negotiations may be remedied by contracting services for traditional union employment in specific areas.

8. Many contracts create revenues for the sport facility manager by requiring a fee or percentage to be paid to the facility for the right to supply a service or lease of space.

9. The frequency with which a service or equipment is needed may be a major determining factor for contracted services. If an item or service is needed frequently, it may be cost-effective to contract for the item.

Although there are considerations for using a contracted service in some areas, there are also reasons for keeping other services in-house (IAAM, 1990):

1. When client service is important, there is an increased value to the promoter when a competent staff is made available through the facility.

2. Facility costs can be controlled, and an overhead fee can be charged, becoming a revenue source.

3. Consistent control over hiring and recruitment methods as well as training and policies can be maintained if the expertise is in-house.

4. A pride factor is always evident when the employees work for the facility as opposed to the contractor's employees.

5. The organization and communication needs are simplified by the fact that everyone works for the same organization.

6. Accounting control is more direct when the services are under the control of the facility manager.

7. There is more control of decision-making when complete control of the staff is provided through in-house policies.

8. Liability may increase if a competent contractor who has the expertise is not available.

Two major items that a facility manager can offer to event tenants are physical structure (building) and the services provided to the tenants while using the venue. It is important that the manager keep the necessary control to operate the facility and services in a way that will insure the service level required to make the event a success. Projecting and defining the needs of the facility when considering in-house or contracted services and extensive research defining the pros and cons as they relate to the quality, responsiveness, and the level of services are all necessary in order for the facility manager to make an appropriate decision.

Recruitment

After deciding to contract a particular service, it is important that a professional company be recruited to provide the service. Recruiting an appropriate company that adheres to the required standards and provides the needed expertise for the operation to run smoothly is of paramount concern. The proposals may be elicited in many ways, but the following guidelines should be followed. The solicitation process for contractors includes developing a list of possible contractors, circulating a draft solicitation and request for proposal (RFP) to the target contract list, and advertising in the local media and trade magazine.

It is important to understand the laws, ordinances and policies governing the facility operation that must be followed in order to contract with private companies. Privately owned or operated buildings usually have more latitude in the recruiting process. It may be possible for the private company to negotiate a contract with a service or products company that appears competent, without having to go through the formal bid process usually required by municipally operated facilities. However, it is a good idea to have a specific plan of action in soliciting a possible contract for the facility.

Request for Proposal

A common tool used in locating contracted professional services is the Request for Proposal (RFP). The contents of an RFP will vary depending on the need, type of recruitment, type of company desired, and specific requests of the facility (Day, 1990). The RFP does not obligate the facility to contract for any services expressed or implied.

Proposal Instructions. Proposals should include a published deadline and place to submit the bid documents. It is important to provide a time frame that will allow the proposers sufficient time to develop and submit their proposals. Additional items to be included in the proposal instructions are

1. **Proposal withdrawal statement:** A proposal withdrawal statement protects the facility and management from inappropriate bids. It allows the bid to be withdrawn once bids have been formally submitted and opened.

2. **Affirmative-action-guidelines:** These guidelines pertain to employment opportunities of minorities and include information pertaining to these requirements.

3. **Non-collusion affidavit:** These are statements that the proposer has or has not caused another proposer to submit a collusive bid of any type.

4. **Litigation information:** This requires that any legal action concerning the construction or interpretation of the contract terms be handled in the court system at a specific location.

5. **Tax and license requirements:** The proposer is required to follow any and all laws in accordance with requirements in contracting for services. Tax and license laws that pertain to the successful bidder should be listed in the document.

The IAAM (1990) stated that the elements of the RFP should include

- A facility contact person, title, address and telephone number responsible for basic information and answering questions posed by the prospective contractors.

- Explanation of proposer responsibility: The RFP does not obligate the facility to pay any costs incurred by the proposer in the preparation and submission of the proposal (Day 1990). It is the proposer's responsibility to cover the expense.

- Rejection of proposal clause: The facility has the right to reject any and all proposals. This clause protects the facility from an inappropriate contract if none of the proposals that are submitted meet the needs or requirements of the services solicited. Proposals that are incomplete or conditioned in any way (i.e., contain erasures or alterations, or do not conform with the law) may be rejected.

It is important that the proposer be aware of the criteria used in evaluating the proposals during the selection process. This information enables the proposer to provide pertinent information on critical items (Day, 1990). The proposer bears the sole responsibility for providing sufficient, detailed, and complete information.

Work Statement. The services sought by the RFP should be specified in a statement that defines the parameters of the contracted service (Day, 1990). Other parts of the work statement should include

- a description of the facilities in which the contractor will be employed, and

- the type of facility, the events, the attendance capacity or square footage, and the prime uses of the facility. This knowledge may encourage interest in some companies that have worked in the industry but are not familiar with the specific facility because of its location or their lack of knowledge of its existence.

- The volume and type of work required of the successful proposer. All pertinent information, such as type of events, the projected number of events, and how many employees are appropriate for different types of events, should be included.

- The essential ingredients of successfully operating the facility. These elements include appearance, attitudes, and service levels that are expected of their staff. The attitude of the facility (i.e., the contractor's staff must project a positive attitude in proving that the goal of the facility is servicing its customers in a professional manner) should be explained. Any proposer that does not prove the ability to deliver the image should be excluded from the evaluation process. The facility retains the right to sever any contract with a company that does not conform to the requirements in this area.

Proposal Content. Other than the required proposal sheet, the format of the proposal can be left to the discretion of the proposer. However, specific information should be required, as a minimum:

1. **Company identification:** Name, address and telephone number of the company; the name, address, and telephone number of each of the owners of the company should be supplied. If the company is a corporation, the names and addresses of the principal shareholders and the corporate officers should be required. This information is valuable for your research into the integrity of the proposer.

2. **Supervision and management:** The names of the proposed local managers for the facility should be presented. Detailed information on the qualifications and experience of these individuals should be supplied, along with the methods of corporate supervision intended, including training and supervisors.

3. **Company philosophy:** A narrative description of the proposer's attitude and understanding of the service being bid on should be required. This should include information specific to the facility and possible situations that may arise in providing service to the facility and its patrons.

4. **Company Training Policy and Procedures:** A concise statement of the proposer's training curriculum, procedures, and policies as they relate to the proposed contract should be required. As many specifics as possible that relate directly to the service should be provided.

5. **Equipment:** Proposer should describe any and all equipment that will be made available to their staff to order to achieve the necessary level of service under the proposed contract. Facility managers should be specific about what equipment may be prohibited, such as weapons, clubs and guns.

6. **Uniforms:** Information should be requested as to the type of uniform and grooming standards the proposer requires. The cost of the minimum uniform should be listed in the contract.

7. **Personnel Pool:** It is important to evaluate the sources from which the proposer intends to recruit. This will provide information as to the caliber of staff that the proposer will make available to the facility. The proposal should include basic charges for staff provided under the

contract or agreement. Also, it is important to find out the rate the proposer will pay its employees. The pay rate that the staff member receives influences the contractor's ability to recruit and retain competent people. The proposal should also include the categories of workers and the proposed charge to the facility for each hour worked.

8. **Proposal sheet:** A specific sheet should be completed and submitted as part of the proposal. Included on this sheet is important quick reference information and the important issues that may make or break the proposal's success. It is a good idea to require an authorized officer of the company to sign the proposal sheet.

Schedule

Facility management needs to define the order and time frame in which the facility will make the selection. This information should include the deadline for proposal submission, bid opening, selection review process, and awarding of the bid to the successful proposer.

A summary sheet at the end of the RFP should remind proposers of the requirements and requested information that make up an appropriate proposal. The proposer should make sure that his or her proposal has complied with all the specifications and requirements included in the RFP. Requirements that must be met by the successful bidder after the selection has been made, such as any performance bonds, licenses, insurance, required forms or any other such items, should also be listed.

Selection of the Contractor

When the solicitation process has been completed, it is necessary to select the appropriate contractor. Using a standard rating method provides an objective score that can be used to eliminate complaints or threatened litigation from unsuccessful bidders.

It is appropriate for the manager of a specific facility area to make the final contractor selection, as he or she has particular knowledge of this facility area and must work with the contractor. Other people involved in the selection process should include a facility employees' representative, because employees will be working alongside the contractor's staff on a daily basis.

It is important that all proposers have their references and background information thoroughly checked. It must be determined that they are reputable and capable of handling the proposed contract work. It is also important to verify the information that has been submitted in the proposal.

After the selected bidder has been notified, all other applicants should be notified as to the actions taken. This will create an atmosphere of cooperation and encourage future proposal submissions. This also protects the facility in case the first choice rejects the contract.

```
┌─────────────────────────────────────────────────────────────┐
│                                                               │
│              FIRST AID SERVICES AGREEMENT                     │
│                                                               │
│        This Agreement is made and entered into on the _____ day of │
│    _____, 199_ by and between Akron General Medical Center dba │
│    CorpCare (CorpCare) and _____ │
│    (Promoter).                                                │
│                                                               │
│        WHEREAS CorpCare is the exclusive provider of first-aid │
│    services for the John S. Knight Convention Center (Center); and │
│                                                               │
│        WHEREAS Promoter has contracted to hold an event at the John │
│    S. Knight Convention Center (Center) on _____, │
│    199_ and is required to obtain the first-aid services of CorpCare │
│    under its contract with Center; and                        │
│                                                               │
│        WHEREAS Promoter wishes to purchase and CorpCare wishes to │
│    provide first-aid services for Promoter's event.           │
│                                                               │
│        NOW THEREFORE, in consideration of the mutual promises, │
│    covenants, and agreements hereinafter set forth, CorpCare and │
│    Promoter, with the intent to be legally bound, agree as follows: │
│                                                               │
│    RESPONSIBILITIES OF CORPCARE:                              │
│                                                               │
│    1)   CorpCare will provide an on-site first-aid station available │
│         to all attendees at Promoter's event during the event and the │
│         set-up and tear-down time.                            │
│                                                               │
│    2)   CorpCare shall provide a duly qualified licensed physician to │
│         serve as Medical Director of the first-aid station. This │
│         Medical Director will provide medical supervision for the │
│         personnel providing first-aid services. Promoter hereby │
│         acknowledges that the Medical Director is not required to be │
│         on-site for the event or the set-up or tear-down time. │
│                                                               │
│    3)   CorpCare shall staff the first-aid station with qualified │
│         Registered Nurse(s).                                  │
│                                                               │
│    4)   CorpCare shall ensure the first-aid station is stocked with │
│         adequate medical supplies.                            │
│                                                               │
│    RESPONSIBILITIES OF PROMOTER:                              │
│                                                               │
│    1)   Promoter shall complete the "Provider Schedule" attached │
│         hereto as Appendix A and made a part of this Agreement. │
│                                                               │
│    2)   Promoter agrees to give Forty (40) days notice of an event and │
│         pay Thirty-Two Dollars ($32.00) per hour for each Registered │
│         Nurse needed for Promoter's event in addition to reimbursement │
│         for all supplies used during Promoter's event. If Forty (40) │
│         days notice is not received by CorpCare then Promoter agrees │
│         to reimburse CorpCare Forty-Six Dollars ($46.00) per hour for │
│         each Registered Nurse needed.                         │
│                                                               │
└─────────────────────────────────────────────────────────────┘
```

FIG 6-1 - SAMPLE FORM CONTRACT

The Service Contract

After the appropriate contractor for the facility's service has been selected, the final stage or negotiations of the contract are then initiated. If the RFP has been used correctly, the signing of the contract by all parties should be a relatively easy task. However, if major difficulties develop during this negotiation phase, it is always possible to break off negotiations and look to the runner-up contractor (Day, 1990). If this situation develops, the initially selected contractor should be provided with every opportunity to respond to the problematical issues and given written notice as to the reasons for severing the negotiation process.

A contract must have mutual benefits for all parties in order for the contract to be successfully carried out. If a contract is lopsided, the slighted party will inevitably become uncommitted and cause problems. A good compromise in negotiations is reached when both sides leave the negotiating table feeling they did not achieve the ultimate agreement yet knowing it was fair. (Laventhol and Horwath, 1989)

Summary

1. Contracts need four elements in order to be valid: mutual agreement, capacity, consideration, time, and form.

2. Services normally contracted out by the facility fall into three basic areas: service, equipment, and supplies.

3. The need for contracted services must be determined by each facility manager, and some of the variables to be considered favoring these services are lower cost; less restrictive policies, laws, and ordinances; protection from litigation; ease of negotiations; and frequency of service.

4. Some of the factors for using in-house services include client service; control over facility costs;   hiring and recruitment; accounting and decision making; decrease in liability.

5. Request for Proposals (RFP) are formal documents used by bidders to submit proposals for various service contracts. The contents of an RFP will vary depending on the need, the type of company desired, and the specific requests of the facility.

6. Once the bidders submit their RFP for the contracted services, it is necessary for the facility to choose the best qualified proposal. Using a rating method provides an objective way to make the selection. This method helps to eliminate most complaints from unsuccessful bidders.

Questions

1. Explain the four elements of a contract.
2. Identify the various contractible services involved in a facility
3. operation.
4. Identify the major elements in projecting contract service needs.
5. Identify at least four reasons for having an in-house operation
6. rather than a contract service.
7. Define an RFP. What are the most important elements of an RFP?
8. Do you feel that the use of a matrix is appropriate to the selection of a contractor? Justify your response.

References

Day, D. (Summer, 1990). Contracting versus in-house. *Facility Manager*, 10-19.

International Association of Auditorium Managers (IAAM). (1990). Course materials from the unpublished proceedings of the School for Public Assembly

Facility Management, Ogelbay, Virginia.

Laventhol & Horwath (1989). *Conventions, stadiums, and arenas.* Washington, DC: Urban Land Institute.

CHAPTER 7

RISK MANAGEMENT

Risk management is an extremely important concept for a sport facility manager to understand. This chapter focuses on the principles necessary to become an effective risk manager in a sport facility.

Definition of Risk

Risk is a peril or the possibility of exposure or harm. The primary focus of risk management is reducing exposure to danger, harm or hazards.(Berlonghi, 1990 and Kaiser, 1986). The most prevalent problem facing a sport facility manager is minimizing financial loss and liability exposure resulting from injuries to patrons. First and foremost then, the goal of risk management is to reduce the possible monetary losses, through lawsuits, while running a sport facility. This goal may sound easy, but it becomes a very complicated and difficult task.

In order to be effective the risk manager should recognize the possible risks, assess the risks, treat the risks, and finally create standard operating procedure.

Identification Stage

In the identification stage the facility must discern the various risks that could potentially cause loss to the facility. Primary and secondary factors need to be addressed in order to reduce losses to the sport facility. Primary factors are included in the daily operations of every sport facility, and each facility manager must consider them while reducing risks. The facility staff are among these primary factors. A well trained staff is the risk manager's best tool in identifying risks, however, but they may themselves become risks. For example, what if a security guard uses excessive force to detain an intoxicated patron? Or if a member of the parking crew uses the facility's "slim-jim" to help himself to a collection of radios, radar detectors and car phones from visiting patrons? What if lifeguards constantly fall asleep in the sun? What if the fitness instructor is more concerned with finding dates than ensuring proper use of the equipment?

Risk identification begins when interviewing prospective employees. The sport facility manager must take special care whom he or she hires for various positions. (A person with a petty theft record would not be a good candidate as a cashier in the parking lot.) Once primary factors are identified, the sport facility manager must be watchful for secondary risks.   A list of secondary risk factors that are applicable to most sport facilities include weather, event or activity type, patron demographics, and facility location. Within each of these secondary risk factors lie identifiable risks. Let us consider one of these and determine what risks may be involved.

The weather affects people every day. Under certain weather conditions various precautions must be taken in order to prevent pending harm. The sport facility manager must use common sense and realize that weather conditions will affect a patron's visit to the sport facility (Kaiser, 1986). For example, if a snowstorm heads in the direction of the sport facility, common sense dictates certain actions. The parking lot and the sidewalks must be cleared and made safe, so patrons do not slip, fall, and injure themselves. The internal staffing must be sufficient to allow the patrons quick entrance into the sport facility to avoid any adverse effects from the weather. The parking staff should be equipped to jump- start any stalled cars and to have sufficient supplies to unlock the cars if their locks should freeze. Upon conclusion of the event, any road closures or travel problems should be announced to the patrons as they are exiting. Finally, sport facilities should provide for patrons to stay overnight if the weather is too bad for individuals to travel.

Using common sense, what risks have been identified? First, the risk of a patron falling in the ice and snow. A patron would hold the sport facility liable if proper precautions were not used to prevent such an accident. Second, patrons may attempt to hold the sport facility liable for conditions such as frostbite or other ailments caused by standing in the cold too long before entering the facility. Third, patrons may try hold the sport facility liable for towing or starting costs if they are unable to start their cars and the sport facility did not assist them. Finally, if the patrons were unable to drive home and the facility management refused to allow them to stay, the patron may hold the sport facility liable for any subsequent accidents on the way home. All of these examples are real life risks that have occurred at various sport facilities.

The sport facility manager has now identified potential risks that may arise due to inclement weather conditions. But as mentioned earlier, risk management is a four step process. The second step is to assess the risk. The purpose of this stage is to determine the severity of loss arising from the risk and the frequency of occurrence of the risk.

Risk Assessment

The two criteria in assessing should be the severity of loss and frequency. The following matrix provides a consistent approach in this assessment process (Mulrooney & Farmer, 1995).

This matrix provides 25 categories in which the facility manager can classify an

	VERY FREQUENT	FREQUENT	MODERATE	INFREQUENT	VERY INFREQUENT
VERY HIGH LOSS					
HIGH LOSS					
MODERATE LOSS					
LOW LOSS					
VERY LOW LOSS					

identified risk. These categories are sufficient to assess any identified risk. With this matrix, classify the risks that were identified in the weather example. Below is the same table with the risks placed in their proper categories.

By placing the identified risks on the matrix, the sport facility manager would

	VERY FREQUENT	FREQUENT	MODERATE	INFREQUENT	VERY INFREQUENT
VERY HIGH LOSS			Slip and fall with injury		
HIGH LOSS					
MODERATE LOSS					
LOW LOSS					Frostbite or other ailment
VERY LOW LOSS		Failure of the car to start or frozen lock			Inability to drive home

have successfully completed the assessment stage. It should be noted that risk assessment is an ongoing process always subject to change. For example, what if snowstorms become more frequent? This would most likely cause an increase in the number of patrons who slip and fall and injure themselves. The sport facility manager must be aware of such changes and assess each risk accordingly. This ongoing process occurs while developing standard operating procedures, which is the final stage in our process (Koehler, 1987). But before one moves to the final stage in the risk management process, each identified and assessed risk must be treated.

Risk Treatment

The next stage, the treatment stage, utilizes the matrix in the following manner:

	VERY FREQUENT	FREQUENT	MODERATE	INFREQUENT	VERY INFREQUENT
VERY HIGH LOSS	Avoid	Avoid	Shift	Shift	Shift
HIGH LOSS	Avoid	Avoid	Shift	Shift	Shift
MODERATE LOSS	Shift	Shift	Shift	Shift	Keep & Decrease
LOW LOSS	Keep & Decrease	Keep & Decrease	Keep & Decrease	Keep & Decrease	Keep & Decrease
VERY LOW LOSS	Keep & Decrease	Keep & Decrease	Keep & Decrease	Keep & Decrease	Keep & Decrease

Avoidance

Risks should be avoided when they cause a high degree of loss and occur frequently. A sport facility should consider not holding an event if there is the possibility of large monetary losses. Scheduling an event or allowing an activity that has caused property damage or lawsuits, or both, at other facilities would not be prudent. These types of events and activities should be avoided altogether. A sport facility manager is also an effective risk manager if he or she does not allow the event or activity to take place thereby eliminating all potential and probable losses (Mulrooney & Farmer, 1995).

Transferring Risks

The treatment of identified and assessed risks usually relies on the sport facility manager's knowledge of when certain losses are likely to occur. Although it is often difficult to determine the severity and frequency of losses involved, a risk matrix can assist in this identification process. Although some risks are identified as problem areas, they should not always be considered immediate concerns, and therefore do not have to be avoided.

The question then becomes, why transfer some risks and avoid others? First, the combination of severity and frequency may not be large enough to warrant avoiding the risk. But it may be large enough to cause substantial monetary damage to the sport facility. The result of this situation is to transfer the risk to somebody who is willing to take the risk. In other words, one should obtain INSURANCE!

This method of transferring risk is very simple. The insurance company negotiates a liability policy with the sport facility to cover certain risks that fall within the facility's transfer zone on the matrix. The sport facility will pay premiums to the insurance company, and in return the insurance company will pay any claims that patrons may have under covered risks, subject to the limits and terms of the policy.

Workers' compensation is another way to transfer some of the liability arising from an injury. Workers' compensation provides benefits to an employee (workers' compensation only applies to employees) of a sport facility who suffers an injury in the course of and arising out of an employee's employment. Sport facilities pay workers' compensation premiums much the same way that they would pay for other insurance premiums. Just as insurance policies have limitations on how much will be paid, workers' compensation claims also have limitations based on the type of injury suffered by the employee.

Keeping and Decreasing Risks

Finally, the sport facility manager can keep the risk and can attempt to decrease the amount of loss the risk that could occur. In the matrix, risks that are kept and decreased, are those that have low or very low potential for loss. A sport facility can keep these risks because there is very little chance of having a substantial amount of loss. This assumes that the sport facility manager takes proper precautions to decrease the occurrence and monetary losses associated with the risk. This can be accomplished through standard operating procedures or SOP's. (Mulrooney & Farmer, 1995).

Standard Operating Procedures

When a sport facility manager develops a strategic plan that will be the most efficient and effective way to decrease the occurrence of the risk, it becomes the SOP. The SOP is a set of instructions giving detailed directions and appropriate courses of action for given situations. SOPs should be developed for all risks, except those that are avoided. The reasons are obvious for developing SOPs. But one may ask why develop SOP's for risks that are being transferred to someone else?

Let us take insurance, for example. If the sport facility manager does not try to reduce the frequency or properly handle the risks that have been transferred, more claims against the insurer of the sport facility will occur (Koehler, 1987). This will eventually cause the insurer to raise the facility premiums to cover the risks in question. By having SOPs to properly handle and possibly reduce the occurrence of risks, the insurer will not raise the premiums the sport facility pays to cover those risks. Thus, sport facilities can save money through properly managing transferred risks.

With the entire risk management process now complete, let us finish the snowstorm example mentioned earlier.

Snow Storm Treatment

From the matrix, it becomes apparent that the sport facility manager should transfer the risk of a patrons slipping and falling and should keep and decrease the risks of frostbite or other ailments, cars not starting or frozen locks, and patrons who are unable to drive home. In real terms, the sport facility manager would obtain liability insurance to cover a patrons slipping and falling on the premises; proper staffing will alleviate the frostbite problem; and adequate maintenance vehicles equipped with jumper cables solves the dead battery problems. However, the final problem of stranded patrons requires a more sophisticated SOP. The sport facility manager's SOP must provide a place for stranded patrons to stay, adequate food, and building personnel to watch over the patrons. The sport facility must ensure the safety of the patrons, their cars, and personal belongings while they

```
┌──────────────────────────────────────────────────────────────────┐
│                                                                    │
│                    SWITCHBOARD              DATE_____          │
│                                                                    │
│               BOMB THREAT PROCEDURE         TIME_____          │
│                                                                    │
│      Keep caller talking - give excuses (can't hear, bad connection,│
│                            etc.)                                    │
│      Caller's message (exact):_____  │
│      _____  │
│      _____  │
│      _____  │
│                                                                    │
│      Where is it?_____  │
│      What time will it go off?_____  │
│      What does it look like?_____  │
│      What kind of bomb is it?_____  │
│      Why are you doing this?_____  │
│      Who are you?_____  │
│      DETAILS OF CALLER                                              │
│              Man / Woman / Child            Old / Young            │
│      Voice:  loud - soft - raspy - high pitch - pleasant - deep -  │
│              intoxicated                                            │
│                                                                    │
│      Manner: calm - angry - rational - irrational - coherent -     │
│              incoherent - emotional - righteous - laughing          │
│                                                                    │
│      Speech: fast - slow - distinct - distorted - stutter - nasal -│
│              slurred - lisp                                         │
│                                                                    │
│      Background Noises: factory - trains - planes - bedlam - animals -│
│              music - quiet - office machines - voices - street - party│
│              - kids                                                 │
│                                                                    │
│      Language: excellent - good - fair - poor - foul               │
│                                                                    │
│      Accent: local - foreign - race                                │
│                                                                    │
│                                                                    │
│              DO NOT DISCUSS THE CALL WITH ANYONE ELSE!!!!           │
│                                                                    │
└──────────────────────────────────────────────────────────────────┘
```

FIGURE 7-1 - SAMPLE SOP FOR BOMB THREATS

wait for the storm to subside.

Keeping and Decreasing Risk Using SOPs

When a facility manager decides to keep and decrease risks, he or she must be ready to develop SOPs that will insure that each situation which arises is handled in a manner that will reduce the chance of liability. No one SOP will work all the time. But the fact that a facility has set policies and procedures to implement when certain events occur is a good indicator, in the case of a lawsuit, that reasonable care was taken to prevent any injury to patrons.

There are two basic times to develop SOPs. The facility manager can develop SOPs either before or after an event takes place. In order to develop SOPs for events that have not yet occurred, the facility manager must take great care to evaluate the potential risks. He or she will want to be relatively certain that the event in question will actually take place. Once this determination is complete the facility manager should develop the SOP. Because the event has not yet occurred, gathering adequate data to develop the SOP will be important. The manager may want to talk to various other facility managers to discover what they have done in similar situations. This will give the facility manager the chance to learn from the mistakes of others as well to capitalize on the correct judgments already made. If the event in question is so unusual that similar circumstances cannot be found, then the manager should ask questions like the following in order to arrive at a plausible SOP:

- What are the costs involved with not handling the risk or event properly?
- Are these costs relatively high or low on the risk matrix?
- If they are high, how many patrons will be at risk?
- Can proper personnel be reached quickly to assist the patrons?
- Are there proper facilities on the premises to take care of the situation?
- If not, is there quick access to the necessary facilities?

These questions do not develop an SOP, but they do make the facility manager aware of the surrounding circumstances.

Risk-Management Summary

This chapter has identified what risk management is, how it relates to sport facility management, and how a facility manager goes about creating a risk-management plan. This has been a general overview of the process. For illustrative purposes, this process has been placed into graphic form.

The Risk Management Process

As readers can see, the four stages are represented by the large arrows. They are all interconnected parts of risk management. The ellipse and arrows represent the concept of risk management as an ongoing process. It is extremely important to realize that risk management is a dynamic process that must continually be analyzed and modified.

Insurance

As previously mentioned, one method of treating risk is to transfer it to someone else. One main way of doing this is to acquire insurance that will pay for losses that occur due to various risks (Hallman & Rosenbloom, 1985). This method is the most certain way to transfer risk. Why? Once the facility manager is able to sift through the legal terminology and the other complexities found in insurance policies, he or she will be able to know exactly what type of risks are covered and how much coverage is available to the facility. There are several ways to insure the facility, and there are different types of insurance. The first method to be examined is self-insurance.

Self-insurance does not shift the risk of loss to another; instead, the facility will allocate funds to specific risks, and these funds will be used exclusively for the payment of claims from this risk. In essence, the facility is simply paying the premium to itself. But this is not as easy as it sounds, nor is the loss minimized efficiently. The facility, in all likelihood, will have to pay more into a risk account than if it were to pay an insurance company to write a policy. For example, to have coverage of $100,000 for each patron who falls on ice during an event, the facility would actually have to set aside $100,000 in an account specifically for falls due to ice. This works out to be roughly $830 per month. If the facility purchased insurance for this same risk, the premium would be much lower for the same coverage. From this example two things should become apparent. First, if a facility manager decides to self-insure some risks, these risks should fall into the lower right hand corner of the risk matrix. These risks should have low dollar loss potential and should occur infrequently. Second, commercial insurance is a more efficient use of funds because the facility will have to dedicate fewer dollars for the same amount of coverage than by self-insuring.

For most major risks, commercial insurance will be the most effective way to manage the risks. Some of the terms relating to insurance are

1. *Adjuster*: a representative of the insurance company who determines the liability of the insurance company if a claim is made due to a specific covered loss.

2. *Agent*: an individual whose primary responsibility is to negotiate and sell insurance contracts to those seeking insurance.

3. *Deductible*: the amount that the insured must pay on a claim before the insurer pays on a claim.

4. *Claim*: the act of the insured requesting payment due to the occurrence of an event included in the policy.

5. *Insurer*: the company that agrees to pay claims according to the terms of the insurance contract.

6. *Insured*: the individual or company that carries the insurance in order to avoid large monetary losses upon the occurrence of certain events.

7. *Liability*: a legal term that for insurance purposes refers to the amount of money that the insurer will have to pay under the terms of the policy.

8. *Premium*: a periodic payment made to the insurer in order to make certain that the policy is in effect and that the contract will be

performed according to its terms.

9. *Policy*: a contract between the insured and the insurer that provides the specific agreements made on events covered, the amount covered, the premiums to be paid, etc.

10. *Policy Limits*: the maximum dollar amounts that the insured is liable for based on the policy terms (Hallman & Rosenbloom, 1985).

There are many types of insurance in existence, and not all apply to the needs of a facility. The following are examples of the types of insurance that facilities must carry in order to provide complete protection from potential risks.

Personal Injury Liability Insurance. As the name suggests, if someone is injured through something that the facility management did or did not do, then the patron was injured personally and can sue to recover appropriate damages. Let us assume that the relevant insurance clause reads: "insurer agrees to pay up to $100,000 on any personal injury action brought against insured." Now, when talking about injuries, the reference is not limited to physical injury, but injury to a person's reputation, or emotional well being, may be sufficient for the patron to recover damages from the facility. A few examples of what would be covered under the insurance policy include

1. A security guard uses excessive force and breaks a patron's nose.

2. A security guard announces to the crowd that the patron in custody is insane and belongs a radical terrorist group. These are untrue statements, and the patron loses business because some of his customers saw the incident.

3. A patron slips and falls on a spill that had not been cleaned up properly, soiling his or her new pants.

All of these incidents would be covered under the personal injury clause of the insurance policy. But, if in Incident #2, the damages caused to the patron are $150,000 and there is no deductible for this part of the policy, the facility would then be liable for the $50,000. It is understandable then that the amount of the policy is extremely low. Although there is no "safe" amount of coverage, adequate coverage may well be in the six-figure range.

Paying the patron is not an automatic occurrence. A cost-analysis process must take place between the facility manager, the facility's attorney, and the insurance company's adjusters. Take the example of the patron whose nose was broken. Assume that the patron started the fight, there are witnesses who will testify that excessive force was not used, and no opposing witnesses exist. Most people would want to go to court because of an apparently airtight case. However, if going to trial would cost the facility $7,500 and the patron is only asking $6,000, would going to trial be the most cost-effective solution? Of course not! Sound awful? If the case is taken to court, the insurance company will pay out $7,500 win or lose. If they settle with the patron, the most they will lose is $6,000, and odds are, in a settlement, the patron would get less money.

Sad as this scenario may be, it is a frequent occurrence. Justice and righteousness take a back seat to dollars and cents in the world of big business, and facility management is big business.

In summary, personal injury insurance is purchased by the facility in order to prevent losing large sums of money when patrons bring a claim against the facility due to a personal injury.

Property Insurance. The facility and its fixtures represent a large investment. This investment is at risk each time an event is held. When people come to the facility certain individuals do not care what they damage or destroy. This is especially true if the event is a rowdy concert where a good portion of the patrons are intoxicated. This combination leads to damage of light fixtures, seats, and anything else not fastened down.

Perhaps these are the types of events that facility managers would want to avoid. But concerts can generate lots of revenue, and profit offsets the amount of damage that the patrons do to the facility. Self-insurance is an option, but as mentioned earlier, too much revenue would have to be dedicated to this type of event, and the profits would drop significantly. The solution is property insurance.

There are two basic types of property insurance to be considered. First is "Named Perils" insurance. As indicated, this coverage will only be for certain events that are specifically mentioned in the insurance policy. The following is a list of the most common perils

- fire
- lightning
- vandalism
- malicious mischief
- hail
- explosion
- smoke
- windstorm

Most of the events mentioned are natural occurrences and virtually uncontrollable. This list of events is rather large, but if more extensive coverage is needed then the "All-Risk" policy is a better choice. In addition to the events listed above, an all risk policy would include

- collapse
- burglary
- freezing of plumbing
- falling objects

Although this list is broader than the "Named Perils" list, items such as ordinary wear and tear, earthquakes, floods and general building deterioration would not normally be included. So the name "All Risks" is somewhat of a misnomer because there will be some exclusions specifically mentioned in the policy.

Listing certain events is only one section of a policy; it also must include what property items are covered. Facility managers may choose one or two types of property insurance. The first policy type is blanket insurance. This type of insurance would be the best in situations where it is difficult to estimate the value of all structures and the contents of each structure. Blanket insurance provides for coverage in a single sum for all structures and their contents.

In contrast, scheduled insurance provides the insured with the opportunity to list specific items within the policy and an associated amount with each item. This type of insurance would be of benefit if the facility manager could easily assign a value to separate structures and the contents of the structure. This increases the likelihood that in the event of a loss, reimbursement for all enumerated items will be more accurate, thereby providing more equitable coverage for the facility. But the benefit of this type of policy may also be a detriment if accurate values are not assigned to each covered item. If the items are undervalued, then the facility manager will not be able to replace the damaged items with the same type or quality item. When choosing either of these types of insurance it makes good sense to overestimate and pay a slightly higher premium than to try to save money with lower premiums and have the coverage fall short if damage does occur to the facility.

The facility manager should also elect either actual cash value or replacement cost coverage. The major difference between the two types of coverage exists in the treatment of depreciation.

Depreciation is a deduction taken from the cost of the asset over its useful life. For example, if a facility manager buys a new satellite system for $15,000 it may have a useful life of 15 years. The facility accounting department would calculate the depreciation for the first year. For example, it may be $1,312.50. This means that after depreciation is deducted for the first year, the satellite dish would have a value of $13,687.50 at the beginning of the second year.

Now, assume that at the beginning of the second year the satellite dish is struck by lightning and destroyed. The differences in the treatment of deprecation of the two coverages, actual cash value and replacement cost, became apparent. Using actual cash value, the insurance company would pay the facility $13,687.50 (the depreciated value of the property at the time of the accident). Under replacement cost, appraisals would have to be made in order to determine what the actual cost of replacement would be. Replacement cost replaces the damaged property, in this case the satellite dish, with property that is similar in type and quality with no deduction for depreciation. This type of coverage is recommended for property that is essential to the operation of the facility because it would be imperative to replace the damaged item with an item that is nearly identical or one that is better.

Workers' Compensation. Workers' compensation exists so employees of a facility can be reimbursed for injuries they suffer in the scope of their employment. In other words, this insurance will pay employees for their medical expenses and disability awards, if applicable, for job-related injuries they have suffered. Awards from worker's compensation usually are limited to the actual damages suffered, unlike personal injury awards, which will almost always include some amount of money for pain and suffering. Also, under workers' compensation there is a schedule for the maximum amount one can recover as damages for a specific injury. For example, if a stagehand loses a finger while setting up a stage for a concert, a workers' compensation table may limit damage recovery to $10,000. Depending on the body part the employee injured, the damage award will vary.

In order to recover under workers' compensation the employee must prove that he or she in fact was an employee and that at the time the injury occurred he or she was acting within the scope or course of employment. This test, in all likelihood, would preclude any employee from recovering for injuries suffered on the way to or from work.

Summary

1. Facility managers should primarily be concerned with providing their patrons with a safe and secure environment in which to enjoy the event; to do so these managers must implement an comprehensive and ongoing risk- management plan.

2. In order to conduct an effective and efficient risk-management plan all potential risks must be identified. These risks can be separated into primary and secondary risks.

3. An assessment of the frequency and severity of each risk must occur after risks have been identified. Using a risk matrix assists in placing the identified risks into their appropriate frequency and severity categories.

4. Once each risk is identified and categorized by frequency and severity, it must be assigned to a specific treatment. These treatments include avoiding the risk, transferring the possible risk to another, keeping the risk and decreasing the possibility of loss, and finally establishing standard operating procedures (SOPs) that will provide specific directions of how to handle and reduce the occurrence of risks.

5. Insurance is the usual method utilized to transfer the risk to someone else. Several types of insurance exist:

    Self-insurance: A budget is established from which the facility will pay off losses to patrons that are low in frequency and also low in severity.

    Personal Injury Liability: The insurance is specific for losses incurred by patrons due to something the facility management did or did not do.

Property: Insurance covers the facility, the fixtures, and the equipment in the facility. Some types of property insurance deal with the various misfortunes that may affect a facility, such as fire and flood, whereas others are specific to the specific pieces of equipment.

6. Workers' compensation is paid to employees for any injuries that occurred to them while they were working.

Questions

1. Identify and define the various stages involved in the risk-management process.

2. Identify and provide an example for each method of risk reduction.

3. Define depreciation and workers' compensation.

4. What are SOPs?

5. Should SOPs be utilized in decreasing or at least stabilizing present facility risks? Justify.

References

Berlonghi, A. (1990). *The special events risk management manual.* Dana Point, CA: Alexander Berlonghi.

Hallman, G., & Rosenbloom, J. (1985). *Personal financial planning.* New York: McGraw- Hill.

Kaiser, R. A. (1986). *Liability and law in recreation, parks and sports.* Englewood Cliffs, NJ: Prentice Hall.

Koehler, R. W. (1987). *Law, sport activity and risk management.* Champaign, IL: Stipes Publishing Co.

Mulrooney, A., & Farmer, P. (1995). Managing the facility. In B. Parkhouse (Ed.), *The management of sport: Its foundation and application* (2nd ed.) (pp. 223-248). St. Louis, MO: Mosby-Year Book.

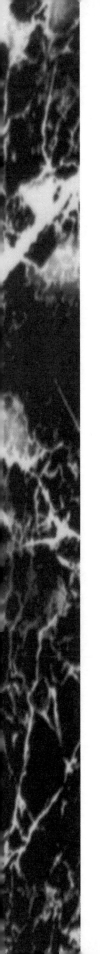

MARKETING,
ADVERTISING,
AND PUBLIC
RELATIONS

CHAPTER 8

MARKETING

Marketing within a sport facility enterprise involves many of the same activities as any other business environment. Through buying, borrowing, and earning media efforts, the facility marketing operation is responsible in great part for putting patrons in the seats and influencing the facility's bottom line.

Marketing, according to O'Shaughnessy (1988),

> Is the process of planning and executing conception, pricing, promotion, and distribution of ideas, goods, and services in order to create exchanges (remuneration) that satisfy individual and organizational objectives. Marketing is those activities that relate the organization to those parts of the outside world that use, buy, sell, or influence outputs it produces or the benefits and services it offers (p.6).

Facility Marketing

Marketing a facility successfully involves a thorough knowledge of the history and purpose of the facility, as well as the local political environment. Facility marketing requires support and input from all individuals and groups associated, directly or indirectly, with the facility. Additionally, today's facilities are mandated to be cost-effective and cannot be in deficit situations. Facility marketing operations provide increased sales and profitability through defining or targeting their market area, developing positioning strategies, researching consumer needs, and developing a sales and advertising support base. These directions can be met by a facility providing a first-class marketing environment that includes advertising, direct selling, image, packaging, market assessment and research, planning, promotion, public relations, and organizational structure to facilitate the process.

Philosophically, marketing attempts to serve the needs and desires of the patrons. Pragmatically, scheduling events, both current and future, is an attempt to satisfy these perceived needs. Facility managers who attempt to meet immediate patron needs and anticipate future changes can provide a more efficient and effective market in which the community patron is satisfied and the facility becomes more profitable.

The primary responsibility of the facility marketing department is to put patrons in the seats for events and to keep them coming back. Although there are many methods of marketing the sport facility, there is no substitute for a satisfied patron.

Sport Characteristics

Facilities that service sport possess several unique characteristics that have a significant impact on marketing efforts. These characteristics are

- Intangibility: Sports by their very nature are intangible, as they cannot be touched, smelled, seen, or heard before the actual activity takes place (e.g., The Super Bowl, World Series, or the Final Four).

- Emotional Attachment and Identification: Spectators feel very real attachment to their team, therefore, in many situations to the facility where the team plays. Studies in the mid-1980's have demonstrated that 95% of U.S. society is affected by sport each day.

- Perishability: Sports are perishable, and the markets for most sports activities fluctuate from season to season. Vacant seats and empty parking lots represent business that is lost forever. This combination of perishability and fluctuating demand creates problems for marketers of facility sporting events, as adjustments are necessary to make the service available during peak periods, as well as during slack times.

- Unpredictability: Sport is inconsistent and unpredictable. This has become one of the main attractions of the sport. No spectators know for certain how or what the outcome will be (Mulrooney & Farmer, 1995).

Mission

The mission statement should provide direction for all facility staff members regardless of their position. An effective mission statement should focus on potential markets, rather than products. It should be realistic, achievable, motivating, and specific and should provide a long-term vision of what the operation is trying to achieve. The development of a mission statement requires the answering of two questions: "What is our business?", and "What should it be?" Answers to these questions will be different for each facility type and community. Other concerns that should be considered are the history of the organization or facility, distinctiveness of the facility, and the environment in which the facility operates (IAAM, 1990).

```
                        JOHN S. KNIGHT CENTER
                    BUILDING RULES AND REGULATIONS


I.  MISSION STATEMENT

    The John S. Knight Center is a multi-purpose, Not-For-Profit facility owned by the City of Akron and
    governed by a Board of Trustees with equal membership appointed by the City of Akron, County of
    Summit and the University of Akron. The Center is leased to the Akron/Summit Convention &
    Visitors Bureau for the purpose of providing a venue for trade shows, conferences and special events,
    and the University of Akron's Continuing Educational Programs. The mission of the John S. Knight
    Center is to provide a first class, affordable facility open to all of Akron and beyond for the purpose
    of business, education, and entertainment which will in turn create jobs, encourage new business,
    promote tourism, increase visibility and gain further recognition of Akron, Summit County and
    surrounding areas as a vibrant and dynamic destination for any type of event.
```

FIGURE 8-1 - SAMPLE MISSION STATEMENT

Objectives and Strategies

Organizational objectives are the mission statement's parameters, refined into a set of specific, measurable actions by which the facility mission can be achieved. To achieve these organizational objectives, the facility must

- develop strategies that focus on improving the position of the facility's present services with its present customer base. This is known as *market penetration*.

- seek new customers or market development.

- develop strategies that would bring new offerings to the present customer base of the facility. This is known as *product development*.

- develop a variety of facility products and services to entice new customers and markets. This area is known as *product diversification* (Mulrooney & Farmer, 1995).

Although each element is important, combining these strategic directions must be feasible and appropriate to the development of the facility.

Situational Analysis

When the facility's mission, objectives and strategies for implementation have been established, the sport facility market should be evaluated in relation to past and present results. This analysis determines future responses and attempts to identify market opportunities and constraints, taking into account market environmental influences. These influences include

- **cooperative environment** in which all parties have a vested interest in accomplishing prescribed goals and objectives

- **competitive environment** which provides entertainment alternatives within the market that rival the facility for resources and sales

- **economic environment** and changes that provide marketing opportunities and constraints

- **social environment** which indicates social trends, norms, and attitudes

- **political environment** which identifies attitudes and reactions of the general public and their effect on image and patron loyalty

- **legal environment** which includes legislation and rules designed to protect the business community and consumers (O'Shaughnessy, 1988).

The development of opportunities for a profitable facility marketing operation can arise only from changes in these environments thus creating new sets of public needs to be satisfied.

Market Research

Market research should be conducted periodically in both local and regional areas. Resultant information should identify

- the public's perceptions of the facility and potential directions that could enhance attendance and revenue,

- possible new markets and revenue sources, and

- potential customer targets.

Results of these research efforts will produce hard data, in the form of demographics or characteristics of population groups (i.e., sex, age), geographic information (i.e., geographic location) and psychographics (i.e., relationships), that are critical in the facility marketing process (O'Shaughnessy, 1988).

In addition to local market research endeavors, it is important to determine the degree and range of the facility's importance throughout the industry. One method to ascertain the image of the facility, as perceived throughout the industry, is to use surveys of event promoters and other industry facilities. This will provide information pertaining to prevalent facility problems. These problems can range from poor building management and undesirable physical facilities to uncooperative and expensive media, labor problems, overlapping and competitive facilities, and excessive facility charges. This type of feedback is necessary to improve facility viability in the local area, as well as to market the facility successfully throughout entire industry.

Event Calendar

A facility must generate income and provide the community with an appropriate sports event and entertainment schedule, if it is to survive. To satisfy the public's perceived needs, a variety of events must be scheduled, in addition to the primary sport bookings. The scheduling of sports events is established as an event framework, at least one to two years in advance. Additional sports or entertainment events, known as "fillers", round out the facility event schedule. (IAAM, 1990)

Marketing Mix

The marketing mix is developed from various elements that must be managed in order to satisfy the defined target market and achieve the established organizational objectives. These key mix ingredients are merchandising or product packaging, pricing, distribution, advertising, and promotion.   In a facility environment this mix is a delicate balance. Each facility and event financially survives on the appropriateness and reaction of the public to this mix (Kotler, 1984).

Merchandising or Product Packaging. Product packaging develops an idea or concept, as a result of market research, into a final product or event for sale to the public.   In the sport-facility industry, marketing areas must be coordinated with other areas (i.e., public relations and retail sales) to provide event packaging. Facilities take on the responsibility to program internal, as well as external or promoter events that will facilitate a reduction in the occupancy problem of the facility. Additionally, each facility or community has potential sponsors that can, with assistance, package sponsorship plans to benefit not only the facility and the proposed event but also the community's budget.

Promotion. Media events, especially when associated with a professional sports enterprise, can provide substantial income from television hook-ups and radio broadcasts associated with these events.   However, even if there is no media generated income to consider, the public relations and marketing benefits, particularly over the long term, will be worth the effort put into these events.

Pricing. The price of a ticket is an important and complex decision in the development of facility sporting events.   Once published, this price should be maintained, to limit public confusion and potential problems. According to the IAAM (1990), ticket price should be determined by

·   public demand;

·   availability, such as seating configuration and capacity;

·   cost of producing the event (i.e., general and fixed costs);

·   the type of product, identifying characteristics such as perishability and distinctiveness (e.g., national basketball championship); and

·   environmental influences (i.e., government regulation and competition).

Distribution. The box office of the facility is the general distribution channel of the event for the buyer or public (Morgan, 1990). This area, further discussed in "Business Operations", works closely with the marketing department of the facility management. The mission of the box office is to facilitate audience selection by providing patron tickets and generating facility income. Additionally, it is one of the initial contacts made with the public and tends to influence a patron's impression of the facility, as well as his or her intention to return for future engagements.

Summary

1. The marketing of a sport facility includes several different variables, but the bottom line is to fill as many seats as possible for each event, with satisfied fans.

2. Sport and entertainment events are unique products that are intangible, perishable, and unpredictable.

3. A mission statement, facility objectives, and strategies are key elements used to establish a marketing plan.

4. Market research is necessary to identify the groups of patron attending facility events, the types of events they are interested in, and the means of improving facility business practices to attract additional event promoters.

5. In order to define the target number and achieve management objectives, a marketing mix must be identified. This mix includes elements that define the product, the price of the product, distribution site of the product, and the methods of product promotion.

Questions

1. Define the concept of facility marketing and say why it is important.
2. Define and discuss strategic marketing and elements.
3. Discuss the role of sponsorship in facility marketing.

References

International Association of Auditorium Managers (IAAM). (1990). Course materials from the unpublished proceedings of the School for Public Assembly Facility Management, Ogelbay, VA.

Kotler, P. (1984). *Marketing essentials*. Englewood Cliffs, NJ: Prentice Hall.

Morgan, L. (1990, Summer). Yes, public relations begins at the box office. *Facility Manager*, pp. 20-21.

Mulrooney, A., & Farmer, P. (1995). Managing the facility. In B. Parkhouse (Ed.), *The management of sport: Its foundation and application* (2nd ed.) (pp. 223-248). St. Louis, MO: Mosby-Year Book.

O'Shaughnessy, J. (1988). *Competitive marketing: A strategic approach*. Boston: Unwin Hyman.

CHAPTER 9

ADVERTISING

Advertising is any paid form of impersonal presentation of ideas, goods, or services by an identified sponsor. It is the communication process that creates messages through words, ideas, sounds, and other forms of audiovisual stimuli designed to affect consumer behavior. For this message to be effective, the idea or message is transmitted from the sender to the receiver or audience through some form of advertisement or public announcement (Patton, Grantham, Gerson, & Gettman, 1989).

The goal of advertising is that the message be understood by the audience and create a favorable impression. In a facility operation there are four elements vital to this process: the product or event, the potential buyer or patron, the seller or promoter, and the box office. This facility advertising operation is a result of advertising either "bought" or purchased from media sources, "bartered" through tradeouts with media and sponsors, and "earned" or free through news media sources.

There are two types of advertising utilized in a facility operation: facility advertising and event advertising.

Facility Advertising

Facility advertising can be described as bought (i.e., purchased with real dollars), bartered (i.e., traded) or earned (i.e., news or publicity that is considered free). Regardless of the methodology, facility advertising attempts to deliver a message to the intended audience while keeping their attention long enough for them to read and understand. Most facilities facilitate their message through brochures with information and pictures that are professionally produced. Although an expensive proposition, brochures are useful for several years. In all materials produced, the facility must be portrayed as a multipurpose venue, catering to each client's special needs and concerns. For example, most sport facilities can

LIGHTED SIGNS ARE A COMMON METHOD OF ADVERTISING IN FACILITIES.

accommodate trade shows, conventions, and concerts as well as reception rooms for dinner or cocktail parties prior to or after sports specific events.

Event Advertising

Event advertising may be the facility's responsibility depending upon the promoter(s) and availability of ready-made or instant media materials. The type of advertising materials used can affect or influence how well the event sells. It is necessary that radio and television spots or commercials be of quality, from a production, as well as public consumption, point of view. Information presented to the public audience should be correct and in a sequence considered appropriate. Other considerations could be the use of appropriate songs, in which particular hooks or lines are instantly recognizable and the music "bed" or soundtrack with voice-over or verbal soundtrack, conveying the desired promotional message.

When developing a series of promotional spots, there must be an awareness of the event parameters and their effect on message timing. Radio spots may require several progressive cuts to focus on specific information targeted at the public. For example, "Event advertising begins on Friday and tickets go on sale on Monday." On Monday the radio spots should be changed to say "tickets now on sale." The week of the event, a change would be made to say "this Saturday night", and on the day of the event the commercial could say "tonight." Monitoring every media spot to make certain of its quality and public message is crucial to the result.

SCOREBOARD ADVERTISING HAS BOTH FIXED, LIGHTED ADVERTISING
AND REVOLVING ADVERTISING WITH THE LIGHTED MATRIX.

Target Advertising

The facility market is divided into three levels. These levels identify local, regional, and national markets (Ray, 1982). From generated demographic, geographic, and psychographic research, the facility can target the "who" and "where" in the market. When advertising the facility, or proposed events, or both, advertisements should be specific for specific markets and audiences. For example, advertising in *Marketing News*, should focus on the marketing aspects of the facility, whereas advertising in *Sports Illustrated* requires sports materials (i.e., pictures of sporting events) as the centerpiece or focus of the message (IAAM, 1990).

A successful method of target advertising to potential clients is through direct mail. This technique provides a much better chance of the information being read and utilized than do others (i.e., address the envelope by hand and mark it personal and confidential). Another targeting method is the use of novelty items (i.e. letter openers, calendars, desk pads, pen and pencil sets, coffee cups, or completed event photos) as giveaways or promotional tools.

Throughout North America, sport facilities compete intensely for sport and event business. To assist in these procurement efforts, the community should be educated about its services, contributions, and specialties that benefit both the facility or the community, or both. For example, a logo communicates the facility name as well as its services to potential users. In Florida, for example, there are facilities in every major city. Regional and local advertising must be able to differentiate facility differences, and a logo assists in this endeavor.

Advertising Agencies

An advertising agency interprets to the public the advantages of a product or service. Facility event advertising is directed to the customer or end user, who buys a product or attends a performance to satisfy his or her own needs and enjoyment. The message conveyed is an emotional appeal that utilizes information developed from demographic research and is then packaged appropriately. This package is usually developed through some form of advertising agency with the goal of providing the facility with effective advertising and an appropriate public message.

There are three advertising options that can be utilized within a sport and public assembly facility: a full-service agency, event advertisers, or an in-house agency.

Full-Service agency. The full-service advertising agency is a contract agency that provides research, creative, and media-buying services for the client. These fee-based agencies can perform such marketing services as sales promotion, publicity, event packaging and design, strategic market planning, and sales forecasting. The advantages of a full-service agency to the sport facility are (a) the availability of individuals with special skills and knowledge; (b) the ability to influence the media; and (c) the ability to coordinate advertising and marketing services. This service usually involves a flat fee commission of 15% on all advertising placed on behalf of the facility.

Event advertisers. Event promoters, such as the Harlem Globetrotters, have their own advertising methods and materials. These companies have the ability to make media contacts independently of the facility or advertising agency (Comte, 1989). At times, these promotional groups may work through the facility organization, especially on the tasks of distributing tickets and developing media trades. It is important to remember that each time a promoter contracts, a charge will be levied for that service to the facility.

In-House agency. Many promoters welcome the opportunity to use an in-house agency, as it makes their job easier. The facility, due to their tremendous event volume, has the ability to purchase media coverage at significant discounts. The facility is a volume buyer and the more media bought, the more bargaining power it enjoys. The in-house agency usually assists with advertising for outside promoters, as well as in-house promotions. These in-house operations usually net the in-house agency a 15% commission on all advertising placed. This financial incentive is the major reason for a facility to develop its own in-house agency, as it impacts the profitability of the entire facility operation.

The responsibilities of an in-house agency are by no means insignificant. If the advertised event is not successful, and substantial losses are incurred, due to inappropriate advertising buys, insufficient advertising budget, lack of appeal in the designated market, inappropriate timing or ticket prices being too high, the facility would have no recourse but to offset the deficit through forfeiture of the advertising commission. As an independent agency, the facility is responsible for all encumbrances.

Trade-Outs.   In the operation of a facility, it has become an industry practice when purchasing radio or television time that a portion of the buy should be in the form of a trade for tickets. Most media have some type of policy that prohibits trading products for services; however, it is usually negotiable. Today, in most markets, trade-outs are a standard procedure. It would be rare if a media source, such as a radio and television station, would not trade for airtime.

The development of the advertising budget of a facility is usually based on a gross buy basis and does not include trades. Trade-outs, although common practice in the industry, provide a vehicle for additional advertising without actually spending real money.

During the course of negotiations with a substantial number of media buys annually, a number of hypothetical situations or proposals can be presented to influence the outcome. These may include

1. An event does not sell out; the available tickets are counted as no value, and used to trade for advertising opportunities. A standard trade-out consists of offering two or more tickets in the front row of an event.

2. A media outlet (i.e., radio or television station) sponsors or "fronts" an event by tying the initial facility advertising purchases to a specific facility promotion or event. A radio station, for example, may offer a front row promotion including limousine service to and from the show, dinner, and front row seats for the event. Other trade-out situations could include event title or co-event sponsorship from a media source in exchange for advertising benefits.

The establishment of solid relationships with media, over time and through substantial media purchases, can facilitate a radio or television station's sponsoring or "fronting" an event. At all times the facility must carefully convey the impression that real dollars can be written off the facility budget if the media becomes involved in trade-outs, deals, and generally help in promoting facility events (IAAM, 1990).

Media Personnel

Facility marketing and advertising personnel should have contacts within all local media organizations. These contacts should include program directors who are knowledgeable about the market and able to assist in evaluating the potential success of an event. In addition sales managers are primarily responsible for effecting trade-outs, deals, or promotions involving events.

Media sales personnel are usually paid by commission rather than by salary. They must be made to realize that trading for airtime is a positive step. Not only do trade-outs contribute to their income in the long run, but radio airtime also is of no value if it is left unsold. This same philosophy applies to event ticket sales. Tickets that remain unsold can be used to generate interest in the event. These unsold tickets may be used as complimentary tickets or as promotional incentives for sponsors and VIPs.

Advertising Budget

An advertising budget is a detailed plan to finance all advertising endeavors. It is usually a part of the facility marketing budget. This financial plan should differentiate among events, markets, media, and specific time periods (Ray, 1982). The advertising budget, which is part of the marketing budget, is determined by one of four methods:

- percentage of sales method or a percentage, usually 3% to 10% of gross event sales generated

- what-can-be-afforded method or an apportionment of the advertising budget based on management's projections

- task or objective method where advertising is an investment or cause of sales

- research budget method where the advertising budget is focused to research findings, such as media reports and surveys

Depending on management philosophy, one or more of these budget alternatives will be responsible for the development of the advertising, and possibly the entire marketing budget.

Sales Promotions

Today, sales promotion has become an important marketing tool. There are three major reasons that people come to watch sporting events: (a) They want to witness a specific promotion; (b) spectators know something of the activity being performed, and (c) the event is socially appealing.

Sales promotion has been defined as those marketing activities, other than personal selling, advertising, and publicity, that stimulate consumer purchasing and seller effectiveness (Bradley, 1992). Sales promotional techniques used in conjunction with sports events are

- contests

- coupons

- child discounts

- advance discounts

- family discounts

- senior-citizen discounts

- season subscriptions

- group sales

- advance mail-order

- corporate sponsorship

- phone solicitation

- on-air interviews

Ticket Sales

There are three basic types of ticket sales: season tickets, mini-plans or partial season tickets and group sales. Season tickets are those seats sold to companies or individuals for the entire season. This package ensures the ticket holder the right to a seat for every event, except play-offs. Season ticket holders may also be eligible to attend special events, such as concert series packages.

Mini-plans are partial season ticket packages, where the ticket purchasers select from groups of games or other events they desire to attend. The individuals are then assured of a seat at only those specified events. The mini-plans are becoming more popular with sports patrons, as all teams do not have local spectator appeal.

Group sales are relatively new, but increasingly important to the facility marketing operation. This is an attempt to sell tickets to various facility events through corporate avenues. These tickets are usually sold in advance of the performance at a discount or group rate. Organizations often involved in this group sales efforts are students, senior citizens, and community groups, such as Boy Scouts and Lion's Clubs.

Summary

1. Advertising is an important method of creating a favorable impression about a sport facility or event by using various media presentations that are paid for, traded for, or provided for free.

2. The message of advertising may be proved by either a full-service agency, or the event promoters, or through in-house methods. Although in-house advertising is undeniably the most cost-effective, certain risks normally taken by the commercial advertisers must now be assumed by the facility management.

3. Trade-outs are an industry-wide practice similar to bartering. The facility usually provides tickets to certain service companies such as radio and TV stations in return for airtime advertising the facility or the upcoming event.

4. Sales promotions are being used as marketing tools to bring more spectators to the facility or specific event. These promotions often take the form of a giveaway or discount.

5. Tickets are generally sold through full-season plans, partial-season plans, or group sales. Various sales promotions may be used in conjunction with these various ticket strategies.

Questions

1. Define advertising and its role in the facility operation.

2. Discuss the differences between advertising options.

3. What are trade-outs? Why would a facility want to use them?

4. Under what circumstances would you use in-house advertising agency, what-can-be-afforded advertising budget and crisis media management?

References

Bradley, M. (1992, July). Leading role players. *Athletic Management*, 17-21.

Comte, E. (1989, March 6). And the tide rushes in. *Sports Inc.*, 42-43.

International Association of Auditorium Managers (IAAM). (1990). Course materials from the unpublished proceedings of the School for Public Assembly Facility Management, Ogelbay, VA.

Patton, R., Grantham, W., Gerson, R., & Gettman, L. (1989). *Developing and managing health-fitness facilities*. Champaign, IL: Human Kinetics.

Ray, M. (1982). *Advertising and communication management*. Englewood Cliffs, NJ: Prentice Hall.

CHAPTER 10

MEDIA AND PUBLIC RELATIONS

Advertising messages must be transmitted through particular communication channels or media, which vary according to efficiency, selectivity, and cost. Selection of the most appropriate media is not an easy task, as numerous types and combinations are available.

The primary media classifications are

- newspapers and direct mail distribution

- electronic or broadcast media, such as radio and television outlets

- position media, such as billboards and signage of all types

- point-of-purchase media, such as message centers, marquees, and telephone selling

Determining the appropriate media type or media combination to use will depend upon various factors. For instance, specific events appealing to specific age demographics should be communicated through very narrow channels; the nature and size of the target market limit appropriate advertising media. Other factors include the advertising budget and media effectiveness and efficiency (Wilcox, Ault, & Agee, 1988).

Public Relations

Public relations (PR) is vital to the development and maintenance of the goals and objectives of facility marketing. Public relations is the management function through which an organization attempts to attract and retain attention, understanding, confidence or support, or both, from the people whose opinions are important to the organization. It differs from advertising in that the organization does not control the actual message or the medium, but is based on the reactions of others to the actions of the organization. All employees in the organization are involved in PR, from the telephone operator to the parking lot attendants.

Publicity or Earned Media

Publicity or "earned media" are unpaid, nonpersonal communications directed at the public. Publicity is usually in the form of news, press conferences, editorial comments, or Public Service Announcements (P.S.A). The facility supports and encourages this type of media, as it does not cost any hard money. However, it does require years of attention and catering to the needs of the media. The facility reaps the benefits of this free media through constant media coverage, reporting of facility events and, it is hoped, increased attendance (IAAM, 1990).

PRESSRELEASE

<Organization> • <Address> • <City, State Zip> • <Telephone> • Fax: <Fax>

For Immediate Release

Date: November 17, 1995
Contact: <Name>
Phone: <Telephone>
Fax: <Fax>

[Title of Press Release]

[City and State of Origin]—

FIGURE 10-1 - SAMPLE PRESS RELEASE FORM

The Publics

There are three publics served by sport and public assembly facilities. These are the known as the client or promoter, patrons, and the media or press. All these publics interact. The actions of one group may significantly impact others. For example, positive relations with clients could result in more event traffic, creating positive impressions with patrons and fostering positive news coverage resulting in an increase in the number of programs at the local civic center. Similarly, negative reactions from patrons due to poor facility appearance and unsatisfactory service can drive down attendance and discourage promoters, which, in turn, results in negative stories about the drop in activity and revenues at the local arena.

Client and promoter relations. The client relationship is one that is durable and has great potential for mutual profit or loss (Wilcox et al., 1988). Public relations activities directed at the client or potential client should be personal and require an investment of time and energy from top facility management. For example, the individual whose calls are not promptly returned may be the representative of a professional sports team. Even if this individual's business is not an attractive proposition for the facility, others will hear about the negative experience. The needs of all clients should be addressed, and the less professional the client the more important to adhere to this strategy.

A detailed plan should be developed to alleviate any surprises, hidden expenses, or restrictions that were not delineated in the initial contract agreement. Realistic expectations should be established so that public relations initiatives directed at potential or current clients, and made on behalf of the facility, would be a realistic projection of the client's event potential. Exaggeration and boasting of unrealistic expectations, such as sell-outs, would be unwise and possibly result in development of unfavorable future relations.

To facilitate a smooth relationship with the client an event coordinator is necessary from the initial planning stages, through event production and event closure. This individual is a required part of a successful and one hopes, recurring facility event.

Patron relations. Creating positive patron relations means creating experiences in the facility for patrons that will ensure their return. An appropriate management philosophy should be "If you like our service, tell your friends; if you don't like it, tell us." A client relationship is shaped by top management; however, the patron relationships usually rests with part-time staff, many of whom work for minimum wage (Wilcox et al., 1988). This makes it all the more important for top management to address service and performance expectations as public relations factors. The patrons' experiences are shaped by three factors: information, environment, and service.

Information. Information provided to patrons shapes their expectations. This information should be accurate, timely, and specific enough to prepare them for the event they are to attend. Information regarding parking, prohibited items, late seating, emergency phone numbers, start time, and event content need to be received before the patron ever leaves. Once at the facility, patrons rely on signage and public address announcements for direction to seating, refreshments, exits, toilets, and specialized services. Complications result when rules for one type of event differ from those for another in the same facility. Lack of adequate information can create patron anxiety, indicating there is something about attending the event that causes discomfort. This discomfort level may result in the patron's refusing to return to another event.

Environment
External and internal appearance of the facility may be the single greatest statement that public relations can make. Regardless of the event, no one enjoys

MEDIA GUIDES HELP TO ENHANCE THE IMAGE OF THE FACILITY
BY PROVIDING INFORMATION AND PROMOTING ITS STRONG POINTS.

WARNING SIGNS HELP TO MAKE ALL PATRONS HAVE A MORE
ENJOYABLE VISIT TO THE FACILITY.

attending a dirty facility. The patron will relate the condition of the surroundings to their sense of well-being. If a facility is clean, safe, well lit, accessible, with moderate temperature control, ambient noise levels, and crowd control, patrons will overall have an enjoyable experience. This good experience will prompt the patron to return.

Auxiliary Service

Auxiliary services are relatively new to the sport and public assembly facility profession. The idea consists of the facility's supplying services that attract patrons who normally could not attend the event. Examples include smoking rooms and baby-sitting services for parents attending a specific event. The Quiet Room is another example. At little or no cost to the facility, the Quiet Room provides a place where parents can wait during events their children are attending (e.g. a rock concert). This area should be comfortable offering magazines, newspapers, television, and light refreshments, for parents while they wait.

Increasing the public's awareness is vital to the success of services such as Quiet Rooms. This space will not be utilized unless the public is aware that it exists. Regardless of the service, a press release should be released to inform the public of its existence. Publicizing a successful service can create a positive public reaction, and provide the opportunity for facility staff to interact with a cross-section of the public (IAAM, 1990).

Media Relations. In times of crisis facilities hope to receive fair and balanced

THE SMOKING LOUNGE PROVIDES AN AREA FOR SMOKING IN THOSE FACILITIES THAT DO NOT ALLOW IT IN THE MAIN FACILITY AREA.

treatment from the media in order to maintain a positive image. Every facility invests time, care, and energy in its development of media relationships. The facility that ignores the media and makes no attempt to manage what is written and broadcast will suffer the consequences of negative media treatments or perhaps no media attention at all. Strategies for cultivating media relationships should be developed through a comprehensive media relations plan. Some of the plans key strategies should be

- attracting media attention through press releases, press conferences, celebrity interviews, media events and critics, and

- preparing for unwanted media attention.

Attracting Media Attention. Every facility should have a Public Relations Director, whose designated position is liaison to the local media. It is the job of this publicist to be familiar with the local working media personnel and to convince the media that the facility events are newsworthy. The PR director accomplishes this task by establishing personal contacts with editors, assignment editors, feature writers, reviewers (i.e., critics), reporters, on-air personalities, and program directors at all the local media centers. The facility with a designated PR director and appropriate local media acquaintances must attract attention that will reinforce the marketing and public relations objectives of the facility.

It is important, even in the smallest facility, that the facility manager not assume the role of PR director, because the facility manager will often be the subject of media attention by virtue of his or her managerial position. The PR person should also be someone other than the facility's advertising placement specialist. The media are universally insistent about separating their editorial coverage from their advertising interest. Facilities that can afford to observe a similar separation of responsibilities within their own ranks will have avoided the temptation to link new coverage to advertising purchases.

The Press Conference. According to W. Peneguy (personal communication, September 18, 1991), press conferences are convened to provide the media with announcements on issues, celebrities, prominent individuals, events, or openings. This event can be as much of a news item as the information itself, especially if the people involved are celebrities or prominent individuals.

When the facility is first notified of the conference, a news advisory, not a release, should be sent to remind the media editor that the event is taking place at a specific location. A follow-up phone call is placed as a reminder. The final notification should be a press release sent to all media outlets. If there is familiarity with members of the media, then a personal (handwritten) note should be attached.

In staging this event, special care must be taken to ensure the conference convenes at the most opportune time. This time is usually between 10 a.m. to 2 p.m., depending on the targeted media audience. If the afternoon newspaper is the primary target, then the press conference should occur early enough in the morning to beat the paper's deadline. If the target is the evening news, an early afternoon news conference will provide adequate time for taping and editing the material presented.

Location of the press conference must provide easy access and sufficient space to host the invited media. The site should offer ample electric power, adequate lighting, and sound (i.e., microphones and speakers), to create an appropriate environment that is intimate and comfortable. Refreshments should also be provided to ensure attendance. All media participants should be greeted at a sign-in table with information sheets, note pads, and a complete press kit or press release. To ensure questions and responses at the conference, staff employees should be supplied with information that includes attendees, titles, order of appearance, purpose of press conference, and any potential controversy.

The actual press conference should normally begin with a prepared statement being read by a visible personality. Following should be special guests and any other pertinent information, along with questions from reporters present. All presentations should be brief and to the point, with the conference being a short 30-45 minute activity, not a drawn-out affair.

The media event. The media event is commonly referred to as a publicity stunt. This staged event commands media attention, due to its unusual nature. Examples include a circus parade down Main Street or a daredevil who will sit atop the facility flagpole. This event usually heralds a larger upcoming event. In addition to the apparent insurance and legal risks, a media event could be unsuccessful and may potentially harm, rather than help, the cause of the upcoming event. This would waste valuable staff time and facility resources, as well as potentially sour relations with the local media (IAAM, 1990).

Unsolicited media attention. Reporters may develop potentially damaging stories to the image of the facility. PR directors and facility managers must insist that all personnel follow specific rules pertaining to relations with the media. For example, the PR director should be the only individual authorized to speak to the news media on behalf of the facility.

According to R. Johnson (personal communication, October 22, 1991), the facility management should develop specific policies and directions to handle media information requests. Such policies will facilitate an orderly transfer of information from legitimate sources by helping direct reporters to the authorized employees who can provide answers. For example, if a reporter has an inquiry, the manager should take the call, noting in detail the reporter's questions. The manager may use any number of plausible excuses for not answering immediately and thus provide more time. Typical responses are "I am not at my personal phone. Let me get back to my desk, I'll look up the information you want and I will call you back"; "I have people in my office. I'll have to call you back later." "I don't have those figures at my fingertips. Let me check the file and I'll call you back." Having noted the reporter's questions and provided the appropriate excuse, the manager should have the time to reflect on the appropriate response. Within a reasonable time the manager should return the reporter's call. However, another set of strategies would be appropriate when returning the call. For example, a summarized response should be provided. The manager should assume control of the conversation. Negative questions should be restated to allow for a positive response, and special care should be taken to avoid technical jargon.

Regardless of the situation, special attention must be taken to avoid making the statement "no comment." This phrase makes it appear that not all is being revealed and there is more to this situation than is being presented. To avoid this, the individual being asked the question must have time to collect his or her thoughts and then proceed with a response strategy in which the manager, not the reporter, has the upper hand. The emphasis must be on managing the questions and by using strategies of restatement, on creating a positive and less hostile environment (IAAM, 1990).

Summary

1. Public relations can be divided into paid communication directed at the public called advertising and unpaid communications called publicity.

2. Facility managers are concerned with maintaining positive relations with three distinct publics: their clients or promoters, their patrons and the media.

3. Facilities that provide adequate information to their patrons through signage, manage a clean building and furnish important auxiliary services ensure the loyalty of these patrons.

4. A public relations director is paramount in dealing with the needs, interests and demands of the media. They should have the appropriate training to conduct press conferences, write news releases and control unsolicited media attention.

Questions

1. Define the elements involved in public relations in a facility.

2. Discuss crisis public relations.

3. What two facility employees are necessary to maintain positive relations with clients or promoters and the media. Which is more important? Why?

References

International Association of Auditorium Managers (IAAM). (1990). Course materials from the unpublished proceedings of the School for Public Assembly Facility Management, Ogelbay, VA.

Wilcox, D., Ault, P., & Agee, W. (1988). *Public relations: Strategies and tactics.* Philadelphia, PA: Random House.

CHAPTER 11

FACILITY IMAGE

Image is the impression and opinion that the various publics form about the organization based on verbal, written, visual, or symbolic messages transmitted. Each consumer has a different impression of the facility. This perception is based on consumers' impressions from the service that they have received. The sum of all of these impressions by the "general public" form the image of the facility.

Images are created by various sensory impressions. To understand the building operation employees should attend facility events and seek information concerning treatment by the parking staff personnel; ticket taking at the facility entrance; impressions of the concessions and novelties; and sight, sound, and smell within the facility. All facility staff, regardless of position, from ushers to custodial personnel, should be asked to contribute information in this image-building process.

The development of the image of the facility is a long-term effort, requiring effort and capital at both the industry and local levels. To achieve the desired image level, the IAAM (1990) suggests that facility organization must consistently be involved in

- industry functions,

- publicity efforts,

- development of a safe, clean, and well-maintained facility environment,

- media accessibility, especially for the local press,

- involvement in community social and political functions, and

- maintenance of good relations with key promoters and event organizers.

According to W. Lewis (personal communication, September 14, 1991), patrons are critical of all aspects regarding a facility from parking to the quality of their seating. Every patron thinks of him or herself as an expert and will give an opinion on any topic and at any time. It is easier to tarnish an image than it is to establish or regain a good image. To cultivate image, four areas need to be enhanced: Public, Press, Politicians or Elected Officials, and Promoters.

The Public

The public or patrons are the reason the sport facility is in operation. Patrons purchase tickets, procure food, occupy seats, and are the facility's strongest supporters or its most vocal critics. The resolution of complaints should be a priority, yet a developmental process. The first step is a phone call from a facility manager to clarify facts and inform the complainant that his or her concern is being investigated. A follow-up letter is then sent to the patron outlining the action to be taken, offering apologies, and possibly offering tickets or some form of incentive to attend another event. These actions will create an image of a sensitive management and, it is hoped facilitate patrons' returning to the facility for subsequent events.

Major image areas important to the public are courtesy, cleanliness, and comfort. Courtesy begins from the patron's first contact with facility personnel, such as telephone operators, ticket takers, ushers, and security personnel. Each of these individuals and groups plays an important role in facilitating the image of the facility. This image is the facility's strongest sales and marketing tool, providing the customer with a positive view of the facility's management, staff, events, and overall facility. To achieve a positive and constant image requires a trained staff who constantly observe the rules of etiquette. The staff are the first contact that a patron will have with the facility (i.e., the receptionist or secretary who answers the telephone). Therefore, probably the most important image-building tool available to the facility is the telephone. Every member of the facility staff who uses the telephone should impart confidence, poise, and a helpful attitude, regardless of who is calling.

Cleanliness can be either a major facility image builder or detractor. Everything else can work like a well-oiled clock, but if the toilets are unclean , any previously cultivated positive image will be destroyed.

Another element is comfort. Comfort applies to seating, temperature control, smoking policies, or removal of unruly patrons. Comfort encompasses anything that provides the patron with a relaxed and trouble free visitation (IAAM, 1990).

The Media

The media can shape and build the facility's reputation. It can also be its instrument of destruction. From day one, credibility and rapport must be established with the media. To satisfactorily handle the media or press and continue image enhancement, it is necessary to keep the following guidelines in mind:

1. Any statement that is "off the record" should never be used.

2. All statements must be complete in their entirety and factually correct.

3. The press should not be able to intimidate any management or staff.

4. One should be truthful. Exaggerations or distortions should be avoided.

5. Adverse publicity may cause frustration, anger, and reaction. The media should not be encourage to dig further into any issue.

6. The staff should keep management informed at all times. The media have the impression that management is always aware of every issue involving the facility. There should be only one designated facility spokesperson.

7. Positive and constant media coverage should be facilitated by creating interesting local angles on stories and events.

8. Impromptu statements should be avoided, and the facts concerning incidents should be researched.

9. All press and media deadline constraints should be considered.

10. Management should keep language simple.

11. When preparing for a television interview, the subject area to be covered should be determined in advance, with the appropriate and official viewpoint established.

12. Management should always attempt to verify the truth of any event or story.

13. When preparing a speech, management should make sure objectives have been delineated. Responses should always appear spontaneous.

14. If planning to use visual and audio, permission from the author of the materials should always be obtained in advance.

PROVIDING NEEDED CUSTOMER SERVICES ENABLES A FACILITY
TO ENHANCE ITS IMAGE.

15. In the area of presentations and situations, there is always the need to present a positive image of the facility (IAAM, 1990).

Crisis Media Management

Events ranging from patron injury, fire, and structural failure to political confrontation with management or a last minute event cancellation are all crisis situations. Every facility manager must have a prepared crisis plan to manage these eventualities. When a crisis develops, the plan is set into motion, leaving management to deal with the content of the crisis without worrying so much about the process. This crisis plan is an attempt to manage public perceptions and reaction to the emergency situation. It should not be confused with operational emergency plans (W. Peneguy, personal communication, September 18, 1991).

Elected Officials and Politicians

Elected officials are those individuals who are chosen by voters. Other groups not elected but considered in the same category are the governor's, mayor's, and city manager's staff. These individuals are influential and can have a positive or negative impact on the operation of a public facility. The success or failure of a publicly run sport facility may depend as much on the relationship with the elected or appointed officials as it does on the success of staged events. This is also true for privately owned or as well as privately managed and publicly owned facilities.

All sport facilities, whether owned or operated by a governmental entity or not, will have some relationship with elected or appointed officials. Areas may include budget, facility control, police protection, garbage pickup, purchasing, and personnel processing, depending on the municipality and degree of political patronage.

Political fund-raisers are the lifeblood of elected officials, and usually require a large space to hold their political functions. Because most public facilities are under some type of political subdivision, politicians will attempt to rent the facility, at a discounted rate. There may be strong temptation to give into the political pressure especially if the official is an incumbent or may be the official who controls the facility.

Several choices are available: (a) The politician may be provided with a favorable situation with management hoping that the incumbent wins and that other politicians and media do not uncover the deal; or (b) a policy can be set that all political fund-raisers must pay the full price regardless of affiliations. The second choice is the appropriate one; otherwise, the facility and management would be subject to negative press and accused of collusion. There is always a risk with elected officials, and facilities should remain neutral, not become involved in political campaigns. A sport facility must be operated without compromising value systems, morals, and ethics, while at the same time maximizing the potential goals, objectives, and image of the facility (IAAM, 1990).

Promoters

The promoters are responsible for bringing the event and entertainment to the community. The image conveyed to this group must be an operation that is well managed, fair, and equitable. If the facility has unions, a smooth working relationship with those unions is essential. Promoters must feel that their problems are understood and their financial interests are being protected. These entrepreneurs are the facility's partners, not its adversaries (W. Peneguy, personal communication, September 18, 1991).

Event Image

The image of the facility is primarily determined by the mix of events. This event mix is determined by a variety of elements such as the financial impact, community interest, political climate, marketplace, and physical limitations of the facilities. Event type and mix will play a major factor in creating good relationships with patrons providing more business and assisting with the bottom line. Management is responsible for image development. It should be deliberate and attempt to create lasting positive perceptions with the paying public.

The Marketing Plan

Every facility manager expects results from his or her marketing, promotional, and public relations efforts. However, what they are, and how they fit into the overall facility direction is defined through the development of a comprehensive facility marketing blueprint. This document, known as the **marketing plan**, is the actual 'game plan' that the facility should follow in the development of a structured document with measurable goals and objectives, expectations, and specific strategies to complete the desired outcome (O'Shaughnessy, 1988). This plan is vital if the facility is to be viable and productive, and maintain marketplace leadership.

This annual plan should be developed in cooperation with all the facility departments or units. Goals and objectives should be delineated, such as increase the number of event days by 10%, increase attendance by 15%, and increase advertising sales by $50,000.00. Budget requirements, and feedback or evaluation methodology are correspondingly developed. The marketing department in any facility is primarily a sales organization, with its goal to generate income for the facility by "putting backsides in seats." For every seat that is empty, facility revenue is unrecoverable.

The elements of booking, scheduling, advertising, sponsorship, box office, food service operations, novelties, and parking are all part of the marketing team effort. Marketing, promotional, and public relations efforts per event are short term, but are the keys to success of the entire sport facility operation (IAAM, 1990).

Marketing Plan Elements

According to the IAAM (1990), there are eight key elements that need to be considered when developing the marketing plan of a facility. These eight elements should provide the reader with an understanding of the elements to be included in any comprehensive marketing plan for the facility, as well as proposed events.

1. **People:** What is the target market for the facility's product(s)? What is its size and growth potential?

2. **Profit:** What is the expected profit margin to be accrued from implementation of the marketing plan? What are the other objectives of the plan and how are they to be evaluated?

3. **Personnel:** What personnel are required to implement the plan? Are these individuals facility personnel, or are outside groups, such as advertising agencies or marketing research firms, to be involved?

4. **Product:** What product(s) will be offered? What variations in the product will be offered in terms of style, features, quality, branding, packaging, and terms of sale and services? How should products be positioned in the market?

5. **Price:** What should be the expected price or prices of the facility's products to be sold?

6. **Promotion:** What methods and in what form will information about the events of the facility be delivered to the target market?

7. **Place:** How, when and where will the products of the facility be offered to the target market?

8. **Period:** What are the expected duration, implementation, and evaluation procedures for the proposed marketing plan?

Planning

The purpose of the strategic plan is to govern and direct the organization's marketing efforts, strategies, and product positioning (Mulrooney & Farmer, 1995). The actual market plan and appraisal attempts to coherently organize the facility's marketing operations, as well as for each proposed event. In each area, advertising, public relations, promotions and image, goals, objectives, budget and evaluations must be established.

Although every facility and event are different, it is important to document the plan that will

· facilitate communication,

· establish measurable goals and strategies,

· identify a focused sales plan,

· quantify the expectations of management and staff,

· establish appropriate budget, and

· develop evaluation procedures (IAAM, 1990).

Although one can easily prepare for planned major annual events, it is impossible to anticipate unexpected events that may occur.

Parameters

An annual facility marketing plan is no different from any business marketing plan. Today, there are many commercially produced market planning tools, both in software and book versions, that can be used to create a viable and comprehensive marketing plan document. Whatever route is chosen, it is important to address the following major plan elements:

- Identifying events and marketing specific programs

- Identifying target groups, such as existing users, potential users, spectators and fans, government sponsors, corporate sponsors, the media, and the general public

- Developing objectives that will address increased public participation, generate revenue, improve or change the public image, and define specific marketing objectives to promote and satisfy the target groups and their needs.

- Completing a SWOT Analysis that identifies the strengths, weaknesses, opportunities, and threats to the facility operation

- Creating the marketing package of sponsors, promotions, public relations, personal selling, advertising, support material, and proposal to interrelate the pieces to enable multiple pay-offs.

- Developing a budget that provides cost estimates for the total marketing effort.

- Developing contingency plans for each activity that includes alternative sponsors, promotional material, and sites.

- Developing an evaluation process to determine if the plan has met the initially established objectives and strategies. This evaluation procedure should take place periodically throughout the year, but should be a definite annual occurrence. The data generated will directly affect future market and facility planning efforts (IAAM, 1990).

Event Marketing Plan

The event marketing plan addresses each event to be staged within the facility. Each event requires a marketing and operational plan that can ascertain not only the potential financial impact per event but also the potential impact on the community and other pertinent entities (Kotler, 1984). The marketing budget for the event, in many facilities, is developed as a specified portion of the income realized on each event. This amount generated could be anywhere from 3% to 12% of the gross revenue. Although there are a variety of methods used to finance events in the annual budget there should be a specific amount allocated to the marketing department as development capital for planned events.

FACILITY MARKETING PLAN
YOUNG'S CHEESE VOLLEYBALL CHAMPIONSHIPS
APRIL 19-21, 1996

FACILITY:	F & M Arena, South City, NC
EVENT:	Young's Cheese Volleyball Tournament
TIME(S):	6 p.m. - midnight Fri., Sat. and Sun.
TICKET PRICES:	$ 12, pay one price
DISCOUNTS:	$ 3 off with Young's Cheese coupon $ 3 off with Hamburger coupon
SALE DATE:	April 19, 1996
TOTAL ADVERTISING BUDGET:	$ 48,000
TARGET MARKET:	Volleyball players, families, spectators and clubs

HISTORICAL DATA

DATE EVENT LAST APPEARED:	May 23-25, 1993
TIMES:	6 p.m. - midnight Fri., Sat. and Sun.
GROSS DOLLARS:	$ 500,000.00
TICKET PRICES:	$ 9.00 w/$2.00 discounts
ADVERTISING BUDGET:	$ 38,000

GOALS

PROJECTED GROSS ($)	$ 743,000
PROJECTED TICKET SALES:	$ 68,000
PROJECTED GROUP SALES ($)	$12,000

SECTION I: PROPOSED ADVERTISING BUDGET

PRINT	$ 3,000
RADIO	$ 20,000
TV	$ 24,000
OUTDOOR/TRANSIT	$ NONE
MISCELLANEOUS	$ NONE
GROUPS	$ 500
PUBLICITY	$ 500
TOTAL	$ 48,000

DATE OF FIRST PRINT AD	April, 8, 1996
TV BEGINS	Thursday, April 10, 1996
RADIO BEGINS	Thursday, April 10, 1996

PROMOTIONS

1. Sponsorships:

a. Young's Cheese: Title Sponsor. Tags with a guarantee of $40,000 in spots over 21 days. $2 discount printed on 2 million coupons with Hamburger. Young's to supply static clings for Seven Eleven

b. Hamburger's:- $2 discounts in 18 South City, NC area locations. Mystery shopper campaign. McDonalds employee who distributes coupon to customer is awarded $5 cash prize on the spot and becomes eligible for $100 grand prize. Tags on $30,000 of media, all radio. One million coupons printed.

2. Reception night: All sponsors and media invited to a reception, April 18 to meet teams and special guests. Not important to continued sponsorship support.

MASS MEDIA

Radio stations: WEZB, WQUE, WCKW, WNOE, WUVE-TV, WYLD, WNOL-TV, and WGNO-TV. These media outlets have been determined to be the strongest and most appealing to the targeted audience and fans. Times and schedules will be developed at a later date. All information will be included on final marketing schedule.

MEDIA DEALS

Earned - Two press releases sent prior to the event. TV assignment editors to be briefed May 11 and each Monday on potential visuals. The Morning Star is scheduled to run information in the sports section. Also interviews with Will Peney and Mark Finney completed May 14 with Jill Anding. Remote WUVE scheduled.

Bought - Same as previous budget $52,000 plus production. WWL-TV has received $11,000 net buy for a matching schedule. Lead station. All other buys will be granted based upon promotional schedules and promotional packages the stations can deliver. More than 60% of paid schedule devoted to two television stations and to CHR and urban radio stations because of their abilities to hit the target market.

Trade - Included in each package. Trade exclusively (no cash) in 50-mile radius outside the city and with Metroscan (traffic reports).

GROUP SERVICES

Not a strong group event over the first 4 years. Schools are on holiday. Concentrated sales to clubs, schools, and churches. Concentration last year to downtown business was unsuccessful (W. Peneguy, personal communication, September 18, 1991).

Summary

1. Facility employees can provide valuable information regarding the image of a facility by attending various events and analyzing the services, sights and sounds and smells from a patron's perspective. Courtesy, cleanliness, and comfort must be practiced constantly.

2. Facility managers must be extremely customer service oriented. Without the patrons there are no events. Without the events there are no jobs. Therefore, dealing with the public in a friendly, courteous manner helps to ensure the continual operation of the facility.

3. Dealing with the press and politicians in a professional and ethical manner will establish solid relationships and positive feedback about the facility. "Deals" and "favors" while providing temporary rewards will ultimately hurt the reputation of the facility.

Questions

1. Discuss facility image and why it is important to a sport facility operation.

2. Discuss the elements and ramifications of developing an annual facility marketing plan.

References

International Association of Auditorium Managers (IAAM). (1990). Course materials from the unpublished proceedings of the School for Public Assembly Facility Management, Ogelbay, VA.

Kotler, P. (1984). *Marketing essentials.* Englewood Cliffs, NJ: Prentice Hall.

Mulrooney, A., & Farmer, P. (1995). Managing the facility. In B. Parkhouse (Ed.), *The management of sport: Its foundation and application* (2nd ed.). (pp. 223-248). St. Louis, MO: Mosby-Year Book.

O'Shaughnessy, J. (1988). *Competitive marketing: A strategic approach.* Boston: Unwin-Hyman.

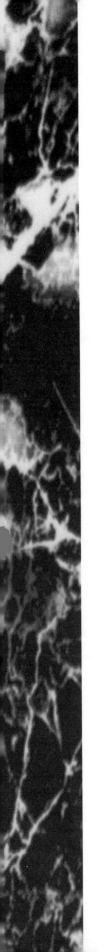

EVENT
OPERATIONS

CHAPTER 12

OPERATIONAL STRUCTURE

Operations is one of the most complex and comprehensive functions within facility operation. Facility operations managers have a variety of departmental responsibilities that include: engineering, event coordinating, security, maintenance, and housekeeping. They must possess an adequate knowledge of budgeting, cost-control, methodology, and negotiation skills to effectively complete their job responsibilities (Mulrooney & Farmer, 1995).

Operations of a facility vary significantly from other businesses, yet the basic principles are similar (Mulrooney & Farmer, 1995). Operations management controls the procedure that converts raw material into finished goods and services. Operations management in a sport facility focuses on how services are produced, rather than their production.

Management Teams

A sport facility is operated under the auspices of a management team. This team, depending upon the facility size and function, is headed by an individual titled General Manager, CEO or Executive Director. Other members of this team involve individuals who oversee Marketing, Public Relations, Advertising, and Operations. This section focuses on management elements, especially policies and procedures, philosophy, mission, organizational elements, booking and scheduling, contracts, the management manual and evaluation procedure (Mulrooney & Farmer, 1995).

Operational Areas

Within a facility there are important operational areas that need to be considered when establishing operational procedures. These areas include:

- administration,
- traffic and parking,

- security,

- first aid,

- safety and medical services,

- building maintenance,

- custodial, janitorial maintenance, and groundskeeping,

- box office,

- concession sales and catering,

- programs and novelty sales,

- building and supplementary personnel (full, part-time, and subcontracted),

- staging of events,

- tenant charges,

- marketing, public relations, and advertising,

- general policies,

- contract permit or lease agreements (IAAM, 1990).

Philosophy

The facility manager's philosophy should provide a basis for establishing guidelines and orientation towards the operations of the facility. This philosophy will provide direction to the staff, predicated on the local situation. It should also produce an environment that will provide the patrons with a high level of service, as well as exhibit fiscal responsibility through control of appropriations and revenues with a break-even or profit motive in mind (Mulrooney & Farmer, 1995).

Mission

The established mission of the building will dictate the management-control system instituted for the entity operating the facility. This mission is based on the following considerations: purpose of the business to be satisfied (i.e., sports events, public events, etc.); functions to be performed to accomplish these undertakings (e.g., housekeeping, equipment set-ups, plant maintenance, and operations); and staff requirements relative to operating costs, number of events, and what is required to provide these services (Thompson & Strickland, 1990).

Policy

Mulrooney & Farmer (1995) described a policy as "...a definitive course or method of action selected from alternatives, and in light of given conditions, to guide and determine present and future decisions" (p. 225). A policy is an outgrowth of the mission statement and the foundation of the operational procedures of the facility (Thompson & Strickland, 1990). "It is the reason or "the why" behind management's decision to function in a designated manner" (Mulrooney & Farmer, 1995, p. 225).

Procedure

Procedures are the established or traditional methods of executing the prescribed policy. They are a prescribed series of steps that need to be followed by the appropriate personnel staff members in a facility if their assigned duty is to be accomplished (Thompson & Strickland, 1990). Prior to the first event in a newly established facility, an operational philosophy, building policies, and operational procedures must be established.

The facility manager should encourage all the facility staff to be involved in the development, dissemination, and communication to personnel of the appropriate policies and procedures. It is important that after the guidelines and implementation strategies have been developed, they must be communicated clearly and effectively to all appropriate facility personnel (Mulrooney & Farmer, 1995).

Evaluation

After all policies and procedures have been documented and prior to publishing them, it is important that each item be evaluated and examined by legal counsel and staff members. The policy manual and the contract are both extensions of management's philosophy, and must accurately portray the facility to the public, clients, and promoters (Luthans, 1989).

After these guidelines have been revised and re-written, it is extremely important that the management team and staff thoroughly understand the facility's operating policy manual and contract. There is a great amount of information that must be interpreted consistently among those using the facility.

Over time, changes in interpretation occur, which can provide the basis for updates and revised versions with new and beneficial policies. Older policies are deleted when they are determined no longer useful. In reviewing, revising, and updating contracts and policy manuals, it is important to utilize input from support staff, patrons, customers, promoters, and clients' through regular feedback or evaluation mechanisms.

Contracts

Contracts with clients, promoters, and vendors are primary areas of concern for the facility. Rather than a document that is merely an outline of building policies, operational procedures should be incorporated into the language of the contract. In any contract all information should be provided as it is much easier to delete a portion or section by mutual agreement than it is to add (R. Johnson, personal communication, October 22, 1991).

Management Manual

In addition to the policies and procedures associated with contractual documentation, it is important to develop a management manual that provides a detailed accounting of standard operating procedures within the facility. There are a number of reasons for having this management manual. It provides the staff with a clear explanation of existing policies and procedures, provides management and

PERFORMANCE EVALUATION	PROBATION REVIEW	COLISEUM EVENT \ SECURITY
Name (last) (first) (initial)		Date of hire _____ 19____
		Rating period from _____ to _____
		Date of evaluation _____ 19____

Performance Dimensions	Ratings			Rater's comments
	Below	Meets	Above	
Dependability, attendance, punctuality & the ability to work all required pos- itions.				
Quality of work, overall motivation toward the job, and initiative. Ability to interact with co-workers & the General Public.				
Personality, personal app- earance, condition of the uniform, personal hygiene, and the use of Building property.				
General knowledge of the building and job responsi- bilites for each post.				
Disposition, temperment, especially his or her rel- ationship with other pers- ons. Ability to grow with the job. Degree of flexib- ility with various events.				

Weak Areas	Suggestive corrective Actions	Most outstanding Characteristics

Comments-

_____ Recommend _____ Do not recommend continuation of employment.

Rater   _____ Date _____ 19 ___

Director _____ Date _____ 19 ___

FIGURE 12-1 - SAMPLE EVALUATION FORM

staff with a tool for teaching and training employees about the facility, protects employees by creating restrictions or limits on their job capabilities, and protects the facility by establishing guidelines that are based on sound legal advice, thereby limiting the liability exposure to outside lawsuits. The manual is also capable of providing peace of mind and reducing the number of management headaches that are caused by excessive meetings due to a lack of procedural understanding among staff members (W. Mulrooney, personal communication, January 9, 1991).

Facility Operations Manager

Depending on facility size and design, the operations manager may be the supervisor for event coordination, security, and maintenance, as well as responsible for engineering. However, this individual is also responsible for the preparation of budgets, cost-benefit analyses, safety and risk-management programs, and labor union negotiations. Operations involves a wide variety of complex decisions ranging from personnel planning to technological and maintenance demonstrations. The following list typifies an operations manager's responsibilities:

- Planning
- Competitive Priorities
- Workforce Management
- Positioning Strategy
- Location
- Process Design
- Technological choices
- Quality Management and Control
- Inventory Management and Control
- Capacity
- Maintenance
- Materials Management
- Layout
- Production and Staffing Plans
- Master Production Scheduling
- Scheduling (Thompson & Strickland, 1990).

This list provides a general understanding as to the focus of an operations manager, but not all these areas apply equally in all situations. An operations manager must be able to deal effectively with a variety of workers, ranging from the coaching staff, field crew, and security personnel to the engineering staff. These departments must cooperate and be in harmony with each other at all times. The operations manager is the key to this coordination of effort.

Event Coordination

Event coordination is the primary responsibility of the event coordinator. This individual must have an overall understanding about facility capability and be familiar with its various departments. When an event, such as an athletic competition, concert, or even a luncheon, considers the facility as a potential site, the first step is the preliminary negotiations between the promoter and event coordinator.

In these negotiations cost is a critical factor. If the cost is too high, the parties must negotiate as to what costs can be eliminated. At this preparatory stage, discussion is centered on the requirements of the event and the appropriateness of the facility. This initial phase is not an easy process, as each event coordinator must understand all phases of event production, budgeting, and cost control, to be able to provide an accurate cost estimate.

Work-orders. After concluding an agreement, the event coordinator prepares an event work order. The event work-order documents **everything** required and requested. These services range from total number of labor hours to amount of lighting required to produce the event. It is vital that all items be documented, for once the event is concluded if items are not documented, payment will not be forthcoming.

The work order document is divided into sections, designating individual department responsibilities. For example, engineering may note what degree of lighting is necessary or the number of speakers required. It is not necessary, however, that the event coordinator be familiar with, and have technical knowledge of, all specific areas, such as wiring (voltage or wattage) requirements. It is however, paramount that good communication exist between the coordinator and the various departments to provide the best service (IAAM, 1990).

The Event. According to Jewel (1992), to undertake an event, and provide the appropriate management of audience support facilities, it is important to maintain "a delicate balance between operations and maintenance" (p.110). Consequently, when an event is about to move into the facility, the event coordinator has the responsibility to ensure that the promoter is receiving every service described in the contract document, nothing less, yet nothing more. If the promoter requires additional assistance items, these must be documented and the appropriate fee determined. During the move-in phase, if the coordinator identifies a problem, acceptable alternatives must be sought quickly.

Before the actual event, the coordinator briefs departments on expectations. Part-time employees, such as security and ushers, are always thoroughly briefed to reacquaint them with rules, procedures, and appropriate details of the facility. During the event, either the coordinator or operations manager is required to make sure that everything is functioning properly until the event has concluded.

The event coordinator's job requires more than just planning skills, as he or she must be able to negotiate, budget, and supervise effectively (IAAM, 1990). Of course, the operations manager is the individual in charge, with the majority of the planning and organizing falling onto the shoulders of the event coordinator. The operations manager is responsible for not only event coordination but also linkages with other departments. The most desirable quality of an individual in this position is the ability to delegate effectively and communicate to subordinates.

Security

In many facilities today, security functions usually fall under the jurisdiction of the operations department. In large facilities full-time in-house security staff are employed. These added duties compound the responsibilities and liability of the operations manager and facility. These in-house security system officers as employees of the facility, raises the legal exposure of the facility substantially (Mulrooney & Farmer, 1995).

It is vitally important that all established rules and procedures be written and accessible to all members of the security department (Connor , 1990). These procedures should provide a clear picture as to their limitations, restrictions, and expected behaviors.

All procedures must be in place before an event occurs. In addition, all employees, from administration to the ticket takers, must have complete understand of the facility's policy and required responses. Any problems that may arise must be quickly resolved with limited public attention. A facility that has stringent policies and procedures that are developed for the protection of the patrons will help reduce liability (Mulrooney & Farmer, 1995).

Emergencies

Emergencies are any incident, situation, or occurrence that has, or could, result in the injury of employees, patrons, or visitors. Examples of potential emergency or disaster situations could be weather, fire, bomb threats, medical emergencies, air crashes, utility loss, and hazardous materials. These situations can occur in a facility at any time, but how prepared are facilities to handle them when the situation arises (Mulrooney & Farmer, 1995, p. 229).

In emergency situations a definite chain of command must be established to maximize coordination and direction (Lloyd, 1990). During any emergency situation in a public assembly facility, a member of the management staff is responsible for making decisions and taking charge when a problem or situation arises. This designated staff member would most likely be the event coordinator or operations manager. It becomes this person's responsibility to ensure that every facet of the emergency plan proceeds according to schedule and that problems are resolved in a timely and professional manner.

Levels of emergency vary, depending on the number of persons involved, threatened, or injured.

Level I emergencies result when the number of persons affected is small and the responding numbers of facility staff are also minimal. For example, a seating problem requires an usher to resolve the problem without any undue effects.

Level II emergencies are situations in which a large number of persons are affected or threatened. Staff response size would still be limited, but substantially more involved. For example, an equipment failure occurs or a substantial ticketing or seating problem develops.

Level III emergencies involve a large number of people, and the entire event staff must be utilized to respond to the emergency. For example, a bomb threat or a relatively large and potentially dangerous fire is a Level III emergency (IAAM, 1990).

Action plan. Before any preparation can proceed or situation arise, a written action plan must be established. This plan is a precedent to establishing policy, responsibility, and requirements for coping with emergencies. The major priority, in any facility, is the prevention of injury and protection of lives (Lloyd, 1990). Security of vital records, money, equipment, and property must be given consideration during any emergency.

Emergency Manuals. According to W. Mulrooney (personal communication, January 9, 1992), a facility emergency manual is developed to make it easy to update information. Inserts that clearly define specific subjects, such as evacuation routes and bomb threats, etc. are essential to an appropriate and complete binder. Emergency manuals should include

- Chain of command to which all employees should adhere.

- Emergency personnel in charge of the situation and designated in the chain of command. All personnel should be identified by a simple identification badge, which should include name, title, function, home phone number, and facility phone number. Any additional information should also be made available.

- A list of names and phone numbers of cooperating agencies, such as police, fire, city, and county officials.

- Telephone contacts of service organizations, such as ambulances, buses, communication, county or city agencies, hospitals, utilities, newspapers, radio and TV, security, federal and national agencies.

- Evacuation routes using color-coded maps on evacuation routes and appropriate building(s). All employees should be tested on this information frequently.

- Paging codes that are defined and listed by location and personnel.

Emergency Response Training. According to Farmer and Mulrooney, (1995)

> Response to an emergency situation by the facility staff must be prompt and professional. The difference between a well-trained response and an erratic poorly-trained response could be the difference between life and death. An emergency response plan should be devised for all perceivable emergency situations. It is vital to thoroughly train all personnel who will most likely be involved in these response procedures. (p. 229).

Examples of developing typical emergency response methodology are

- training sessions within each facility department

- role playing and practice drills

- departmental staff briefings prior to events

- prompt-cards provided to event staff containing reference notes detailing emergency level, location, and assignment of pivotal personnel

- written and practical tests on the facility's emergency response plan

- outside training sessions with professional organizations

- posting of reference information for different emergencies

Emergency response procedures. Every facility is different. Consequently, each facility must develop its individual emergency-response plan and procedures. The plan must be able to detail elements, such as staffing, physical properties, event classification and type, and specifics concerning event emergency medical personnel. It is imperative that all medical response personnel be strategically placed, in constant communication with management, with access to appropriate supplies and equipment and the ability to respond properly (R. Johnson, personal communication, October 22, 1991).

To ensure maximum safety in all facility operations, an evacuation plan must be developed, understood, and implemented. It is imperative that if these procedures are to be successfully implemented, they be practiced. These procedures are vital especially in situations pertaining to a mechanical failure, bomb threat, fire, or riot.

Safe evacuation of patrons, in a professional and orderly manner, will minimize panic and resultant injury. In most large facilities, ramps and other non-mechanical egress measures are employed in these situations. No elevators or escalators should be used under any circumstances. When an unusual situation develops, where no specific plan has been established, management must select the most appropriate and efficient response choice (Mulrooney & Farmer, 1995).

Summary

1. Operations are the framework by which a sport facility is managed. The philosophy of the facility establishes the guidelines for the staff. The mission establishes the purpose of the facility. The policies provide the way the facility functions and are developed from the mission. The procedures are how policies will be carried out.

2. The facility operation manager is ultimately in charge of the overall event. This person prepares the budget, assists with risk management, and deals with various individuals associated with the event.

3. The event coordinator takes care of the specific details of each event. This person is in personal contact with the promoter, assists in establishing the cost estimate, and organizes the work order.

4. Establishing an emergency plan is extremely necessary and important for facility management. Representatives of all agencies (law enforcement, parking, ticket taking, cashiers, crowd, concessions, and facility management) should have input to its design. It must be understood, implemented, and practiced by all groups operating at the facility.

5. An emergency manual must be developed as a tool for those employed at the facility. Each employee must receive one and understand how his or her actions impact the success of the entire plan. Emergency training must occur with each employee.

Questions

1. List and describe the four components of Operations Management.

2. Identify the operations manager's responsibilities.

3. During the process of coordinating an event, what are considered the important elements, from an operational perspective?

4. In the development of an Emergency manual, list the important elements that a facility manager should be concerned with.

5. What measures need to be taken to ensure prompt and professional emergency response training for facility staff?

References

Connor, B.   (September, 1990).   Safe in their seats.   *College Athletic Management*, 44-46.

International Association of Auditorium Managers (IAAM). (1990).   Course materials from the unpublished proceedings of the School for Public Assembly Facility Management, Ogelbay, VA.

Jewel, D. (1992). *Public assembly facilities*. Malabar, FL: Krieger Publishing Company.

Lloyd, C. (Summer, 1990). When disaster strikes. *Facility Manager*, 22-34.

Luthans, F. (1989). *Organizational behavior*. New York: McGraw-Hill.

Mulrooney, A., & Farmer, P. (1995). Managing the facility. In B. Parkhouse (Ed.), *The management of sport: Its foundation and application* (2nd ed.). (pp. 223-248). St. Louis, MO: Mosby-Year Book.

Thompson, A.., & Strickland, A. (1990). *Strategic management concepts and cases*. Boston: BPI/Irwin.

CHAPTER 13

CROWD AND ALCOHOL MANAGEMENT

Modern crowd management involves many facets and is one of the most vital components of event and facility management. Every element of the event, from the design of the facility to the game itself, is part of crowd management (Antee & Swinburn, 1990). Crowd management is often included as part of the duty facility managers owe their patrons. Management must protect their patrons from unreasonable risk caused by other individuals (van der Smissen, 1990). In addition a facility manager must recognize the importance of an effective crowd management plan in order to protect the image and reputation of a sport facility. However, such a policy must be created to assist in *managing* crowds, not in trying to *control* them. Trying to control a crowd is a very difficult and potentially dangerous endeavor, whereas managing a crowd is more achievable.

Managing crowds at sport facilities often is an enjoyable and pleasant experience; however, as previously stated, some fans are prone to violent behavior. The frequency and the intensity of spectator violence is increasing, as several incidents have shown in the past few years:

- Monica Seles stabbing incident in Hamburg, Germany

- Soccer riots in England and Italy

- Post-game victory riots after recent Super Bowls and Stanley Cup Finals.

An additional example of violent behavior was displayed when a football game between the Eagles and Cowboys was delayed because of snowballs thrown by fans. A referee was knocked down by the icy missiles; the doctors trying to assist him were pummeled; and the cheerleaders were driven from the field ("Brotherly Love", 1989). In another situation 69 people were injured, 7 critically, when students rushed the field at Camp Randall Stadium after the University of Wisconsin beat the University of Michigan in a collegiate football game ("Badger players," 1993).

These incidents, though not common in sport, are increasing in number, and in order to effectively combat these situations a detailed management plan must be implemented.

CROWD CONTROL BEGINS THE MOMENT PATRONS START ENTERING THE FACILITY.

Crowd Management

Components of a Plan

Every facility should design, implement, and practice a crowd management plan (Antee & Swinburn, 1990; Appenzeller, 1993; Baley & Matthews, 1984; Miller, 1993; Sharp, 1990; van der Smissen, 1990). This plan provides the blueprint for a safe and enjoyable environment for all spectators. Providing a safe and secure environment for all patrons should be the philosophy of sporting event facilities and the crowd management policy should parallel this precept. A proper plan may be accomplished through the implementation of four important procedures:

1. Trained staff

2. Ejection policy

3. Effective communication network

4. Sufficient signage

Initially, a trained and competent staff must be employed to carry out the crowd management policy. Using personnel who have progressed through an orientation program provides the facility director with better qualified employees. These orientation sessions should provide employees with an understanding of the facility layout including the location of first-aid stations, rest-rooms, telephones, and the lost and found. Employees must also be shown the correct techniques utilized when dealing with intoxicated, disruptive, or unruly patrons. Employing trained personnel also may serve as partial protection against frivolous lawsuits, as the judicial system recognizes this training as an effective means of providing knowledgeable employees.

Second, a crowd management plan should address the specific procedures used to eject intoxicated, disruptive, or unruly patrons. It is important to mention that the facility ushers should not be used in this undertaking; their responsibilities should be to enhance communication and customer satisfaction (Miller, 1993). Because ushers are not trained to handle these disruptive behaviors, they may injure themselves or cause the problem to escalate if they attempt to become involved in an ejection (van der Smissen, 1990). Ejections should remain the primary responsibility of the crowd management staff.

As previously mentioned, the prime focus of an effective crowd management

CONTROL OF ALCOHOL CONSUMPTION HAS A GREAT DEAL OF IMPACT ON WHETHER OR NOT CROWD MANAGEMENT TACTICS WILL WORK.

plan should be to provide for the safety and security of the fans, which includes protection from violent third parties. Although a facility operator is not responsible for all injuries that occur at his or her stadium, the operator must take reasonable precautions (Wong, 1988). Therefore, the removal of any disruptive or intoxicated fan will provide a safer environment for the remaining spectators and help to protect the stadium director from potential litigation.

A crucial step in the ejection process is documentation of the incident, as it serves to protect the crowd management employee and facility administration from subsequent litigation.   Additionally the person being ejected should be photographed. This technique provides an accurate depiction of the condition of the ejected patron and further protects the employee from unnecessary legal harassment.

The third component of an effective crowd management plan is the

COLISEUM INCIDENT REPORT

DATE _____ 19 ___ TIME _____ M

EVENT _____

NAME OF PERSON INVOLVED _____ AGE _____ SEX ___

ADDRESS _____ PHONE _____

EMPLOYED BY _____

TYPE OF INCIDENT _____

PLACE OF INCIDENT _____

CAUSE OF INCIDENT _____

REPORTED BY _____

DESCRIPTION OF ILLNESS OR INJURY (IF ANY) _____

AID RENDERED _____ BY WHOM _____

DISPOSITION _____

WITNESSES: NAME _____ NAME _____

        ADDRESS _____ ADDRESS _____

        PHONE _____ PHONE _____

COLISEUM EMPLOYEE(S) WHO SAW OR HAVE KNOWLEDGE OF INCIDENT _____

COMMENTS (WHAT-WHEN-WHY-WHERE-WHO) _____

SIGNATURE OF PERSON OR OFFICER MAKING THIS REPORT _____

FIGURE 13-1 - SAMPLE INCIDENT REPORT

implementation of an effective communication network. Communication appears to be a critical aspect in guaranteeing the safety, enjoyment, and security of facility patrons (Berlonghi, 1990). The use of a centralized area for representatives from each group (facility, medical, security, and law enforcement) involved in the management of an event will provide the opportunity to facilitate communication and improve decision making. This command post should be located in a position to view the overall event and is critical for effective communications. Depending on the facility, the command post will normally be placed in, or on top of, the press box.

Multi-channeled radios are integral elements in the implementation of such a communication system. These types of radios allow simultaneous communication between various employees.

In addition, by using binoculars, the command post operators may identify disruptive or intoxicated patrons. The patron's location can then be communicated over the radios to the responsible crowd management team. Also, medical emergencies, and traffic congestion can also be observed from the command post. Experience has shown that patrons will recognize the serious tone the crowd management plan conveys, when these potentially dangerous situations are dealt with in a swift and firm manner.

The fourth component of an effective crowd management policy involves the use of signage. Directional signs have a number of important uses. As spectators approach the facility, road signs are used to indicate the correct exits. In addition, these signs assist in providing parking information. Other signs serve to indicate the correct gate or portal, as well as direct the ticket-buying patrons to the box office. There are a number of important questions asked by patrons regarding the location of concession stands, first-aid rooms, telephones, and rest-rooms, and signage will help to provide the answers.

Informational signs regarding prohibited items in the facility assist patrons in making decisions upon entry. Cans, bottles, backpacks, weapons, food, recording devices, and sometimes cameras are not allowed in many facilities. Spectators appreciate being treated fairly and will normally abide by facility directives if previously informed.

Duties of a Facility Manager

A facility manager is expected to take reasonable care to avoid foreseeable actions that may lead to injuries. An additional concept that permeates liability relates to the fact that the facility management does not guarantee a patron's safety; the duty of management is to provide a safe premises (Berry & Wong, 1986; Champion, 1990; Wong, 1988). If an injurious situation has occurred in the past, then "foreseeability" dictates the circumstances may occur again and "due care" needs to be implemented.

The topic of foreseeability was examined by a midwestern state court, when a male plaintiff attended a high school football game during which he was beaten and robbed. He sued the school district for not providing safe premises. The state court found there had been no prior attacks; therefore, there was no duty to protect the patron against the unforeseeable violence (*Gill vs. Chicago Park District*, 1980). The court determined that although a duty of care existed to provide safe premises for patrons, that duty of care to protect did not extend to unforeseeable acts committed by third parties (van der Smissen, 1990).

The *Bearman vs. University of Notre Dame* (1983) case was a landmark decision regarding the issue of foreseeability and had far reaching implications for facility managers (Berry & Wong, 1986; Miller, 1993; Sharp, 1990; van der Smissen, 1990; Wong, 1988; Wong & Ensor, 1985). In October 1979, Christenna Bearman attended a Notre Dame football game and, upon leaving, was walking across a university parking lot with her husband. An intoxicated spectator fell on Bearman from behind, breaking her leg. No security or facility personnel were present at the time of the accident. Bearman sued Notre Dame stating she was an invitee and the university had a duty to protect her from the negligent acts of a third party. The university maintained the incident was an unforeseeable accident. The Indiana Court of Appeals, however, disagreed and stated that Notre Dame allowed alcohol to be consumed during "tailgate" parties in the parking lots. With the presence of alcohol it was foreseeable that some individuals could become intoxicated and pose a general danger to others. Therefore, the court found that the university had a duty to protect their "invitees" from negligent third-party acts.

The duty of care owed to facility patrons depends on their status. Most fans and athletes enter onto facility property with the owners encouragement and these "invitees" usually provide the facility with monetary benefit. These individuals are owed the greatest degree of care from any known defects, and from injurious acts caused by third parties. Facility management does not guarantee spectators an injury free experience, however management has a duty to protect patrons from risks that should have been discovered by exercising reasonable care (Wong, 1994).

Alcohol Policy

Every crowd management plan should include a comprehensive alcohol policy. Alcohol is served at many sport and entertainment events throughout the United States, and although most spectators drink alcohol responsibly, a few are irresponsible. Because intoxicated patrons cause many problems because of the safety concerns brought onto themselves and others, facility and event management staffs must be aware of the potential problems that exist with large events and alcohol abuse. Patrons' personal enjoyment of alcohol may present liability concerns for the facility. If the sale and consumption of alcohol are managed properly, a few problems may occur; if improperly managed, a serious litigation may occur (Berlonghi, 1990).

Alcohol Legislation

Two statutes make it essential that facility managers implement alcohol management strategies to prevent their patrons from drinking too much. Statutes in many states allow injured plaintiffs to bring suit against the defendant, in addition to the owner of an establishment that allowed the defendant to become drunk. Some states allow plaintiffs to sue liquor establishments under these statutes, often called "dram-shop laws"; others allow recovery by common negligence theory and some states allow both (Chafetz, 1990; Miller, 1993).

A second ordinance for sport facility managers to monitor is "social host liability." This type of statute provides injured plaintiffs the opportunity to prefer charges against both the host of the party, where the defendant became intoxicated, as well as the inebriated individual (Chafetz, 1990). Significantly, however, not all courts follow this line of thinking.

In one case, a 16-year-old girl was knocked down by a drunk at a sports

ALCOHOL MANAGEMENT PROGRAMS ARE A MAJOR FACTOR IN A
FACILITY'S ATTEMPT TO PROVIDE A SAFE AND ENJOYABLE ENVIRONMENT
FOR THE PATRONS.

pavilion. She sustained a catastrophic injury from the incident. The court found
that because the facility did not serve alcohol, neither the injury nor the intoxicated
patron was foreseeable (Miller, 1993). In a similar case, a superior court in New
Jersey ruled that an intoxicated fraternity student, at a Rutgers football game, was
responsible for his own injuries because Rutgers did not serve or sell alcohol at its
football games (*Allen vs. Rutgers The State University of New Jersey*, 1987). Two
crowd management techniques limit these types of situations from occurring.
Trained crowd management personnel can be deployed at the facility entrances and
prohibit intoxicated individuals from entering the facility. Second, these crowd
management employees prevent patrons from entering the facility with alcoholic
beverages. These two procedures assist in controlling alcohol consumption, thus
protecting the facility from social host liability suits.

Reasons for Selling Alcohol

Some programs, especially those at universities with small attendance figures,
find it difficult to generate a profit if alcohol is not sold at home events. Many
individuals involved in sport management throughout the United States argue that
alcohol sales are worth the risks, due to the substantial revenue generated. Other
types of facilities have determined alcohol not to be worth the liabilities associated
with the increased revenue. The NCAA, for example, banned the sale of alcohol
at all championship and tournament events in the 1970s, and in the 1980s many
municipal stadiums began selling only 3.2% beer and offering their patrons seating

in alcohol-free sections (Wong & Ensor, 1985).

Foreseeable Risks

Foreseeability is a key determinant in most court decisions involving alcohol-related incidents. The facility management's ability to foresee harmful alcohol risks is an important way to potentially reduce liability (Miller, 1993).

Documenting incidents and reviewing records to determine the problems that occur more often than by random chance are means of measuring foreseeability. Preventive measures that guarantee these incidents do not reoccur must then be undertaken. If facility managers adequately use all procedures at their disposal, liability resulting from foreseeable risks will be greatly diminished (Maloy, 1988).

For example, a man and his companion, while bowling, became involved in an argument with a group of intoxicated individuals in the next lane. The bowling-alley management was notified by the plaintiff about the unruly individuals. Upon leaving the facility, while still in the parking lot, the plaintiff was savagely attacked by one of the drunks. The decision rendered by the United States Court of Appeals in the ensuing case created serious implications for managers of many various facilities. The court stated the bowling alley failed to protect the plaintiff from an obvious and foreseeable danger. The bowling-alley management should have ceased alcohol sales to the intoxicated group and should have provided safe passage for the plaintiff to his vehicle (*Bishop vs. Fair Lanes Georgia Bowling Inc.*, 1986).

Bearman vs. University of Notre Dame (1983), a case described earlier in the crowd management section, is a landmark case pertaining to foreseeability and its relation to alcohol policies. During ensuing litigation the facts of the Bearman case demonstrated that intoxicated individuals may pose a general danger to university patrons.

Alcohol Training Programs

Training individuals who serve alcohol or handle intoxicated patrons is an extremely important facet of a successful alcohol strategy and a crowd management plan. Within the past 5 years, two national programs have received awards for their effective impact on alcohol-related situations. Training for Intervention Procedures by Servers of Alcohol (TIPS), a program funded by General Motors, received the National Commission Against Drunk Driving Award for Education and Prevention (Chafetz, 1990). Techniques for Effective Alcohol Management (TEAM), formed in conjunction with the International Association of Auditorium Managers (IAAM) and several other organizations, also provides successful training to individuals in effective alcohol management (Antee & Swinburn, 1990).

In order to administer an effective crowd management plan, the plan and its associated alcohol strategies must treat spectators in a humane fashion and assist in providing a safe environment. Incorporation of designated driver programs provides a popular service by building rapport with event patrons and increases individual awareness of the need to drink responsibly. The Miller Brewing Company (1992) provides brochures and other written information about designated driver programs for interested facilities. These tips remind fans of their own alcohol limitations and describe how to make patrons recognize the problems with alcohol abuse, thus reducing alcohol-related accidents.

Criteria to Control Alcohol Problems

Because of the obvious potential for litigation involving alcohol, many facility managers have eliminated alcohol sales. Chafetz (1990) believed this reaction is analogous to eliminating cars because of their potential to be involved in accidents. He states that individuals learn to drive responsibly; therefore they can learn to drink responsibly as well.

A comprehensive crowd management plan containing equally extensive alcohol management policies provides the framework for a successfully managed sport facility. Various crowd management measures, when implemented, will assist the facility manager in curtailing irresponsible alcohol-related actions (Miller Brewing Company, 1992). A few of these measures include:

1. Management should be aware of the type of crowd attending the event; the time of day and weather will often affect the crowds mood and attitude.

2. The appropriate use of signage makes spectators aware that responsible drinking is the only type of drinking allowed in the facility.

3. The emphasis should be kept on the sport, not on the drinking.

4. Servers and security should be TIPS or TEAM trained.

5. IDs should be thoroughly checked and everyone who is legal to drink should be wristbanded.

6. The number of beers sold to one person at one time should be limited.

7. The size of servings should be reduced to 12 ounces.

8. Beer sales should end at a specific point during the event.

9. Food and nonalcoholic beverages should be offered.

10. Families should be encouraged to attend and troublemakers, to be on good behavior.

Summary

1. An extensive crowd management policy containing comprehensive alcohol management strategies should be written by facility management.

2. Trained employees should be hired to provide crowd and alcohol management services. These employees should be required to participate in facility training and orientation sessions on a quarterly basis.

3. Facility management should establish written policies regarding the ejection of unruly, disruptive, or intoxicated fans. Documentation should accompany each of these ejections, describing in detail what actions preceded the ejection. In addition a picture of the ejected patron should accompany each incident form.

4. The facility manager should design and implement a communications system linking the various agencies involved in event management. It is recommended that this communications net be accessed through the use of multi-channeled radios. During events the facility should provide a command post, where representatives from the various agencies are in communication with each other.

5. Various signs should be used around the facility to (a) direct fans from major streets to the facility and parking, as well as to other locations and services; (b) identify what items are prohibited from being brought into the facility.

6. Depending upon the philosophy of the facility, the facility manager should decide if alcoholic beverages will be sold during events.

7. If alcohol is sold, policies regarding the consumption and sale of alcoholic beverages should be created, including limitations on the size and number of beverages permitted per sale. These sales should cease at some common point before the end of the event.

8. Alcohol management training such as TIPS or TEAM should be provided by the facility management to those employees involved in alcohol sales.

9. Alcoholic beverages should be prohibited from being brought into the facility; anyone judged to be under the influence of alcohol should be denied entry to the facility.

10. "Tailgating" should only be permitted in parking lots under supervision from law enforcement officials.

Questions

1. Discuss the existence of violence in sport today. Are crowd management policies justified?

2. List the four components of an effective crowd management plan and give specific sport examples of each.

3. What duties does a facility manager have to his or her patrons?

4. Should facilities serve alcohol at athletic events? Support your argument with specific examples.

5. What is the difference between dram-shop laws and social host liability?

6. Foreseeability is a key determinant in cases regarding alcohol. Discuss the concept of foreseeability and explain why it is important in crowd and alcohol management.

7. Construct a crowd and alcohol management policy and provide reasoning for the various components.

References

Allen vs. Rutgers, The State University of New Jersey, 523A. 2d 262 (NJ. Sup. Ct. 1987).

Antee, A., & Swinburn, J. (1990, January-February). Crowd management: An issue of safety, security, and liability. *Public Management*, 16-19.

Appenzeller, H. (1993). *Managing sports and risk management strategies.* Durham, NC: Carolina Academic Press.

Badger players, fans came to rescue. (1993, November 1). *Columbus Dispatch*, p. D7.

Baley, J. A., & Matthews, D. L. (1984). *Law and liability in athletics, physical education, and recreation.* Boston: Allyn & Bacon.

Bearman vs. University of Notre Dame, 453 N.E. 2d 1196 (Ind. App. 3 Dist. 1983).

Berlonghi, A. (1990). *The special event risk management manual.* Dana Point, CA: Alexander Berlonghi.

Berry, R. C., & Wong, G. M. (1986). *Law and business of the sports industries: Common issues in amateur and professional sports* (Vol. 2). Dover, MA: Auburn House.

Bishop vs. Fair Lanes Georgia Bowling, Inc., 803 F. 2d 1548 (11th Cir. 1986).

Brotherly love on ice. (1989, December 23).. *The Economist*, 30.

Chafetz, M. E. (1990, January-February). Managing alcohol in public facilities: Caveat manager. *Public Management*, 20-21.

Champion, W. T. (1990). *Fundamentals of sport law.* Rochester, NY: The Lawyers Cooperative.

Gill vs. Chicago Park District, 407 N.E. 2d 671 (Ill. App. 1980).

Maloy, B. P. (1988). *Law in sport: Liability cases in management and administration.* Indianapolis, IN: Benchmark Press.

Miller, L. K. (1993). Crowd control. *Journal of Physical Education, Recreation and Dance, 64*(2), 31-32, 64-65.

Miller Brewing Company. (1992). *Good times: A guide to responsible event planning.* Milwaukee, WI: The Miller Brewing Company.

Sharp, L. A. (1990). *Sport Law.* National Organization on Legal Problems of Education (Whole No. 40).

van der Smissen, B. (1990). *Legal liability and risk management for public and private entities.* Cincinnati: Anderson Publishing Co.

Wong, G. M. (1988). *Essentials of amateur sports law.* Dover, MA: Auburn House.

Wong, G. M. (1994). *Essentials of amateur sports law.* (2nd ed.). Westport, CT: Praeger.

Wong, G. M., & Ensor, R. J. (1985, May). Torts and tailgates. *Athletic Business,* 46-49.

CHAPTER 14

HOUSEKEEPING AND MAINTENANCE

Housekeeping and maintenance are important areas of responsibility that ensure a clean and functionally operational facility. These functional areas should not be minimized as they are one of the most influential factors that keeps the public returning to the facility.

To develop appropriate planning for facility housekeeping and maintenance functions, it is important to take facility type, traffic access, usage level, identification of various user groups, available labor, and funding or revenues into consideration. Once the facility mission has been defined, a plan for housekeeping and maintenance should be established. This plan will provide for the establishment of guidelines and staffing requirements. The IAAM (1990) and Mulrooney & Farmer (1995) suggest specific planning elements that should include

- *Purpose*: To provide a clean, well-organized, and safe facility with available equipment for events, lessees, and patrons.

- *Operation*: To operate an effective facility that has an acceptable level of cleanliness, appropriate space and equipment to accommodate contracted events efficiently and in a timely manner. All attempts should be made to prevent safety violations. At the close of any event all equipment should be secured; all refuse containers should be emptied; and spaces and equipment should be cleaned and returned to original status; and all deficiencies should be reported and corrected in a timely manner.

- *Equipment Storage*: To provide for quick inventory and identification, maximum space utilization, convenience to using area, protection against tearing, bending, scarring, water or dust accumulation, broken parts or damage of any kind, proper spacing, and safe handling.

Operations Staff

This operational area should include: Housekeeping and Arrangements, Engineering, and Technical or Audio-Visual. These may be further subdivided:

- Housekeeping and Arrangements involves the actual physical cleaning and arrangement of the facility and furnishings. It involves vast and varied areas, such as bleacher seats, portable seats, large restrooms, loges, carpets, tile floors, concrete floors, stairwells, and elevators. Crews usually consist of a foreman and few full-time personnel. For the most part, part-time workers are usually employed. At times these crews work 7 days per week in 3 shifts, with 8 hours per shift. Housekeeping and Arrangement could structured into two groups such as (a) setup and striking events;   and (b) deep cleaning, who would complete scheduled major cleaning tasks, such as carpet shampooing, tile stripping and waxing, and glass washing.

- Engineering could include painting, plumbing, welding, carpentry, and parking lot and grounds maintenance.

- Audio/Visual section might involve lighting, sound, projection, television, and telephone areas (Mulrooney & Farmer, 1995). According to Jewel (1992),

> Custodial [housekeeping] by its very nature is often not conducive to high employee morale...adequate training, good equipment, proper materials, and pleasant working conditions are factors that can improve the attitudes of these staff members...[as well as] their roles in the overall facility performance (p.110).

Maintenance and housekeeping differ markedly in both function and responsibility. "Maintenance components include structural maintenance, equipment maintenance, setup and breakdown of events, as well as custodial functions. Maintenance management requires awareness and adherence to federal and state regulations, as well as the ability to implement preventative maintenance and safety plans within the facility." (Mulrooney & Farmer, 1995, p. 231)

In any facility, regardless of size, management should develop housekeeping and maintenance procedures similar to those suggested below:

- Cleaning equipment and supplies, should be issued, by employees signing the items out at the beginning of the shift and signing them in at the end of the shift.

- Daily work responsibilities should be assigned to all personnel.

- Frequent building tours should be conducted to detect damages and other problems.

- Damages attributed to previous facility events should be noted and directed to the attention of the director of housekeeping.

- Employees should be constantly supervised, and motivated to complete the job properly.

- Appropriate company and work rules should be maintained.

- Employees should be notified of appropriately authorized breaks and times to return to work.

- All management personnel should attempt to find less expensive, less difficult ways of cleaning and more cost-effective methods of maintaining the facility (IAAM, 1990).

CONCOURSE RESTROOM MAINTENANCE

CONDITION OF RESTROOMS AT THE START OF SHIFT

MEN EAST_____	WOMEN EAST_____
MEN NORTH_____	WOMEN NORTH(2)_____
MEN WEST_____	WOMEN WEST_____
MEN S.E._____	WOMEN SO.(2)_____
MEN S.W._____	WOMEN S.W._____

RECORD OF MAINTENANCE DURING SHIFT

RESTROOMS	TIME Maintained and/or Checked				
MEN EAST					
WOMEN EAST					
MEN NORTH					
WOMEN NORTH (2)					
MEN WEST					
WOMEN WEST					
MEN S.E.					
WOMEN S.(2)					
MEN S.W.					
WOMEN S.W.					

MAINTENANCE NEEDED OR REPAIRS TO BE MADE:_____

ATTENDANTS ON DUTY: _____   DATE: _____

FIGURE 14-1 - SAMPLE HOUSEKEEPING/ MAINTENANCE REPORT

Summary

1. Patrons will normally return if they have a safe and enjoyable experience in a well-managed and maintained facility.

2. The cleanliness of a facility is a direct reflection of the emphasis management places on customer service. Housekeeping and maintenance assist in providing

```
                        LOGE RESTROOM MAINTENANCE

    CONDITION OF RESTROOMS AT THE START OF SHIFT
    LOGE 1 NORTH                        LOGE 1 SOUTH
    MEN_____         MEN_____
    WOMEN_____         WOMEN_____
    LOGE 2 NORTH                        LOGE 2 SOUTH
    MEN_____         MEN_____
    WOMEN_____         WOMEN_____


    RECORD OF MAINTENANCE DURING SHIFT

    RESTROOMS              TIME Maintained and/or Checked
    LOGE 1 N MEN

    LOGE 1 N WOMEN

    LOGE 1 S MEN

    LOGE 1 S WOMEN

    LOGE 2 N MEN

    LOGE 2 N WOMEN

    LOGE 2 S MEN

    LOGE 2 S WOMEN

    NOTE OF MAINTENANCE TO BE DONE OR REPAIRS TO BE MADE:
    _____
    _____
    _____
    _____

    ATTENDANTS ON DUTY:                        DATE:
    _____
```

**FIGURE 14-2 - SAMPLE HOUSEKEEPING/
MAINTENANCE REPORT**

functional operations in a healthy environment.

3. As with all sections of facility management, a written housekeeping and maintenance plan should be designed, implemented, and utilized.

Questions

1. Define the following terms, housekeeping, maintenance, engineering, and structural and equipment maintenance.

2. List all of the elements of a maintenance and housekeeping plan.

References

International Association of Auditorium Managers (IAAM) (1990).   Course materials from the unpublished proceedings of the School for Public Assembly Facility Management, Ogelbay, VA.

Jewel, D. (1992). *Public assembly facilities*. Malabar, FL: Krieger Publishing Company.

Mulrooney, A., & Farmer, P. (1995). Managing the facility. In B. Parkhouse (Ed.), *The management of sport: Its foundation and application* (2nd ed.). (pp. 223-248). St. Louis, MO: Mosby-Year Book.

CHAPTER 15

BOOKING AND SCHEDULING

According to Mulrooney & Farmer (1995), the area of

> event booking and scheduling is one of the most important areas
> in the operation of a facility. In fact, because the facility is revenue
> producing, the booking and scheduling of events is considered the
> 'lifeblood' of a facility enterprise. In reality, a facility without
> events has little purpose. (p. 226)

These facility event and revenue generation functions, as well as the public
relations efforts, are the actual operations responsible for shaping the image of the
facility.

To understand the booking and scheduling function, it is necessary to discern
the mandate of the facility. Each facility is different. This difference is not only by
mission and function but also in the management approach. By example, a public
facility is obligated to provide for the scheduling of community events, whereas a
private facility may limit charitable and non-profit activities (Mulrooney & Farmer,
1995).

An important element of a private facility operation is that private facilities have
the ability to promote their own events and "...will aggressively attract events
through bidding or presenting comprehensive proposals to the various event
promoters" (Mulrooney & Farmer, 1995, p. 226). Although today, many
municipally operated facilities are being operated like their private operation
counterparts, there is still the tendency, due to the layers of bureaucracy, to be
conservative in the promotion of their own events. University-operated facilities,
however, are mandated to meet the needs and requirements of the student
population. As a result, this type of facility must give priority to university-
sponsored events (IAAM, 1990).

Booking

"Booking is the act of engaging and contracting an event or attraction" (Mulrooney & Farmer, 1995, p. 226). Regardless of facility mission, the guiding principle in attracting and promoting events is to reserve "...a specific space, within a specific facility, for a specific date, at a specific time, for an agreed upon amount of money" (Mulrooney & Farmer, 1995, p. 226).

From the outset, the facility attempts to secure events that provide the facility with a positive public image. An initial step is the development of an attractive and appealing facility brochure. This informational publication should be easily accessible to those interested in the facility. This publication should provide details of facility specifications, staffing, desired events, classifications, and event suitability. It should be updated annually, or as often as considered necessary (Mulrooney & Farmer, 1995).

Other aspects considered important in attracting events include maintaining facility visibility within local, regional and national markets, as well as with appropriate event promoters. This may include visits to appropriate trade and convention functions and networking with other facilities. Success in booking an event is more probably a result of management's network, not walk-in trade (Mulrooney & Farmer, 1995).

Scheduling

According to Mulrooney & Farmer (1995), "scheduling is the reservation process and coordination at all events to fit the facility's available time space" (p. 227). To provide the best possible event mix and full use of the facility, a variety of events must be properly spaced and should under no circumstances overlap. This scheduling responsibility falls to experienced individuals who have an in-depth knowledge of the facility's operational functions, as well as the ability to secure the appropriate number and right type of events. Management must be cognizant of the fact, that if the facility is to book and schedule events successfully, management must not overtax the staff, overwork the building, overspend the budget, or satiate the market (Mulrooney & Farmer, 1995).

It is imperative that the scheduling process be under the control of one individual responsible for the process. This individual should be the only individual to physically input or erase information from the scheduling book or primary booking mechanism. All changes in arrangements and notification of event alterations should be the sole responsibility of this designated facility scheduler. It is important to realize that this process can be a manual operation using a scheduling book or a modern facility scheduling computer program (Mulrooney & Farmer, 1995; IAAM, 1990).

Reservation Process

Within a facility operation, there are two categories of space reservations. A tentative or tentative-hold reservation process indicates that a specific organization or group has requested a specific date, time, and facility usage area. When an event is considered tentative, there is no actual contract document and that chosen date can be challenged by another event. If another organization desires this same date and time, and has the earnest money, the facility scheduler will contact the originally 'tentatively' scheduled organization to request their intention (Mulrooney & Farmer, 1995).

After communication with the tentative organization, confirmation will be requested and a contract developed. It is possible to have a series of first, second, and third tentative holds on a specific date or time period. It is quite usual for these dates to be secured more than a year ahead of time. If there are any changes in the schedule, the facility will notify the scheduled organization of the resultant schedule changes.

An organization that has agreed to a date, and time, placed a deposit and begun contract negotiations is known as a confirmed or contracted reservation. It is in the best interests of each facility to develop policies that establish appropriate time allocations for a tentative hold and confirmation period. However, they should be sensitive to need of their clients and their reputation. Every event is different. It is reasonable to assume that different events differ in confirmation periods and deadlines. Any facility that hopes to maintain its integrity must adopt a reservation system which is fair, equitable, and reasonable (Mulrooney & Farmer, 1995).

Scheduling Techniques

Most facilities use a manual scheduling technique, with all pertinent event information documented by hand. This information is usually located in a bound volume with each page representing a single calendar day. Computerized scheduling tools, however, are in the process of being implemented in facilities throughout the country.

Many scheduling directors prefer the manual method as the information is easily accessible and visible, and by physically placing the information on the calendar it is easier to personally recall at a later date. It is thought by industry members that this physical method has less margin for error. It is important to remember that any method involving human beings is subject to error by virtue of human frailties.

For example a promoter calls the facility to book a specific date for an upcoming attraction. The date is open, and the facility can accommodate that type of event without any apparent conflicts. The information required to hold a date will be recorded:

> Contact name
> Phone numbers-work and home
> Company name
> Act or event, and
> Date called

A (T) is placed at the top of the information to signify that the date is being tentatively held.

Meanwhile, another promoter telephones to schedule the same date. The sponsor is informed that another event is already scheduled for that day. The sponsor inquires as to whether a challenge for that day is appropriate. If a challenge is requested, the same information is recorded and (2nd Hold) is placed at the top of the page. The first promoter is notified of the challenge and is given the choice to "firm" the date by placing a deposit or selecting another date. If the first promoter confirms that original date, the (T) becomes an (F) and a contract is sent to the sponsor for review. The event is then considered contracted.

Contracting

Following confirmation of the tentative hold, the next order of business is the negotiation of the contractual agreement. According to Mulrooney and Farmer (1995), five requisites required to develop a contract are:

FIGURE 15-1 - SAMPLE EVENT BOOKING FORM

1. Consideration is legal value (money) and bargain by partner.

2. A valid offer and valid acceptance must be present.

3. The substance of the contract must be legal.

4. A specific duration is set for the contract.

5. The contract must have a proper form, either written and/or verbal.

As with all contracts only appropriate and qualified individuals should develop the contractual agreement document. An understanding of the facility's policies, goals, and objectives of the facility is paramount if the implementation is to be successful.

As attorneys are relatively expensive, many facilities do not have a full-time attorney available. Thus, when a new facility event contract is proposed, a boiler-plate contract or standard contract form is used. "The boiler-plate contract is similar to an apartment lease, with all language in standard form and appropriate 'fill-in-the-blanks' to address specifically agreed-upon terms" (Mulrooney & Farmer, 1995, p. 227).

Standard language enables boiler-plate contracts to provide consistency. Language modification and contract clause addenda and eliminations customize the standard form. It is imperative that every modification be mutually agreed upon by both parties; otherwise, potential problems will develop.

Although contracts have the reputation of being complex structures, it is important that these documents be as simple as possible. Simplicity avoids confusion and allows the contractual process to proceed. Due to the variety of events in large facilities, there are three rudimentary boiler-plate contract forms utilized.

Events that are open to the public and require tickets obligate language addressing the issues of ticket sales, proceeds, and personnel. Contract addenda usual address insurance, additional financial and promotional issues. Facility events involving patron and building security issues require more decisive contractual procedures and language.

The less complex nonticketed or closed events are considered reduced-liability activities. Banquets, conventions, and trade shows are examples where there is no ticketing and limited public attendance.

Contracts for small events are usually simple. Event types that require minimal space and employee numbers, are proms, seminars, and conferences.

The main objective in any contract negotiations is to maintain facility control and direction before, after, and during the event. Control is effected by providing personnel, such as "...security, ushers, ticket takers, first-aid, and special insurance arrangements. This control element definitely reduces facility liabilities" (Mulrooney & Farmer, 1995, p. 228).

Priority Policies

All facilities, whether private, municipal, or university owned, have specific scheduling priorities. However, at many municipal facilities, clear scheduling

Display Rental

Mail or Fax to:

JOHN S. KNIGHT CENTER

"Fax us both sides of this form for quick, convenient service"

Exhibitor Information

Company: _____   Contact: _____

Address: _____   Voice#: _____

_____   Fax#: _____

Event Name: _____

Date(s): _____   Booth#:_____

TERMS:
All orders must be prepaid and received 14 days prior to event or 15% surcharge will be added to invoice total. For your convenience, Visa and MasterCard will be accepted. Please include appropriate information in the space below. If mailing order form with company check, please include P.O. number on check.

CANCELLATION POLICY:
Items cancelled less than 14 days prior to event will be charged at 50% of price. Items cancelled after installation or any custom panels or graphics cancelled after start of construction will be charged at 100% of original price.

Method of Payment

☐ Company check to follow fax or accompany order

   Check # _____

☐ Please charge to my Visa/Mastercard # _____

   Expiration Date: _____

   MasterCard users enter the four digits above name:_____

_____   _____
Cardholders Name   **Cardholders Signature**

_____
Street   **City**   **Zip**

FIGURE 15-2 - SAMPLE FORM CONTRACT

priorities are not clearly defined. Most facilities today have as their primary objective revenue generation. As a result they develop programs and seek events that produce the most revenue.

Many times a facility will decline an event because of conflicting dates, such as scheduling priorities. For example the City of New Orleans declined to bid on the SEC Football Championship game scheduled for December 5, 1991 because two conventions were previously contracted (W. Racek, personal communication, October 14, 1991). Not only do conflicts arise with facility time and date availability, but the host city also, especially within the hotel industry, can reasonably accommodate only a limited number of major events.

Smaller facilities tend to have requests for events that are inappropriate for their space. A facility as large as the Superdome or Astrodome has few events deemed inappropriate, and an underlying philosophy is "If they can pay, they can play." University facilities, such as the Reily Student Recreation center at Tulane University, turned down a rock concert because of inadequate space. The main gymnasium was not considered conducive as back-up in case the rock concert were to be held indoors due to inclement weather.

When an event reserves space, two days should be reserved for setup and breakdown of equipment and supplies. The demand on facility personnel would be overwhelming if one event moved out and another moved in on the same day. For example, the Superdome, New Orleans, Louisiana, declined a Paul McCartney and Wings concert due to a prior commitment to a specific convention. Although the date of the concert was the day after the convention, removal and set-up would have been extremely difficult and would have placed an inordinate amount of pressure on the facility and personnel. The convention group was considered a good and steady client and not considered appropriate for such treatment (W. Racek, personal communication, October 14, 1991). In other facilities multiple events can be accommodated on consecutive days. At the Richfield Coliseum, Cleveland, Ohio, it was common to have a hockey game and a basketball game on the same day.

Scheduling Conflicts

According to Racek (personal communication, October 14, 1991), there will always be conflicts in scheduling if a facility processes a substantial amount of business. The manner in which the facility handles these conflicts molds its image and reputation.

A facility that has athletic events as its first priority must hold all possible dates open that the team may require, including post-season or tournament games. This is usually an expectation of the governing bodies of both amateur and professional athletic associations.

The primary users of the Superdome are the New Orleans Saints, a professional football team (NFL), and Tulane University's football team. These two attractions are given priority over all other events in any given year. Tulane University has a tentative schedule of 5 to 10 years coordinated with the Superdome and other university football programs. The National Football League (NFL) and the New Orleans Saints coordinate schedules on a year-to-year basis. All available home game dates are clarified by these two organizations by April of each year. However, the Superdome must hold dates open for possible NFL post-season play, in case the New Orleans Saints may be host. These play-off dates are always in January and change annually as the NFL experiments with game schedules and priorities.

The Superdome's third priority is the Noika Sugar Bowl events. The Noika Sugar Bowl Basketball Classic is at the end of December, whereas the Noika Sugar Bowl Football Game is held on New Year's Day. These events have been fixed and secured for many years to come.

After these first-, second-, and third-level priorities have been met, the Superdome then attempts to accommodate an event mix. For auxiliary events, January, February and March offer various types of events like trade shows. These events do not require a stage (i.e., the home and garden or a sportsman's show). The Superdome's two best attractions, which provide high revenue and long-time patronage, are the Boat Show and Truck Tractor Pull. In spring, Disney on Ice and The Fun Fair, an indoor version of a carnival, are the highlighted events. Summer attracts mostly religious conventions, because this is considered low season, especially for the local hotel industry.

In sport event-oriented facilities, scheduling policies, that are consistent with their mission and operational direction are established in written form. For example, the Reily Center Student Recreation (Tulane University, 1991) scheduling policy states:

First Priority Scheduling

- University informal sport programs

Second Priority Scheduling

- Organized university recreational sports programs

Third Priority Scheduling

- Instructional classes

Fourth Priority Scheduling

- Intercollegiate athletics

Fifth Priority Scheduling

- Community groups

Another scheduling example is the Civic Arena, Pittsburgh, Pennsylvania. This facility is privately operated by Spectacor Management Group. The arena's scheduling priority is both family entertainment events and professional sporting events, (i.e., Pittsburgh Penguins). After accomplishment of these priorities, the arena can service any type of event ranging from concerts to graduations. As a privately operated facility, owned by the taxpayers, events generating a profit are highly sought after.

Facility-Client Relationship

If an event has been previously booked by the facility and has promptly paid its debt, it is considered a good client. This event and the facility have developed a good working relationship; therefore, the event should receive priority in future scheduling. For example, a particular event may be important because it has been held every year since the facility opened its doors. However, this year, two dates were being held in the month of January to host the event. Although confirmation of the specific date was expected soon, other events were interested in contracting with the facility on either of these two dates. Even though these additional events were revenue producing and facility management desired the additional business, the policy of the facility was to provide booking priorities for the original event because of its consistency and loyalty as a client (IAAM, 1990).

Qualifications for Reserving Space

According to Racek (personal communication, October 14, 1991) once scheduling priorities have been established, events must meet several qualifications to be eligible for facility space. These elements should include

· Availability of the specific date and time

· Appropriate confirmation for the space

· Sufficient availability of facility staff to meet the demands of the organization requesting space

At times established facility priorities may conflict with revenue generation efforts. For example, a women's university basketball team was prevented from playing host to a second-round basketball tournament due to the scheduling of a significant revenue-generating event (i.e., Sesame Street Live). Even though this popular event produces far more revenue than a women's basketball game, the facility must follow its established written priority policies. If the facility does not adhere to its priorities, the facility risks losing credibility with its clients.

Another example that illustrates poorly handled scheduling was a conflict at a major stadium in the south. In 1992, this stadium was to host a major convention, which required the entire month of August for preparations. The major league baseball team who played at this stadium, had a month of home games already scheduled at the facility. The stadium had been aware for some time that the facility would host the major convention and a month was needed for preparations. However, the facility did not make any effort to resolve the conflict until confronted by the media. The general manager of the stadium stated the team would play their home schedule at another stadium in a different state, yet, this other stadium replied that it could not accommodate the entire home schedule. The players union also had an agreement that a team is not permitted to play a 30-day road trip. The problem was finally resolved with the assistance of other facilities.

Scheduling conflicts can be prevented by adhering to three basic principles when booking and scheduling the facility:

1. Managers should not lose control of the scheduling book and process.

2. Managers should be fair when dealing with all events when holding space and changing booking dates.

3. Managers must understand and be knowledgeable of the scheduling priority policies of the facility.

These essential elements, when in place and operational, enable a facility to schedule numerous events, without an overworked staff or building and with a healthy budget and satisfied marketplace.

Summary

1. Booking deals with contracting a specific event for the facility while scheduling has to do with reserving a date for the event on the facility calendar.

2. Reservations may be tentative or confirmed depending upon if a deposit has been placed for the specific date.

3. Even in today's modern business world, many facilities still manually schedule future events in a large book shaped calendar.

4. Only those individuals with a thorough knowledge of the facility philosophy and mission should contract with event promoters.

5. Each facility needs to establish specific scheduling practices. These priorities usually pertain to athletics, curriculum, intramural, community non-profit and profit types of events.

6. Scheduling conflicts will invariably occur, how the facility deals with these conflicts will reflect upon their image and reputation.

Questions

1. Define booking and scheduling.

2. Describe the reservation process and state weather or not you think that this process is not fair with reasons for your judgment.

3. How does the mission of the facility influence its reservation decision making process?

4. How would you alleviate a problem between two sport promoters desiring the same date and time?

References

International Association of Auditorium Managers (IAAM). (1990). Course materials from the unpublished proceedings of the School for Public Assembly Facility Management, Ogelbay, VA.

Jewel, D. (1992). *Public assembly facilities.* Malabar, FL: Krieger Publishing Company.

Mulrooney, A., & Farmer, P. (1995). Managing the facility. In B. Parkhouse (Ed.), *The management of sport: Its foundation and application* (2nd ed.). (pp. 223-248). St. Louis, MO: Mosby-Year Book.

Reily Student Recreation Center. (1991). *Facility reservation policy and procedures* (Brochure). New Orleans, LA: Author.

CHAPTER 16

BUSINESS OPERATIONS

Business operation is an essential unit in every sport facility. In small sport facilities one individual might be in charge of business operations while many of the other managerial functions are usually contracted to an outside entity. General accounting and finance concepts, for the most part, will be left to other courses that deal specifically with these functions. This chapter will focus on the essential elements that are the core of the facility business operation: types of budget, budgeting process, budget issue papers, event settlement, auditing, and bad debts collection.

Overview of Business Operations

The facility business operations are where all financial policy, statements and forecasting, expenditure review and approval, payroll, purchasing and billing, invoicing and event settlement, tax preparation, and budget development reside. These operations, because of their extremely complex nature utilize highly sophisticated computer software programs to complete these tasks. Depending upon the facility type, size, and function, this department can range from one employee to several accountants and staff, overseen by a manager. The manager of the operation can take on many titles, but is usually known as the comptroller, the vice president of finance, or the business manager.

Mission Statement, Goals and Objectives

The operation of the facility, as stated previously, is directed by the mission statement. Although many facility organizations, especially those related to governmental and large corporate entities, are extremely formal in their missions, other facilities operate under very general guidelines. These mission guidelines help to construct the budget of the organization.

Goals and objectives are support elements that assist in justifying the mission or statement of purpose of the facility. These statements of direction should be devised by knowledgeable managers, and compiled from input from all operational personnel, regardless of rank or position. A participatory or "bottom-up" management approach is preferred to a traditional "top-down" approach, as it is vital that all personnel develop and support the mission, goals, and objectives of the facility. According to Rummel (personal communication, October 22, 1991), the success or failure of any facility operation is a direct result of the support generated for the purpose and established guidelines of the facility.

Budgets

The most important element of the facility business operation is the development of the budget document. Budgets are an estimate of receipts and payments for a given period of time (Davidson, Malver, Stickney, & Weil, 1988). They are important predictive tools, as they can not only anticipate the flow of revenues and expenditures but can also be used as tools of control. This written expression of income and expenses is established for a fixed period of time, usually 1 or 2 years. It is a guide to the financial expectations of the facility and an expression of management's plans (Mulrooney & Farmer, 1995).

Government budget process. Many sport facilities today are involved in some way with government. The general manager, must have some knowledge of the political process to the public budgeting process (Mulrooney & Farmer, 1995)

Many state and local governments operate on periods of one to two years (biennium). Using the biennium as the sample time period, budget requests for public sport facilities are usually submitted one and a half years prior to actual budget appropriation. This projected budget is limited in scope and detail, and is often inaccurate. Many times the expenses are inflated and income is deflated due to the numerous hearings, volatile economies and political nature of the budget process (Mulrooney & Farmer, 1995). Although the approved budget is difficult to change, if the desired amounts are not appropriated, political advocates can lobby for an adjustment to the approved budget. The system is extremely cumbersome and complex. (W. Rummel, personal communication, October 22, 1991).

Operational budget process. Regardless of private or public operation, the submission of the bureaucratic request will not hinder the internal budget operations. "Operational budget submissions and approval are usually prepared up to 60 days before their actual implementation. This time limitation provides limited flexibility when compared to the governmental product." (Mulrooney & Farmer, 1995, p. 241).

Budget Cycle. The four phases of the facility budget cycle are budget preparation, presentation and adoption, execution, and postexecution and audit phases (Davidson et al., 1988).

Budget preparation begins with the establishment of the facility's mission, goals, and objectives. It is important that this initial phase be as inclusive as possible, with all facility personnel providing input. Review of previous years budgets, current financial information, and associated rationale should be presented concerning personnel, wages, benefits, materials, supplies, utilities, and various projected facility services. The resultant draft document should be considered a well-balanced program. This document is then submitted for management approval.

The presentation phase of the budget document is a political process, especially in large facilities. Initially, the budget document is circulated amongst proactive supporters for their input and approval. This document should be clear, precise, and include any supporting documentation, (i.e., as letters, charts and comparative statistics, etc.) that may provide the reviewer with insight and understanding (Mulrooney & Farmer, 1995). After all supporters have reviewed the document and suggested changes, the revised document is then circulated amongst the management group. At this time, those preparing the budget must be ready to defend and justify the document. As soon as the document is approved and adopted by the governing board, it is ready for interpretation and execution.

According to W. Rummel (personal communication, October 22, 1991), once the budget has been adopted by senior management, it is then disseminated to the various departmental entities. Departments, such as Operations or Engineering and Maintenance, are obligated to maintain a control on spending. In fact, methods of budgetary control, such as monthly statements, are developed to maintain this level of control and expenditure direction. Monthly meetings should be convened to ascertain whether budget goals and objectives are being met, or are in need of adjustment (Mulrooney & Farmer, 1995). It is important to remember that budget limits are an essential part of each budget document. However, flexibility should be incorporated in every budget document. It is important to remember that any substantial shift in facility goals and objectives will require a formal budget review. The budget document and resulting implementation must be altered accordingly. However, the prime directive, regardless of potential alterations, is to achieve the stated mission, goals and objectives of the facility established at the outset of the budgeting process (Mulrooney & Farmer, 1995).

This procedure simply evaluates whether the stated budget assumptions were achieved and the portion of the mission fulfilled. In any facility budget, whether public or private, overspending is simply unacceptable. The evaluation process actually determines the current level of success and the outcome is used in the development of the next budget document. This budget process is similar to painting San Francisco's Bay Bridge: When you think you have finished, the process begins again.

Types of budgets. There have been many budget systems developed that were supposed to solve the problems of accountability and fiscal control. In the 1940's and 1950's the Line Item or "object of expenditure" budget method was developed. This method listed all objects of expenditure by item, which are then placed in a specified category. This relatively simple budget approach recorded expenditures by classification, such as travel, salaries, supplies, enabling the reader to obtain easy access and scan the operation quickly. This budget method, however, did not provide an in-depth informational analysis.

The 1960's saw the development of performance-based systems. These systems endeavored to focus on the spending activity and include activity classifications, narrative, justifications, and unit costs. This type of budget was cumbersome, and in the case of most sport facilities not practical, especially when the unit costs are not known until after the event has concluded. This budget process also increased the levels of bureaucratic red tape and complexity of the process.

Performance-based systems were followed by the Programming, Planning and Budgeting System (PPBS) and Management by Objective (MBO). In the 1970's Zero-Based Budgeting (ZBB), developed by Texas Instruments, attempted to build a budget annually, from the ground floor, justifying each step and expenditure. All these methods exist and are prevalent in sport facilities today (Davidson et al., 1988).

Throughout the 1980's and 1990's there has not been a predominant budgeting philosophy developed by a governmental genius or proposed by the nation's business schools. As there has been no dominant budget style or concept, the most common approach has been to use whatever works best. With the advent of rapid technology changes in computers and tailor-made software programs, most organizations are able to develop budget programs specifically designed to meet their needs.

Zero-Based Budgeting

ZBB is a process that requires an organization to review and evaluate all of its programs and activities in terms of their effectiveness and efficiency (Mulrooney & Farmer, 1995). The best way to describe ZBB is to contrast it with a line-item budget. A line-item budget takes the previous year's figures and projects either an increase or decrease in each line item. A ZBB does not start from a current base level, but instead evaluates all programs and considers the budget request as a series of supplemental requests up to a current level. ZBB is a managerial tool that looks at programs, levels of service, and impact as a result of dollars spent.

The basic steps of a ZBB include identifying budget units, determining the varying levels of service within each budget unit and resources required, and then ranking the service levels based on their relative importance. The following is an example of a ZBB for a small arena:

1. Organization- Sports Arena

2. Budget Unit- Setup crew

3. Arena Operations (1 of 3): positions - 20: cost - $185,000. Setup and tear down, general cleaning.

4. Custodial Service (2 of 3): positions - 5: (total 25) cost - $70,000 (total $255,000) Daily cleaning

5.   Special Services (3 of 3): positions - 2: (total 27) cost $15,000
(total $270,000) Provides special services.

The final step would be to rank the service levels within this unit in
terms of their relative importance. The highest level would be at the top
with the least important level at the bottom (W. Rummel, personal
communication, October 22, 1991).

Budget problem solving or issue paper. According to the IAAM (1990), "issue
paper" is a management tool used to identify and correct problematic situations
that may develop within a facility operation. Although used in the budget-
development process, it can also be used in other problem situations. This
somewhat complex process involves all facility staff who have pertinent and
appropriate information about the specific issue or problem. The issue paper
develops through various stages:

Stage 1.   The initial phase attempts to identify and define all problematic areas,
such as facility access for patrons with disabilities or smoking in the
facility.

Stage 2.   This phase develops a specific situation that requires focus on an issue
and initiation of a problem solving approach. Take for example the
federal legislation known as the Americans with Disabilities Act (ADA).
This act states that all public facilities must provide access and
participation to all individuals regardless of their disability. The law
requires that

·   A visually impaired individual must be provided with the means
to comprehend the event that he or she is attending.

·   A hearing-impaired participant must be provided with an
interpreter.

·   All disabled patrons purchasing tickets, regardless of price, must
be accommodated in a price-related section that provides
accessibility and functionality for that individual's needs (i.e.
seating, ramps, elevators, restrooms, and access to concessions).

The effect of this mandate is that every facility must redevelop its
facilities to comply with the letter of the public law. To achieve
compliance, substantial financial expenditures may be needed.
Noncompliance could result in considerable penalties.

Stage 3.   After the problem has been identified and evaluated Stage 3 determines
the appropriate action to be taken. This action could be in the form of
documentation generated to facilitate changes in budget direction and
requirements, or in non-budget-related measures.

As presented, the issue-paper process provides management with a tool to
identify the problem and subsequent solutions while staying within the facility's

mission, objectives, and most important the budget.

Facility Accounting

Accounting within a sport facility is similar to that of any business. The only exceptions are governmental operations because these operations need not be responsive to stockholders, as is necessary at a private facility operation. Facility accounting procedures generally involve three fundamental accounting areas:

1. Managerial or internal accounting guides the management decision-making efforts. It is developed through information and projections from facility income and financial data.

2. Financial or external accounting primarily involve the income, balance sheet, and a cash-flow statements. These reports are subject to auditing procedures and conform to the generally accepted accounting principles (GAAP). These reports are not tax reports.

3. Tax accounting reports are compiled in accordance with the guidelines of the Internal Revenue Service.

All of these accounting procedures are subject to an annual audit by an independent auditing firm. This auditing procedure is an unbiased and objective report on the financial status of the organization and helps to maintain the confidence of the public, as well as stockholders and bondholders.

Depreciation. Depreciation is simply an accounting tool that shows how much of the usefulness of an asset has already been consumed (Gibson & Frishkoff, 1986). To illustrate, assume a battery is purchased. The price of this new battery was $100. After the battery has been used for a month it is discovered that 50% of its power has been used. Translating this into financial terms, it could be said that $50 of the cost of the battery has been also used. This $50 represents depreciation.

Two benefits of depreciation should be mentioned. First, depreciation will lower income on the accountant's ledgers, but not in reality. Depreciation expense is considered a charged expense not a paid expense. An example of a charged expense would be a $100 per month phone bill. This means that the customer pays the phone company $100 per month. Conversely, with depreciation expense, there is nobody to pay it to. Instead, this expense is charged against income on the books of the facility.

The second benefit is related to the first. Because depreciation helps to lower income, taxes for the facility will also be lower. So, it is advantageous to own equipment, because of diminishing of depreciation effect on income and taxes.

Sport facilities involved with the government do not use depreciation methods because these facilities generally do not own any equipment. However, an understanding of this concept is important because there are private facilities and buildings, within the facility network, that definitely employ depreciation methodology.

Event settlement.

The event settlement process utilizes procedures normally involved in cost accounting or managerial accounting. This procedure is used to compute the operational costs of producing an event. Evaluation of this data guides management decisions which in turn affect future events (Mulrooney & Farmer, 1995).

The event settlement procedure involves two costing systems. The first is process costing, which primarily identifies the expenses of the entire operational process. The second is job-order costing, in which expenses, such as labor and overhead, are identified by the job. The job-order costing method is more appropriate to the needs of a sport facility (Davidson et al., 1988).

The reasons sport facilities should analyze cost data before and after an event settlement are that they will (1) provide an operational measure in terms of dollars generated, (2) assist management in economic and negotiating decisions, (3) justify the need for greater funding, resources and reimbursement, and (4) accountability. Also, if in the development of a settlement estimate at the end of an event an item is overlooked, the facility or management group will have to suffer the loss, as recuperation will be impossible (Mulrooney & Farmer, 1995).

Any event expenses, such as stagehands, light operators, utilities or production, will be utilized in determining the cost of the event. Some elements are known as "house expenses", such as a plumber to unstop toilets and alleviate potential flooding situations; specific facility setup configurations, such as a basketball floor or ice rink; and the security guard assigned to the box-office window to protect the deposits of the facility from theft. These services cannot be charged to the event promoter, as they are the responsibility of the facility and are not recoverable cost items.

A cost accounting system itemizes detailed contractual elements of the event and those that define the responsibilities of the management of the facility (Garrison, 1982). These expenses must be organized and documented, otherwise facility management will have to absorb these costs rather than pass them on to the promoter. The event settlement process, especially at a concert usually begins about midway through the performance and may conclude before the end of the show if all goes well. One major concern after completion of settlement is that the show does not run over the projected time allotment; otherwise, the facility will be responsible for the additional staffing costs.

The major problem in this process is that if the settlement procedure has not been completed by the conclusion of the event, the probability of procuring additional expenses is minimal. Events that have good reputations and have been dealt with successfully over the years develop a level of trust. These settlements are usually resolved within 10 days of the end of the event. With other events, the facility would normally require a significant deposit in advance; in fact, it would be expected in the majority of cases that the rent be paid 30 days in advance or up-front, rather than after the event (W. Rummel, personal communication, October 22, 1991).

Policies covering settlement procedures are event specific and part of the facility management philosophy. The bottom line is that every penny the facility expends for the event must be accounted for, and hopefully, will be fully recovered by the facility (Mulrooney & Farmer, 1995, p. 242).

Payroll

Payroll is the process by which compensation is paid to employees on a regular basis in a sport facility operation. The majority of employees are part time or seasonal (37 hours per week). These employees are usually paid on a weekly or biweekly basis for an hourly wage. Full-time employees (40 hours weekly), are paid biweekly or monthly are paid overtime (1 1/2 times the regular hourly wage) when an employee works more than 40 hours in a week. Unionized employees are sometimes reimbursed at higher rates. Full-time employment is classified as either staff or management, with staff usually being hourly employees, whereas

FIGURE 16-1 - SAMPLE SUPPLIES INVOICE FOR EVENT SETTLEMENT

Form **W-4** Department of the Treasury Internal Revenue Service

Employee's Withholding Allowance Certificate

▶ **For Privacy Act and Paperwork Reduction Act Notice, see reverse.**

OMB No. 1545-0010 **1995**

1 Type or print your first name and middle initial	Last name	2 Your social security number
Home address (number and street or rural route)	3 ☐ Single ☐ Married ☐ Married, but withhold at higher Single rate. *Note: If married, but legally separated, or spouse is a nonresident alien, check the Single box.*	
City or town, state, and ZIP code	4 If your last name differs from that on your social security card, check here and call 1-800-772-1213 for a new card . . . . . ▶ ☐	

5 Total number of allowances you are claiming (from line G above or from the worksheets on page 2 if they apply) . 5

6 Additional amount, if any, you want withheld from each paycheck . . . . 6 $

7 I claim exemption from withholding for 1995 and I certify that I meet **BOTH** of the following conditions for exemption:

- Last year I had a right to a refund of **ALL** Federal income tax withheld because I had **NO** tax liability; **AND**
- This year I expect a refund of **ALL** Federal income tax withheld because I expect to have **NO** tax liability.

If you meet both conditions, enter "EXEMPT" here . . . . ▶ 7

Under penalties of perjury, I certify that I am entitled to the number of withholding allowances claimed on this certificate or entitled to claim exempt status.

Employee's signature ▶ **Date** ▶ , 19

8 Employer's name and address (Employer: Complete 8 and 10 only if sending to the IRS)	9 Office code (optional)	10 Employer identification number

Cat. No. 10220Q

FIGURE 16-2 - SAMPLE W-4 FORM

management is usually paid a salary.

An employee paycheck consists of both salary and deductions. Some of these deductions include social security, federal income taxes, state and local income taxes, state disability insurance, unemployment compensation, and any voluntary employee deductions. The employee's net or take-home pay is the difference between gross pay (wages earned) and all the appropriate taxes and deductions. At the end of the financial year all employees will receive a W-2 form prepared by the accounting division of the facility (W. Rummel, personal communication, October 22, 1991).

Payroll is one of the largest costs of any facility. Payroll records must be maintained in order to prepare annual taxes and for auditing purposes. Today, many facilities are moving away from a manual payroll operation to prepackaged payroll software applications. These applications can be customized to meet the specific needs of the facility (Mulrooney & Farmer, 1995).

Bad Debts and Collections

In any business operation, bad debts are a part of doing business. According to W. Rummel (personal communication, October 22, 1991), the steps employed to avoid the problem and methods of debt collection are important topics for a facility manager to know.

For example, a concert was to be held at Facility X. The promoter of the event was new, having never promoted an event before. This individual was a businessman from another large urban area, and his partners were similarly inexperienced. The main act for the concert was a well-known superstar, and the promoters anticipated a sold-out crowd.

The promoter sent a cash deposit, in the form of a wire transfer to the facility after signing the contract. A check was not acceptable due to the unproven track record of the promoter. Once the cash was deposited into the facility's account, the promoter was allowed to proceed with the concert arrangements.

As the event date approached it became increasingly clear to the facility management that the concert had not sold sufficient tickets to pay the bills. This information was determined by observing the daily ticket-sale figures generated by the box office. The promoters were contacted and asked to pay another wire transfer as a guarantee, so that management could continue to hold the concert as planned. The promoter was warned that if this cash transfer did not take place, the show would be canceled. After not receiving the cash transfer, management decided to cancel the show.

By employing these tactics the facility management avoided collection problems. Without the promoter's deposit it was extremely unlikely that if the show had proceeded, the facility management would have recovered their investment.

The facility business manager must constantly be aware of the status and problems surrounding an event. He or she must make arrangements to collect as much of the money in advance, or face the major problems of collecting after an event has been completed. By working with well-known promoters, requesting deposits in advance, and employing strict operational procedures a facility will limit its potential for bad debt.

Collections

Sometimes even with using strict procedures facilities must try to collect outstanding debts. The first step in any recovery procedure is to secure the assistance of a lawyer. If initial legal steps do not produce the repayment of the debt, then a lawsuit should be filed in the local civil court. It is hoped that, the results of such civil action would be the payment of the debt, to include attorney fees and probably some additional penalty. If, even after going through all these steps, there is no recoverable money or assets, the debt must be written off as an expense against facility revenues, thereby reducing the profit margin.

For example, a restaurant owner paid $4,000 by check for souvenir programs from a sports event, for display in his establishment. The owner sold the programs and retained the proceeds, but the check bounced. Even though the check was resubmitted a number of times it went unpaid. The sport facility's attorney sent a number of letters to inform the individual of the amount of money owed and the legal steps to be pursued if payment was not promptly received. According to the laws of the state, the fraudulent use of a check made the owner liable for triple the value, attorney fees and court costs, and a possible jail term. The judge awarded the facility a judgment of $12,000 and court costs. The total amount to be reimbursed was now $16,000 plus 16% interest, and a lien was placed on the owner's business. In addition, if this amount was not paid within a specified time period, the restaurant owner could be placed in prison, as well as lose his restaurant. The facility manager and the legal counsel are responsible to pursue this matter to its inevitable conclusion.

This costly and lengthy bad-debt collection process is why so much care is taken with event development. Credit checks of the promoter help to determine the promoter's reputation and whether or not he or she pays his or her bills and incurred obligations. Other prevention techniques include accepting only cash from promoters, rather than any other form of payment. Most facilities do not accept checks, and in fact, many buildings do not to take a certified or cashier's check. A cash-wire transfer to the facility's account or hard currency is the preferred method to secure the services of the facility. In most situations these transfers are nonrefundable.

In order for a sport facility to survive financially, it needs to be able to host a variety of events in addition to sporting events. When looking at these auxiliary clients, several factors are taken into consideration to establish a preferred ranking order:

1. Concerts with first class promoters and an event history

2. National events with visible or eminent contractors

3. Local contractors

4. Touring shows with out-of-town or country promoters

5. Religious conventions and events (W. Rummel, personal communication, October 22, 1991).

Remember, the individual/promoter who contracts and pays the bills, rather than the star or performer, is responsible for any and all liability of the event. Once the event has concluded the promoter will move on to the next tour stop while the facility manager remains.

Revenue Sources

Traditionally, there are five sources of revenue that enable the facility to be maintained and operate successfully. These areas are facility rental, food and beverage concessions, novelties, parking, and box office.

Facility rental. In any facility, whether sport oriented or not, rental income is a standard means of deriving income. There are three standard rental-income agreements: percentage of the gross, which applies primarily to ticketed events; a flat rent, which is usually reserved for nonticketed or nonprofit groups; and rental based on a specific dollar amount per square foot basis, particularly when dealing with events known as flat shows (convention or trade shows). Additional income can be derived from creative bookings and co-promoting events. For example, with small meeting-room rentals for functions, such as luncheons and dinners, a flat fee per person is built into the catering fee. Rental income can also be realized through trade-outs for goods, services, or favors, and the rental of storage space to tenants and outside companies. All these rental agreements should have a nonrefundable minimum deposit policy to insure against event cancellation.

Concessions. Income is derived from such entities as concession stands at events, event catering, special-event catering, and special-function catering. Additional income can be derived from managing the food and beverage operation (in-house); procuring catering contracts in other facility locations or for private functions; managing a full-service restaurant; operating a mobile catering service; supplying food and beverage vending machines for the employees; subcontracting part of the concessions operations to outside food service vendors; altering and upgrading concessions stands with updated equipment and enhanced toilet facilities; and providing portable concession stands in the parking lot to accommodate outdoor events.

Novelties. Extra income can also be realized through the management of a novelty operation. The income can be derived from a percentage of gross sales or a flat rate per event combined with a specific dollar amount per patron. A permanent facility novelty store that holds the prime tenant's product lines (e.g., Mazda Cannons) and local merchandise can be developed. The facility novelty units can be open during facility tours and events. Also, investment in and resale of novelty items for one-time events, such as concert tours and the World Cup Final, can yield a sizable surplus.

Parking. According to R. Rummel (personal communication, October 22, 1991), there are usually three revenue generating methods utilized in facility

PRESENTATION AND SELECTION HAVE A GREAT DEAL TO DO
WITH THE AMOUNT OF NOVELTY SALES A FACILITY HAS.

parking operations. The first is a direct collection method on an individual or per car basis. The second is flat rate per ticket issued, and the final is a flat rate for specific events. Other sources of parking revenue are

- preferred, personalized parking spaces
- per event, all-event, season, or annual parking passes
- valet parking for VIP parking at a standard fee per automobile
- marketing parking lots for car, ski or boat shows, motor homes, carnivals, food festivals, auto races, driver safety school, and swap meets (Jewel, 1992; Mulrooney & Farmer, 1995).

Box office. There are four revenue-generating methods used in box office operations. The first is a percentage of the gross. The second involves billing the promoter for actual costs. The third is a flat rate or percentage of the actual revenue generated, up to a prescribed amount. The final method is a combination arrangement which is a percentage of the gross on advanced sales, added to the actual event-day costs (Jewel, 1992).

Additional box office revenue can be realized:

- by the facility becoming a vendor for events at other venues,
- through the sale of transportation tickets (i.e., bus or train),
- by the facility becoming an agent for lottery tickets,
- by prepackaging events through the selling of series, season, or yearly ticket subscriptions,
- through a ticket-service charge system from the use of the telephone, credit cards, direct mail, and other ticketing outlets,
- by selling souvenirs at the ticket windows,
- by selling advertising on ticket backs and ticket envelopes, and
- by subcontracting the box office management to other venues who are without an established box office for a major event or spectacle.

Additional Revenue Sources

Although the preceding information identifies income sources from established facility entities, there are also nontraditional facility enterprises that can produce substantial income for the facility operation. These include advertising, administrative fee services, facility name, luxury suites and miscellaneous areas (W. Mulrooney, personal communication, January 9, 1992).

Advertising. Through the operation of an in-house advertising agency the facility can generate up to a 15% service royalty. Other income opportunities include developing in-house production facilities for mass media and desk-top publishing; selling inside and outside advertising through static signs or reader board messages; obtaining sponsorship for all events; specialty advertising associated with sports teams, and trade-outs for goods and services (W. Peneguy, personal communication, September 18, 1991).

The administrative arena. The administrative arena provides the facility operation with opportunities to obtain additional income. Some of these methods include

- the opportunity to invest event-derived income and manage cash flow (depending upon operational rules and regulations of the facility),

- the implementation of an administrative fee for event staffing;

- charges for a site origination or television-connection fee;

- development of chargeable public services, such as a parents' waiting room, and baby-sitting service for patrons or performers' children, and

- the issuance of a special-event insurance policy, and an underwriter's fee (IAAM, 1990).

Facility name. The sale of the facility name and or parts of the facility, such as special rooms, locker rooms, fountains, walkways, to corporations, companies, or individuals or donors who desire not only recognition but also advertising clout is a viable method of procuring additional revenue. This type of revenue has been used successfully in higher education for years and is an appropriate development for highly visible public-assembly and sport-facility operations.

Luxury suites. In recent years, the development of upgraded and luxury suites has become somewhat commonplace. Income opportunities from this luxury accommodation can be derived from rental; sublease from owners who initially purchased the suites; catering prior, during, and after events; fees for media hook-ups for television, radio, fax, and telephone; additional ticket-sales outlets; and cleaning services (Jewel, 1992).

Miscellaneous income. According to R. Johnson (personal communication, October 22, 1991), other areas from which the facility could derive income may include

- joint ventures with professional sports teams and enterprises, such as the New Orleans Saints and the New Orleans Superdome,

- development of a community health and fitness center for corporate executives or individuals for an annual fee,

- financial donations for specific projects,

- bond refinancing,

- lobbying of political entities and officials for capital improvement projects and additional budget funding, and development of the facility's own series of special events (i.e., Christmas Show, food festival, and special sports events) and holiday celebrations (IAAM, 1990).

Summary

1. The overall operations of a facility are guided by the mission statement. Although most privately managed facilities are profit driven, some municipally operated facilities are more interested in nonprofit community programs.

2. Budgets are a tool for managers to use to organize their revenues and expenses over a period of time.

3. Budgets usually contain four cycles. These include

   1) Budget preparation: The budget is prepared based on the mission and philosophy of the facility management.

ALL FACILITIES HAVE AN ADMINISTRATIVE AREA FOR HIGH LEVEL MEETINGS AND DECISION-MAKING THAT CAN INCREASE INCOME LEVELS OF THE FACILITY.

   2) Presentation and adoption: The budget is communicated to various supports and once approved is adapted by senior management.

   3) Execution: The budget is communicated to everyone in the program and carried out according to its structure.

   4) Postexecution and audit: Feedback and evaluation on the success of the budget is necessary for future situations.

4. Line item, PPBES and ZBB are several of the budgets used in the process. Zero based budgeting (ZBB) is used by a great many facilities because every expense starts from zero and must be justified before acceptance.

5. Issue papers are a management tool that facilitates use to identify problems and then take the corrective steps necessary to overcome them.

6. Depreciation is used to determine how much of a product has been consumed at a specific point in its life cycle.

7. Event settlement occurs during every event usually near the end. The promoter and facility representative sit down and discuss the financial status of the event. Bills are presented, expenses are divided, and profits are shared. Because in most cases the promoter moves on with the event to the next step, it is imperative that any differences be settled before event completion.

8. Bad debts can be alleviated by working with well-known promoters, requesting significant deposit in advance and utilizing strict budgeting principles. If a debt is incurred, legal services should be employed to recapture outstanding debt.

9. Traditional revenue is generated by a facility through building rental, ticket sales, parking, novelties, and food and beverage concessions.

10. Additional sources of revenue for facility managers include selling the facility name, renting luxury suites, administrative fees, and advertising.

Questions

1. Define and describe a budget.
2. How does the political/government budget process differ from the private/operational budget?
3. Describe the phases of the budget cycle.
4. Describe the various budget types that can be involved in a facility budget.
5. Identify and describe the phases of a White Paper. How does this apply to a sport facility?
6. Describe how event settlement works in a sport facility.
7. Why is it important to develop collections procedures?
8. Identify traditional revenue sources and operational segments in a facility.
9. List additional revenue sources.

References

Davidson, S., Malver, M., Stickney, C., & Weil, R. (1988). *Managerial accounting.* Chicago: Dryden Press.

Garrison, R. (1982). *Managerial accounting.* Plano, TX: Business Publications

Inc.

Gibson, C. & Frishkoff, P. (1986). *Financial statement analysis.* Boston: Kent Publishing Co.

International Association of Auditorium Managers (IAAM). (1990). Course materials from the unpublished proceedings of the School for Public Assembly Facility Management, Ogelbay, VA.

Jewel, D. (1992). *Public assembly facilities.* Malabar, FL: Krieger Publishing Company.

Mulrooney, A., & Farmer, P. (1995). Managing the facility. In B. Parkhouse (Ed.), *The management of sport: Its foundation and application* (2nd ed.). (pp. 223-248). St. Louis, MO: Mosby-Year Book.

CHAPTER 17

Box Office Management

The box office is one of the important operational and revenue-generating areas in sport facilities. Although this area is not perceived as a complicated operation, it is linked to the business office, marketing, public relations, and actual operation of each facility event. The box office is also the public's initial contact with the facility (Mulrooney & Farmer, 1995).

According to Rummel (personal communication, October 22, 1991), too often the box office is the most neglected, especially when planning facility construction. Often this neglect is based on the assumption that patrons will tolerate confusion and discomfort to buy a ticket for an event of their choice. Although this may be partially true, the patrons should also feel good about spending their money to view the event.

To market services to the public, the box office should be organized and accessible to the consumer. The size of the box office area should accommodate the sale, pick-up and distribution of tickets. An adequate number of windows should be available to handle an unexpected number of "walk-up" sales. It is suggested that the sales windows should be located on all sides of the facility rather than just a main box office area at the main entrance to the facility (Mulrooney & Farmer, 1995).

The primary facility entrance, as a rule of thumb, should contain at least 40% of the ticket-selling windows. Also, the box office lobbies should be of sufficient size to enable patrons sufficient space to line up for tickets (G. Lewis, personal communication, September 14, 1991).

Each sales window, to serve the public satisfactorily, should be able to retail various priced tickets for each facility event. For example an 18,000-seat arena should have 18 to 24 ticket windows available for the sale of tickets. This number is based on 400 to 700 tickets available per window. This is an optimum number of windows and probably would not be present at sport facilities. This ratio of windows to projected sales, along with historical sales data, provides a functional estimate of the number of windows required for a specific event (IAAM, 1990).

Covered areas ranging from 30 to 50 feet in front of the ticket windows should be made available for the convenience of patrons. In addition to inside ticket windows, outside ticket windows should be provided. This distribution will provide patrons with the opportunity to purchase tickets from several locations, as well as keep lines from interfering with patrons entering the facility via the turnstiles. An outside ticket-selling window location is also useful for pre-sale tickets for future events, without having to open the facility.

All box office locations should be located in easily accessible areas. These open and accessible windows tend to generate repeat business and promote sales of future facility events. It is important to identify specific windows located away from the main entrance for "will-call" and reservations (Mulrooney & Farmer, 1995).

THE BOX OFFICE AREA SHOULD HAVE AMPLE WINDOWS AND SPACE
TO ACCOMMODATE A GREAT NUMBER OF PATRONS.

Box Office Personnel

The box office, although an important operational unit, employs a minimal number of full-time staff. These include the box office manager and two or three assistants as the only full-time staff members. The remaining employees are usually employed on a part-time basis (Morgan, 1990).

The box office manager is responsible for the operation and supervision of all personnel in the box office. This individual is also responsible for the ordering, distribution, and sale of event tickets, as well as production of the final box office statement.   Additional responsibilities include policy development, personnel selection, placement, safety, discipline of employees and working closely with promoters and facility operational personnel (Mulrooney & Farmer, 1995).

Box Office Policy

The box office normally is staffed and operational from 9:00 a.m. to 5:00 p.m. on nonevent days.   On event days, however, the box office should continue operations at least until half-time or intermission, depending on ticket demand. Box office policies should be relatively simple and uncomplicated with the ultimate goal being to provide an efficient, secure, and service-oriented operation. with employees being instructed about appropriate dress and attitude (Mulrooney & Farmer, 1995).   Box office policy areas, according to Mulrooney & Farmer (1995), include

· patron courtesy,

· event seating familiarity, and

· efficient ticket processing.

Equipment operation

Box office equipment includes
· ticket counters that can apportion tickets into numerical sequencing and price breaks,
· cash drawers,
· computer terminals and printers for printing computerized tickets,
· cash registers, and
· telephones or answering machines to provide messages and record ticket orders (Mulrooney & Farmer, 1995).

Ticket Purchases

The numbers of tickets purchased by the patron for a specific event is at the discretion of the box office manager in agreement with the promoter. Generally, there is usually no set limit to the number of ticket purchases for athletic events, whereas many concerts limit patrons to 8 to 10 tickets. This policy attempts to diminish the scalping of tickets.

Refunds and exchanges

Regardless of the facility,   a general rule should be that NO refunds or exchanges should be given at any time. All sales should be considered FINAL. It is imperative that the public be aware of this policy, both through signage and verbal communication. The facility is an agent for the promoter and cannot make the rules or exceptions; therefore, any refund or exchange policy would have to be approved in writing by the facility contractor or promoter. (G. Lewis, personal communication, September 14, 1991).

Telephone and Mail Orders

Both of these procurement methods should be contractually agreed upon by the promoter and facility personnel. A few important guidelines can insure effective administration. Examples of these guidelines include

- On sold-out events, a ticket for a specific seat should be held for only 3 days;

- Telephone ticket orders should be acceptable if the promoter and facility management have both agreed upon this sales method; and

- All transactions should be recorded as a cash transactions (Mulrooney & Farmer, 1990).

For most events and for the convenience of patrons, tickets should be made available through the mail. This method creates an inexpensive opportunity to sell tickets for future events. It also provides the patron with information via advertising, within or on the envelope (IAAM, 1991).

Will Call

A will call location should be established in every facility. This location provides patrons with the opportunity to pick up pre-paid tickets prior to, or on the day of, the event. For security reasons and to limit problems when the patron arrives to pick up the ticket, proper identification should be produced before the tickets are released.

Lost Tickets

As mentioned previously all ticket refunds or exchanges are subject to agreement of the facility and promoter. However, in the case of a ticket lost, prior to the event, the ticket manager should be empowered to issue a seat replacement pass, voiding the original ticket. If, however, "the ticket manager decides that the patron should purchase new tickets, then if rediscovered the original tickets could be returned to the box office for a full refund, prior to the performance. This lost ticket policy impacts the facility's image..." (Mulrooney & Farmer, 1995, p. 234).

Scalping

Scalping is the illegal sale of tickets for more than the face value shown on the ticket. Most local policies and laws address this problem through arrests and fines. This situation is problematic, and although the facility and box office can do little to combat scalping, placing a limit on the number of tickets purchased may help a little (IAAM, 1991).

Ticketing Variables

There are various elements associated with ticket sales operations that should be kept in mind. According to Mulrooney & Farmer (1995), these include

Capacity. Each event and resultant seating configuration are different. To maximize revenue the facility must be able to sell every available seat.

Seating. Facility seating arrangements, without regard to configuration, fall into two classifications:

1. **Reserved seating,** where a patron may select a specific seat. This type of seat-selection-process seating provides a systematic method, especially when involved with concerts and athletic events.

2. **General admission**, where all patrons may purchase seating on a first-come, first-served basis. Some concerts may sell **festival seating**, which is a misnomer because no actual seats exist. The area in front of the stage is void of seats, and after the doors open the patrons crowd as close to the stage as possible. Although many dangers arise because of the potential for injuries, many promoters like the setup because it allows them to sell additional tickets. Also many of the bands like these types of configurations because they bring the crowd closer to the stage.

Ticket Type. On the back of every ticket purchased is a printed contract between the promoter and facility management, and the purchaser. A ticket is a license, and being a license it may be revoked at any time by the promoter. When selecting ticket producers, the box office manager should deal only with reputable and bonded ticket companies. All ticket stocks should be ordered in advance, to reduce the chance of error and ensure patron satisfaction. Today, computerized tickets are the trend. Although more expensive than traditional ticket stock, there are certain advantages. Event information, sponsoring organization, ticket price, program name, performance date and time, facility name, seat location, and advertising can all be printed on the computerized ticket stock (Mulrooney & Farmer, 1995).

Ticket-Sales Strategy

In most facilities ticket-sales strategy should be a joint operation between the marketing department and the box office. However, primary responsibility for its success or failure lies solely with the box office operation. According to Lewis (personal communication, September 14, 1991) strategic ticket-sales issues include

Pricing. The box office will develop appropriately priced ticket options, in conjunction with the marketing department and promoter. Decisions concerning ticket pricing should be made with two issues in mind: (a) **house scale,** where pricing is established solely by the box office, and (b) **performance scale,** where the event promoter indicates the ticket price.

Incentives. There are many types of sales incentives utilized today:

1. **Discounted tickets** make use of unusual seating areas, such as standing room or special circumstances;

2. **Group sales** enable an event to be sold at lower cost to groups for a reduced price. A group sales policy is useful when an event has low sales; and

3. **Season tickets** are used predominantly for athletic or theatrical events based on the seasonal nature of the activity.

Information Service

The box office is the primary public-information area of the facility. All box office personnel should consequently be trained in courtesy and be able to provide information regarding the facility, personnel, and upcoming events. Additionally, the box office should have a 24-hour-a-day pre-recorded message, informing the public about upcoming facility events. This message serves as a cost-effective way to provide public information without additional personnel.

Records

To provide an efficient and organized box office operation, records need to be maintained and appropriately filed. These records, by event types, are important especially when conducting a facility audit, reviewing procedures, and looking at issues such as facility access.

The single most important element is the daily transaction report. This form should be completed daily, providing management with a record of the daily transactions performed by the box office operation. Items that should be included in this document are ticket sales, mail orders, and anything else deemed relevant by the facility management.

Event Summary

Another required document, completed under the authority of the business office, is the event summary. When tickets are sold, a record is required for all transactions. Upon conclusion of the event it is vital that all ticket sales, whether sold, unsold, or complimentary tickets, equal the revenue generated. The event-summary information for each event is calculated as follows:

FACILITY CAPACITY - TICKETS SOLD = UNSOLD TICKETS + COMPLIMENTARY TICKETS + RECORDS (IAAM, 1990).

Computer Ticket Management

According to Jewel (1992), "the computerized ticket industry estimate they sell more than $2 billion in tickets annually" (p. 115). Computerized ticketing systems have recently been developed in an attempt to minimize personnel costs and eliminate unwieldy operational procedures. Although each system is different the following information can be provided:

- point-of-sales patron information by ZIP code or subscriber numbers;
- computerized mailing lists,
- updated daily financial information,
- solicitation of patron response for specific events,
- monitoring of ticket sales versus marketing efforts, and
- ability to compare demand fluctuations to the type of advertising or marketing program employed (IAAM, 1990).

Gift Certificates

As in many other business enterprises, gift certificates can provide incentive for patron participation. The idea of gift certificates becomes especially attractive when associated with a cultural event. However, it should be used infrequently and with approval of the event promoter.

Box Seat

In all events, certain seats will be more highly sought after than others (i.e., front row for a boxing match or the 50-yard line for a football game). These designated seats are considered the best in the house and will sell for a premium. The pricing for these seats should be determined by the box office manager, in conjunction with the promoter, based upon historical data of like events.

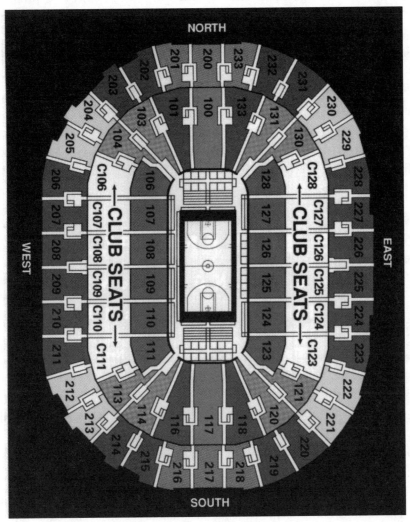

SEATING PLANS ALLOW PATRONS TO SEE WHAT TYPE OF SEAT THEY WILL GET BASED UPON HOW MUCH THEY ARE WILLING TO PAY FOR A TICKET

Summary

1. For most patrons, the box office is the first contact they have with the facility. It also provides a central location for individuals with questions, problems, or concerns.

2. Though one main central location should exist, ticket windows should be provided for the public in various locations around the facility.

3. Although most box office employees are part time, the box office manager and his or her assistants are full-time employees.

4. Refunds are rarely given by the box office. In most instances the promoter is the owner of the event and therefore ultimately responsible for all moneys generated by the box office.

5. Scalping is the illegal sale of a ticket for more than face value. Though illegal, scalping is an extremely lucrative venture that is experiencing widespread growth throughout the country.

6. Various strategies exist regarding the sale of tickets. Some of these include house vs. performance scale, discounted tickets, group and season ticket sales.

7. Tickets for most athletic and entertainment events are printed by computer. The actual ticket is called *stock*.

Questions

1. Describe why the box office plays an important role in the facility operation process.

2. Identify the important components of the box office operation.

References

International Association of Auditorium Managers (IAAM). (1990). Course materials from the unpublished proceedings of the School for Public Assembly Facility Management, Ogelbay, VA.

Jewel, D. (1992). *Public assembly facilities*. Malabar, FL: Krieger Publishing Company.

Morgan, L. (1990, Summer). Yes, public relations begins at the box office. *Facility Manager*, 20-21.

Mulrooney, A., & Farmer, P. (1995). Managing the facility. In B. Parkhouse (Ed.), *The management of sport: Its foundation and application* (2nd ed.). (pp. 223-248). St. Louis, MO: Mosby-Year Book.

CHAPTER 18

CONCESSIONS AND MERCHANDISE

Jewel (1992) states that "food and beverage services have today become a major factor in a development of successful facilities" (p.103). In fact, if a facility desires to operate with a profit, a comprehensive food service operation is a necessity. Food services are the business operation that prepares, delivers and sells food and beverage items to patrons. Under this food service title are concessions and merchandise.

Here are some interesting facts concerning facility food service operations:

1. Beer and alcohol account for the highest percentage of concession profits.

2. Popcorn is a large revenue producer, with the cost of a box of popcorn around $.05 whereas patrons pay $2.00 to $2.50 per serving.

3. Concession sales are usually constant one hour prior to the game with 80% of sales taking place at half-time. The remaining 20% takes place after half-time.

Food Service Arrangements

According to the IAAM (1990), in most facilities there are three types of operations: **In-House, Full Contract** and **Management Contract**.

In-House. The in-house operation has the facility management controlling the entire food service operation, from procurement of supplies and employees to supervisory control, scheduling and the resultant profit or loss. Advantages of an In-House operation are that the facility exercises maximum control over food service operations, and controls price, product, and quality. This type of operation can result in a higher profit potential, and it would not be necessary to change food service companies because of poor performance. Disadvantages are numerous. All employee and administrative problems are those of the facility management. The facility operation also has little regional or national network of expertise. If the facility is a public operation, the political and bureaucratic red tape will be substantial.

Full Contract. The full-contract option involves contracting an outside contractor to manage the entire food service operation. This arrangement usually nets the facility anywhere from 30 to 52% profit, depending upon variables such as the facility size, stature, and negotiated contract. The food service contractor controls the entire operation with a contract ranging from 5 to 10 years in length. Advantages of this arrangement are that volume purchasing enables the vendor to provide quality products at reduced prices as well as provide the facility operation with efficiency, expertise, and capital equipment. In-house management, staff, purchasing, maintenance, inventory, and storage are all the contractor's responsibility.   There are few for the facility regarding employees and their associated problems, such as workers' compensation, equal opportunity, hiring or firing; and national expertise. Liability lies with the concessionaire, rather than the facility in this situation. Additionally, there is little political interference when compared with an in-house operation.

Management Contract. This third option, the management contract, is a combination of the previous options. A management fee provides an in-house food service operation, with an outside manager contracted to administer the operation.

CONCESSIONS IS A MAJOR MONEY MAKER AND MANY FACILITIES
WILL CONTRACT THIS SERVICE OUT.

This option provides the facility with maximum control of the employees and purchasing as well as uses contracted professional management who have expertise in the food service industry.

Selection of a Food Service Operation

When considering contract options, there are a number of factors to be taken into account. These include the amount of capital investment the contractor is willing to provide for the facility operation. Other elements in this decision would be the contractor's financial stability, strength of reputation, quality personnel, and most important the intended percentage split with the facility operation (J. Neeley, personal communication, January 11, 1992).

After selection of a contractor to manage the food service, it is important that the facility have some input and control over the pricing structures, menu, number and kind of food service stands operating at events, and use and control of volunteer groups associated with the food service operations.

Concessions

The term *concessions* and food service are synonymous, often being used interchangeably. A well-operated concessions operation plays a vital role in the financial success or failure of a facility operation, because very often food and drink go along with recreation and sports (Jewel, 1992). For example in 1989-90, the Superdome in New Orleans, Louisiana, reported that concession revenue amounted to $7.5 million, which represented almost 60% of its operating revenue (Mulrooney & Farmer, 1995).

If a facility concessions operation is to thrive, management must be more concerned with serving good food and beverage at a reasonable price. Management must possess a knowledge of marketing, financial management, business planning, purchasing, inventory management, business law, insurance, advertising, and personnel.

Stocking

Stocking is the maintenance of the materials and goods to be utilized in the facility food service operation. It is an important component of any concessions operation. The process begins with the manager's deciding which products or brands to purchase based upon quality, price, service, and customer acceptance. It is common for the facility staff to taste-tests items to determine the most salable products. When deciding on the quality of items, past records should be scrutinized carefully (Mulrooney & Farmer, 1995).

Nonperishable items, such as cups, napkins, and other paper goods, should be purchased in large quantities for the entire season whereas perishable or time-sensitive items (i.e., hot dogs and buns) should be ordered fresh per event. In large facilities, restocking can take up to one week to complete, whereas in smaller venues it may require only five hours.

Convenience Foods

Foods in the concession stands are known as convenience foods. The three types of convenience foods found in facilities today are frozen, dehydrated, and powdered foods.

Frozen foods range from fruit juices to meat. Sizes vary from individual servings to large volume servings. One of the problems with frozen foods is that they usually must be consumed after thawing which requires the concessions manager to be accurate when estimating demand. Dehydrated and powdered foods are appropriate for facilities as they can be stored for long periods of time without spoilage. They are often pre-packaged and require only water and/or a short period of cooking for re-constitution. Dehydrated and powdered foods available in facilities today are spices, seasonings, soups of many varieties, milk, pastry mixes, sauces, gravies, and beverages (Mulrooney & Farmer, 1995).

When considering convenience foods, variety is a key that enables concession stands to present the public a varied menu and allow employees with limited knowledge and training to prepare appetizing fail-safe dishes. Convenience foods provide concessionaires with savings in money, time and labor, especially in the areas of cleaning, trimming, packaging, storing, cooking, and serving foods.

Efficiency of these food service operations has been realized through the development of disposable packaging, containers and utensils. Disposable products in use today include: semi-rigid foil pans, plastic pouches, foil and plastic packets, foam containers, cardboard containers and other disposable items, such as plates, cups, eating utensils, doilies, aprons and uniforms. "Boil-in-a-pouch" foods as well as chemically generated foods have also been developed to reduce both the cooking time and cost. Other developments involve foil and plastic packets. These items encase individual servings of condiments (i.e. tomato sauces, mayonnaise, salt, pepper, etc.), and provide foam and cardboard containers pre-shaped for specific carryout items. Disposable products enable a variety of finely prepared convenience foods to be served by minimally trained labor, with minimal equipment (Mulrooney & Farmer, 1995). These products are easy to stock and dispense, and can reduce resultant sanitation problems.

For concessions operations to be successful ventures, they should not only use good food but also have adequate storage space and be appropriately positioned for spectator access. In most facilities there should be sufficient numbers of concession stands to serve the total number of seats, with each patron being able to reach the nearest the stand within 40 to 60 seconds of leaving his or her seat.

Advertising

All concession operations should be bright, colorful, and well lit. Menu boards should have prices and attractive pictures of the food and beverages being served. Signage should be in neon, instead of blending with the color of the facility structure. If a facility serves recognizable brand-name products (i.e., Coors beer and Coca-Cola) questions about the quality of the merchandise would be

CONVENIENT AND CLEAN CONDIMENT STANDS ENHANCE THE IMAGE
OF THE FACILITY.

eliminated. Simple food combinations should be listed in large readable print to provide customer direction, eliminate complex orders and limit the amount of time patrons wait in line for food and beverage service. Additionally, all prices should be rounded to the nearest $0.25 or $0.50 to limit time spent at the counter.

Concessions should be well-organized with clear indications of where patrons should line for service. Equipment, food, and cash registers should be conveniently located so that items can be quickly served by a single person. It is important that all employees be trained to manage large crowds and keep lines moving. However, they should also be encouraged to increase sales through suggestive selling techniques, trying to convince the customer that all items are reasonably priced and buying a larger size actually results in saving money (Mulrooney & Farmer, 1995).

Maintenance

To encourage patrons to return to the facility for future events, they must feel comfortable and find the facility clean and well maintained. Concession operations are no different from the rest of the facility operation. To ensure cleanliness and compliance with health guidelines, floor drains as well as adequate ventilation and exhaust systems must be installed in stand and kitchen areas.

A concessions supervisor should not allow any employee to leave work until the stands are spotless. At some large facilities nonprofit groups, (i.e., girl scouts, church groups, etc.) volunteer their labor and receive a percentage of sales.

At the conclusion of the event, employees must dispose of large amounts of waste from disposable products. This debris should be eliminated through various methods. One method is incineration, which requires a minimal amount of space, and reduces disposable paper items and plastics to ash. A second method uses a shredding machine that converts plastics and paper into a pulp, by removing the water and shredding the fibers. The third method, compression or dumpsters, packs refuse under pressure thereby reducing its size to aid in ease of removal. Today, many of these products are being replaced by recyclable products that can be reused and are considered environmentally safe.

Hawkers and Vendors

A financially successful part of the concession operation are "vendors" or "hawkers." These individuals are responsible for taking food or beverage directly to the patrons in the seating area. This service generates substantial sales as many patrons will utilize this convenience to purchase food and beverage, rather than miss any of the event action.

Trends

Recent trends in concession operations now provide name-brand products, such as Taco Bell and Pizza Hut, being sold in facilities. These operations provide the facility with a percentage of sales for little cost expenditure. In the near future, many items served in these concession stands will be health oriented, such as soup, salads, and yogurt (Mulrooney & Farmer, 1995). Additionally, there will be specialty operations, such as sweetshops with a large assortment of candies and chocolates or hot-dog specialty shops offering several hot-dog combinations. In the

PORTABLE STANDS PROVIDE AN ALTERNATIVE TO THE MAJOR
STANDS AND PROVIDE A LIMITED NUMBER OF ITEMS.

beverage area, there has always been a demand for 'fast-bar' service. Computer-operated services have been developed to satisfy this demand and can mix and pour up to 1,000 beverage servings in 4 seconds, with uniform liquor content in each drink poured.

Another recent innovation is frozen foods being placed in a timed oven drawer. After the specific time has elapsed, the oven automatically turns off, the door opens, and the food is ready for serving. The main advantages of this cooking equipment are that it saves time and space compared with conventional equipment.

Along with these aforementioned trends, new packaging has been developed. For example, the prototype package of the future may be a rigid aluminum foil dish and cover with a pull tab, containing a hot dog, onion rings, condiments, and napkins. Pulling the tab before opening the cover will break a heat capsule which, after 30 seconds, would bring the contents to eating temperature (Mulrooney & Farmer, 1995). Another innovation could be the development of an unusual condiment. For example, odorless garlic. Originally developed in Japan in 1988 and is now being used commercially in the United States. This processed garlic, soaked and then dried, has the characteristic odor before ingestion but not after.

Food Safety and Sanitation Practices

Food services attract all types of bacteria, insects, and animal pests as they provide food, water, and warmth, the three basic ingredients necessary to sustain life. To control food contamination and limit the spread of disease, all employees must possess basic knowledge of food safety and sanitation practices (Mulrooney & Farmer, 1995).

Other precautionary measures should be the regular inspection of delivery vehicles to ensure appropriate refrigeration and sanitary conditions. Crates or boxes should never be stored outside when unloading as insects could infest the products and contaminate the food service environment. Further, all spills should be removed as soon as they occur.

Another important factor to control food contamination is personal hygiene. Hands are a source of contamination. Every time an employee scratches or coughs, he or she is exposing his or her hands to bacteria that will spread to anything that is touched. All employees should practice basic hygiene methods, and eliminate unhealthy practices (e.g., beards, uncontrolled long hair, unnecessary jewelry). Finally, ill employees should not attend work as they can expose the food preparation and service areas to bacterial contamination.

In most communities legislation and rules have been enacted that oversee community (facility) food service operations. All food service employees are mandated to pass some form of medical examination, such as a tuberculosis test, and satisfactorily complete some form of written examination concerning the handling of food products.

Projecting Operational Costs

In the budgeting for a facility concessions operation, sales projections are a crucial and difficult task. It is virtually impossible to know how much revenue will be generated from event to event. However, past experience can provide relatively accurate projections.

From the beginning of any facility concession operation all operational costs must be recorded. However, after a period of time the operations will become more streamlined and efficient, thereby developing a solid reputation for serving consistent quality products.

To ascertain the appropriate levels of inventory, a projection of total sales must be determined. It is important to budget material costs, food and beverage costs, not necessarily actual costs, but the percentage of cost. This figure is derived by dividing the actual cost by the total sales, resulting in a percentage.

Another crucial item is determining labor costs. Management salaries will be a fixed monthly cost, whereas the employee-salary expense is a variable cost that fluctuates with total sales. Employee labor costs should have a break-even point where labor costs are covered by profit from sales. Rent and insurance are also fixed operating costs. The rent is a fixed monthly figure, but can include a percentage of the total sales or pretax profit amount. Insurance costs, which cover such items as insurance premium amounts, such as fire, theft, liability, and workers' compensation, should also be included.

Finally, general operating costs, such as labor and other taxes; repairs of equipment or building or both; advertising; promotional expense; equipment rental; licenses; travel; social security; federal and state unemployment tax; local taxes; sales taxes; cost of scheduled maintenance and emergency repairs; expense of all business and government licenses (e.g., operating licenses, health permit, liquor license) and the cost of business travel, should be established.

Computation of total expenditures is achieved by the addition of all the total budgeted expenditures. Net profit is realized by subtracting total budgeted expenditures from total sales. Projected pretax net profit percentage will be calculated by dividing the total net projected profit by total projected sales. Finally, to determine the gross net profit, total material costs should be subtracted from total projected costs (IAAM, 1990).

Merchandise

Merchandise includes anything sold within the facility not related to food and beverage. These items may include T-shirts, hats, programs, pennants, posters, or other souvenirs that are event and facility related.

The popularity of the artist, athlete, or sport team is an important element in attracting audiences to the facility, thus impacting the sale of merchandise. As in other facility areas, each facility management will dictate the procedures to be used in merchandise sales. Each of these performing artists owns the rights to his or her likeness and the merchandise produced as a result. This is one reason why cameras are rarely allowed into events; the promoter or merchandise representative holds the copyright on all images produced from the event. Simply stated, the promoter wants the patron to pay for the pictures, not take them for free (J. Neeley, personal communication, January 11, 1992).

Splits or Deals

If an event threatens to relocate to in another facility, the local venue often will attempt to rework the contract and develop a better division of profits or "split" between the facility and the promoter. There is no standard formula to follow, as competition will dictate the requirements and generate the business.

The success of merchandise sales depends upon the application of the appropriate formula to each specific situation. The following are four different merchandise formulae traditionally used:

1. **Flat Fee:** The flat fee is a designated amount, collected in advance, which may be part of the promoter's deposit. It is paid directly to the facility. This arrangement is most often employed for a nonticketed event, such as meetings, graduations or religious services.

2. **Percentage of Vendor Sales:** This formula requires the vendor to pay the facility a percentage of the sales. The percentage may range from 5% to 20% of sales, depending upon the vendor, facility, and event.

3. **Percentage of Facility Sales:** This method requires the facility to be responsible for all inventory and sales. This method is more often preferred, as the facility receives a significant percentage of total sales. The facility controls the merchandise operation and knows the approximate amount of inventory available. At the end of each event, the vendor will receive a percentage of sales that can range between 55% and 75%. The facility then pays the sellers from its percentage of sales.

4. **Fee per Person:** This method requires the vendor to pay the facility a fee, per ticket sold, including complimentary tickets. This contracted fee can vary by event and the type of merchandise item. Collection of this fee should be in advance or completed early in the event based on ticket sales or house capacity (IAAM, 1990).

Bootlegging

At most major events a federal injunction is obtained to protect against copyright infringement. This allows police with the authority to arrest bootleggers or confiscate unauthorized merchandise. In addition, local city ordinances governing the sale of items can be most beneficial in eliminating bootlegging operations (R. Johnson, personal communication, October 22, 1991).

Sales Personnel

Training can make a difference in many areas, including appearance, uniforms, and attitude of the vendors. However, training on how to sell is extremely important if the facility embraces a profit oriented philosophy. Another factor is the employment of experienced merchandise sales personnel. Although anyone can sell T-shirts or souvenirs it takes special ability developed by experience to generate the type of sales desired in merchandise operations (Mulrooney & Farmer, 1995).

Shop-lifting is a major problem in today's society. Merchandise personnel should be recognize possible shoplifting situations, and reduce opportunities through proper product display. Events such as concerts are prime targets, due to the large numbers of people purchasing T-shirts and other items (Mulrooney & Farmer, 1995).

Product Liability and Liability Insurance

Product liability suits are a main reason that a facility may contract out their concession operations to an independent contractor. Due to high visibility, a relationship with the community, and perceived deep pockets, many facilities are frequent targets of lawsuits.

Because of these problems, each facility management must secure large amounts of insurance coverage. Although each contractor carries its own coverage, it is the facility with the most to lose. When a patron suffers an injury injured as a result of a defective or misused product or illness resulting from a consumed product (e.g., cotton candy or snow cones), the facility will probably be the first to be sued, regardless of fault. Facility management, therefore, should make certain their liability insurance covers these types of claims.

Responsibility

Regardless of the status of food service management, it is important for facility management to maintain some control over the operations. This can be achieved through experienced management personnel who know their product mix, have sound policies and procedures, employ competent reporting and accounting systems, and maintain the profitability of the operation.

Summary

1. Food service management includes food and beverage sales (concessions) as well as the sale of merchandise.

2. Concessions may be done in-house, where the facility controls everything, or they may be contracted to an outside company. When these services are contracted out, the facility management maintains a certain degree of control to insure product quality.

3. Concession stands must be attractive and well maintained business operations with trained and energetic employees.

4. Recent trends in concession management include (a) name-brand products, (b) computerized beverage machines, and (c) self-heating prepackaged food.

5. Safety and sanitation are important concerns for a successful concessions operation.

6. Merchandise includes many items such as poster, jerseys, T-shirts, hats,

pennants, and programs.

7. The division of profit or deal between the event and the facility should be mutually agreed upon. This split should not become a factor in whether or not an event is scheduled.

Questions

1. Explain the following terms: in-house food service management, concessions, stocking, convenience foods, and hawkers.

2. Describe the circumstances that would warrant you to contract an in-house food service management operation.

3. How do you project an operational inventory?

4. Explain the following terms: novelties, bootlegging, and merchandising deals with sport teams and athletes.

References

International Association of Auditorium Managers (IAAM). (1990). Course materials from the unpublished proceedings of the School for Public Assembly Facility Management, Ogelbay, VA.

Jewel, D. (1992). *Public assembly facilities*. Malabar, FL: Krieger Publishing Company.

Mulrooney, A., & Farmer, P. (1995). Managing the facility. In B. Parkhouse (Ed.), *The management of sport: Its foundation and application* (2nd ed.). (pp. 223-248). St. Louis, MO: Mosby-Year Book.

CHAPTER 19

EVENT PLANNING AND PRODUCTION

The preceding chapters have provided the reader with an understanding of the development of a facility and have described various management segments responsible for the various facility operations. This section on event production is designed to provide information on the development and staging of a sport-facility event.

Producing and Staging a Sport-Facility Event

Producing and staging an event in a sport facility is not drastically different

GROUNDS CREWS WORK DILIGENTLY TO CHANGEOVER AND PREPARE
THE FACILITY FOR THE NEXT EVENT.

from producing and staging events in other facilities or environments (Graham, Goldblatt, & Delpy, 1995). The process is two-fold and although these two processes are similar, they have significant differences. The first area involves development and implementation of the event from the facility point of view. The second process is the event viewed from the perspective of the organizers.

Facility Perspective

The types of events held in a sport facility are varied and can range from charitable activities, such as local high school football games and Special Olympics, to major events, such as NBA, NFL or Major League Baseball games. Each event, although different in form and procedure, is similar in its organization, development, and operation. Each event is the lifeblood and primary income source of the facility. Income is generated from various sources, such as tickets, concessions, advertising, and sponsorships (R. Johnson, personal communication, October 22, 1991).

Event Progression

All events held within a facility are similar in sequence and organization. Each and every event begins with a concept (Berlonghi, 1990). As with any idea, the event requires planning if it is to be implemented. Elements of this planning and implementation process include

- the establishment of the event hold date
- information exchange between the promoter and facility management
- budget development
- research
- market analysis
- negotiations
- equipment and personnel requirements
- booking and pricing confirmation
- contract and deposit completion
- promotional and public relations (publicity) campaign development
- implementation
- ticket development
- event work-orders and contractual changes
- facility preparation
- concessions and catering
- load-in
- show call

- personnel orientation
- event begins
- box office operation termination
- event settlement
- load out
- clean-up
- evaluation

Organizational Event Structure

It is imperative that the management staff of each sport and public-assembly facility be identified by their title and function. The individual in charge is usually titled CEO, managing director, or facility director. This individual is responsible for both the venue and event production. Within all facility organizations, various managerial personnel are charged with decision-making tasks, especially within their specific areas of expertise. This level of authority provides for event changes, authorization of expenditures, and enforcement of policy and procedures, without additional bureaucratic interference.

The primary responsibility for the complete organization of an event is that of the event coordinator. This individual, usually a full-time operations staff member, is charged with the coordination and supervision of the proposed event. After assignment of an event coordinator, the facility team is assembled. This team includes representatives of the business operations (and box office), marketing and public relations, security, parking, engineering, and concession areas. As the event date approaches the event coordinator, along with members of this team, develops the plan and coordinates its implementation with the promoter's representative (G. Lewis, personal communication, September 14, 1991).

Event Hold Date

The initiation of an event formally begins when the event promoters or client(s) contact the facility to determine availability for a particular date to hold a proposed event. Once the date is deemed available, a hold is placed by the facility for the client(s) and the specified event (Berlonghi, 1990). At the time of the hold date or placement the facility requests information, both financial (including credit) and event history, to determine if the event is appropriate to be held in the facility.

Event Research

Event research refers to a number of areas that affect the booking and scheduling, as well as financial feasibility of the proposed event. According to R. Johnson (personal communication, October 22, 1991), the first elements to consider are the reputation, quality, and trustworthiness of the event and its promoters. This information is gathered from other facilities in the network (i.e., other facilities in other states and locales) that may have had contact with the event or promoter. This information is important to determine if the planned event is appropriate and worthy of the interest of the facility.

The second element is the classification of this tentative event. This classification is based on the event or promoter's ability and willingness to pay their debts. The following is a preferred list of clients, in order of qualifications and ability to pay:

- Promoters or contractors that pay in cash
- Events with quality promoters and event history
- National events with visible and eminent contractors
- Local promoters or client(s), or both
- Touring events with out of town or country promoters
- Religious conventions and events

Negotiations

After the client and facility have exchanged information, the facility and client(s) negotiate the terms of the contract. This includes not only the price but also the deal or split of income from tickets, concessions, advertising, and other income areas. Other elements of the negotiation phase are types, skills, and numbers of tradesmen, laborers, ticket-takers, box office personnel, security and engineering personnel. Indications as to whether the labor will involve union or non-union workers should be determined. Any and all specifics should be discussed at this stage; however, they can be modified at any time up to the event and settlement (R. Rummel, personal communication, October 22, 1991).

Facility Equipment and Personnel

The extent and demands placed on the facility by the event will depend upon the type and size of the event planned. The facility, due to its multi-use nature, is capable of hosting most events. If special equipment or personnel are required, planning for these eventualities is paramount if the event is to be successful. To oversee the event and coordinate or communicate between the facility and the event and promoter(s), an event coordinator is assigned who is able to speak for management in the majority of problem situations that may arise.

Event Coordinator

According to A. Chetta (personal communication, September 18, 1991), the event coordinator is probably the most important person associated with the development and execution of a facility event. This individual, usually a member of the management team, has the authority and job description to coordinate the various facility departments into one effective unit (Berlonghi, 1990). This unit is organized based on the negotiations between facility management and the event promoter. These negotiations are usually done months in advance. The event coordinator is responsible for all elements of production, regardless of the area. It is important to note that while one event is being conducted, a second one is being developed, and a third is in the discussion phase.

Booking, Scheduling, and Pricing Confirmation

If the client(s) and the facility are satisfied with the proposed event type, date, tentative schedule, and the resultant negotiations (i.e., financial outcome and personnel requirements), the proposed event booking and scheduling is confirmed. In conjunction with the booking confirmation, the facility cost estimate is confirmed (W. Racek, personal communication, October 14, 1991).

Contract Execution and Deposit

The next stage in the event development is the execution of the contracts between the facility and the lessee. The documents normally are simplified generic contracts similar to apartment leases, called boiler-plate contracts. Deposits are usually demanded at this stage, depending upon the past relationship of the facility and the client. Some clients are asked to pay the entire amount for the facility lease and event at this stage, depending upon what information had been gleaned during the facility's research of the event's or client's background.

Marketing and Promotional Strategy Development

> During the negotiations stage, the promoter(s) and facility marketing organization should be in contact to determine the type and extent of facility involvement with the proposed event. The level of facility involvement will hinge upon the event type and the promoter's approach to marketing the event (Mulrooney & Farmer, 1995, p. 228).

At times, the client will take on the entire marketing operation, from media outlets to facility promotions on the day of the event. This type of control is dependent upon the promoter's experience while developing the event. Client controlled marketing efforts limit the event cost to the facility, and therefore reduce revenues due to the facility at the time of settlement.

Most promoters will not be familiar nor developed ties, with the local community and media. In this instance, promoters will want the facility marketing department to organize the entire event marketing campaign and develop a marketing plan (W. Peneguy, personal communication, September 18, 1991).

Commencement of Marketing Efforts

Contacts with local media begin after determining the type of event to be held and analyzing the results of the marketing research. This initial contact determines the level of media purchased (i.e., bought), and sets up some form of trade or promotion with these media sources. Advertising through the media should be targeted at the appropriate audience (Graham et al., 1995).

At the same time, the group sales department attempts to contact business corporations and service groups, in an attempt to sell group tickets and bookings for the upcoming event. Promotional activities, such as press conferences and star athletes visiting key publics, commonly known as earned media, should be planned and executed (Mulrooney & Farmer, 1995). According to W. Peneguy (personal communication, September 18, 1991), these type of public awareness promotions should take place near to the date of the actual event, whereas the initial media contact meeting could be as much as a year in advance.

It is important to remember that every element of broadcasting the event has a potential to the potential sponsor. These elements, including advertising, merchandise, ticket impressions, message board, TV and radio commercials, outdoor advertising, and signage, have a value to the potential sponsor.

Tickets and Sales

After an agreement has been reached between facility management and the event client, the printing of the tickets and their distribution are authorized. This process must be completed in conjunction with marketing efforts, to ascertain the sponsors and advertising messages that need to be placed on the ticket stub and other associated publicity. Once the tickets have been produced, they are dispatched to the box office and other distribution outlets for disbursement. This process involves a number of facility departments as well as outside contractors or entities, and must be closely supervised by the event coordinator.

It is important that as soon as these tickets are available for sale, the facility box office personnel and other distribution sites are informed as to the details (i.e., where, when, and who) of the planned event. This is important because the ticket buyer's first contact with the event is with these individuals. These personnel are also representatives of the facility and need to be sufficiently informed in order to provide the public with appropriate information and a positive impression.

Final Changes

As the event organization between the facility and the promoter becomes coordinated, deficiencies become apparent. At this juncture, the original contract and arrangements are reexamined. Technical riders and specifications are added, after negotiation, to the document. In addition to the additional expectations by the promoter, the facility adds its requirements, as well as additional charges.

Work Orders

After the final draft is produced, the event coordinator meets with all facility management representatives involved with the implementation of the event. Although some of these individuals may be involved in the formulation phase, the team is now assembled and ready to undertake the final phase, the event execution.

At this stage, the various management or department heads issue directives for their specific area of responsibility. These directives affect all personnel involved in the event. Operations contact and organize their personnel, who include ticket takers, security, parking, technicians, and the field crew.

In-house and contract equipment requirements, as well as planning and specifications for the preparation of the physical set, stage, or field, are finalized with the event coordinator and a representative of the client. Engineering and housekeeping are advised and personnel lists and requirements established. Personnel rosters are developed and posted with operational hours and event parameters.

The box office will ensure that all sales personnel, both in-house and contract, understand the event type, configuration, ticket price, and parameters involved with the event. Box office hours of operation, specific event rules, and personnel schedules are established and posted. Marketing, having developed a specific event plan, will maintain a predetermined schedule. It is at this juncture that the development of news stories and opportunities is examined (i.e., earned media or publicity), along with developing media credentials, invitations to all media and sponsors, as well as catering arrangements for the media center and VIP areas. It is important that any positive publicity opportunities that present themselves be utilized to publicize the event as well as the facility.

The final area to be addressed, yet one of the most crucial, especially in financial terms is food service management (i.e., concessions, catering, and merchandise). This unit will ensure that its stocks are sufficient, the event-specific merchandise has been ordered in sufficient numbers (i.e., T-shirts, basketballs, collectors cards, pins and posters), and working personnel have been scheduled. It is important that the concessions operations be clean, and this requires coordinating efforts with housekeeping (W. Mulrooney, personal communication, January 9, 1992).

Event Execution

Prior to any event, all facility-management personnel participate in an orientation and organizational meeting. This meeting, for many, is the first time that they have sat in the same room discussing the event. Prior to this meeting, the event coordinator is the conduit and is responsible for the information flow.

This meeting not only orients the group to the event but also addresses specific problems in specific areas (Berlonghi, 1990). It is expected that collectively these individuals are able to resolve any potential areas of difficulty. At the termination of the meeting, all managers are expected to speak with their specific personnel. This orientation takes place prior to the event, to ensure that all personnel understand their duties, responsibilities and expectations in the pre-event, event and postevent periods.

Preparation and Setup

Depending upon the number of events scheduled, the facility set, stage, or field is preset to certain specifications. This involves the load-in of materials by vehicles and members of the operational crew. Potential setup problems are kept to a minimum by completing the setup well in advance of the actual performance. At this time all sound and special effects are assembled and thoroughly examined.

PARKING PERSONNEL   POSTING SHEET

EVENT: _____   DATE: _____

SUPERVISORS: _____   SUPERVISORS: _____

_____   _____

CASHIERS: ATTENDANTS:
  WEST: (1)_____   EAST#1: (1)_____   (5)_____
        (2)_____   (2)_____   (6)_____
              LEADER   (3)_____   (7)_____
        (3)_____   (4)_____   (8)_____
CENTER: (4)_____   EAST#2: (1)_____   (5)_____
        (5)_____   (2)_____   (6)_____
              LEADER   (3)_____   (7)_____
        (6)_____   (4)_____   (8)_____
EAST#1: (7)_____   WEST: (1)_____   (5)_____
        (8)_____ LEADER   (2)_____   (6)_____
EAST#2: (9)_____   (3)_____   (7)_____
        (10)_____   (4)_____   (8)_____
        (11)_____ LEADER   NORTH: (1)_____   (5)_____
NORTH: (12)_____   (2)_____   (6)_____
        (13)_____   (3)_____   (7)_____
        (14)_____ LEADER   (4)_____   (8)_____
        (15)_____
TIME OUT: CENTER (1)_____   (5)_____
EAST#1: (1)___ (2)___ (3)___   LOT: (2)_____   (6)_____
EAST#2: (1)___ (2)___ (3)___   (3)_____   (7)_____
WEST# : (1)___ (2)___ (3)___   (4)_____   (8)_____
NORTH# : (1)___ (2)___ (3)___
CENTER: (1)___ (2)___ (3)___   NORTH   (1)_____   (2)_____
Misc Info: RESERVE:
_____ _____ _____   LOGE: (1)_____   (2)_____
_____ _____ _____   POINT: (1)_____   (2)_____
_____ _____ _____

FIGURE 19-1 - SAMPLE EVENT STAFFING SHEET

All field-crew personnel must complete their assigned tasks, in the prescribed time allotment. It is important that in all positions, experienced personnel be a part of each and every organizational unit, to alleviate the headaches that always appear in any complex organization. All concessions and merchandise operations, catering for media and VIP areas, and any special considerations are finalized at this time (W. Mulrooney, personal communication, January 9, 1992).

Personnel Orientation

At this point all personnel involved in the event production, such as ticket takers, parking, security, field crew, box office, technicians, custodial, media relations, and management are briefed as to their responsibilities. This takes place under the auspices of the event coordinator, but in small group meetings (Berlonghi, 1990). The emphasis at this meeting is that each facility employee should complete his or her assigned responsibility in a timely and appropriate manner. However, it should be impressed upon employees, that their specific duty is to be courteous and welcome the patrons to the event, as well as recognize of any

CLASSIFICATION	4 HOUR CALL	6 HOUR CALL	8 HOUR CALL
EVENT _____ STAFFING SHEET			
DATE _____			
HEAD TICKET TAKER			
ASST. HD. TICKET TAKER			
TICKET TAKERS			
HEAD USHER			
ASST. HEAD USHER			
USHER SUPERVISORS			
USHERS			
COURTESY DIRECTOR			
COURTESY SUPERVISORS			
COURTESY OFFICERS			
NURSES			
AMBULANCE			
TELEPHONE OPERATOR			
UNIFORM ROOM			
MATRONS/PORTERS			
EVENT CREW/SWEEPS			
HOUSEKEEPERS			
STAFF SUPERVISOR			
DEPUTIES			
PARKING MANAGER			
CASHIER MANAGER			
PARKING SUPERVISORS			
CASHIERS			
ATTENDANTS			

FIGURE 19-2 - SAMPLE EVENT STAFFING SHEET

IN MULTI-PURPOSE FACILITIES, STORAGE AREAS ARE NEEDED TO HOLD ALL
OF THE EQUIPMENT USED FOR OTHER TYPES OF EVENTS.

```
COLISEUM-COURTESY BOOTH-ACTION REPORT

DATE:_____        TIME:_____

PATRON'S NAME: _____

TELEPHONE #:    _____

PATRON'S CONCERN:_____

              _____

              _____

              _____

RESOLUTION:   _____

              _____

              _____

              _____

OFFICER'S NAME: _____   TIME COMPLETED:_____


DATE:_____        TIME:_____

PATRON'S NAME:_____

TELEPHONE #: _____

PATRON'S CONCERN:_____

              _____

              _____

              _____

RESOLUTION:   _____

              _____

              _____

              _____

OFFICER'S NAME: _____   TIME COMPLETED:_____
```

FIGURE 19-3 - SAMPLE ACTION REPORT

potential risk-management elements that may exist .

The Event

After all the preparations are completed, the event is ready to begin. The doors to the facility are opened, and the patrons proceed to their assigned seating. Regardless of the performance, the patrons should be constantly supervised by ushers and security, as well as have access to food services. Soon after the start of the performance or event, the box office closes, and receipts are accounted and deposited.

Event Settlement

Event settlement is the final settlement between the promoter and the facility

RELEASE

I REQUEST EMERGENCY ASSISTANCE WITH REFERENCE TO MY VEHICLE. IT IS
UNDERSTOOD THAT I ACCEPT FULL RESPONSIBILITY FOR ANY DAMAGE INCURRED
TO MY PROPERTY DURING THE COURSE OF THIS EMERGENCY ASSISTANCE.

I FURTHER AGREE TO HOLD HARMLESS THE COLISEUM,

            (AND THEIR REPRESENTATIVES) OF ANY AND ALL CLAIMS ARISING

FRCM BEING PROVIDED THIS EMERGENCY SERVICE.

NAME_____

SIGNATURE_____

MAKE OF VEHICLE_____

MODEL_____

LICENSE NO._____

TYPE OF ASSISTANCE_____

DATE_____

REMARKS:

FIGURE 19-4 - SAMPLE RELEASE REPORT

AFTER ALL OF THE PRELIMINARY WORK IS DONE, THE EVENT CAN
FINALLY TAKE PLACE.

representative (usually the business manager). This topic is covered in the "Business Operations" chapter.

Load-Out

After the event concludes, the patrons are assisted in leaving the facility and departing safely. The set, stage, or field is broken down. This material is then removed in the "load-out" procedure by the operations crew on available transportation. The facility is then thoroughly cleaned and readied for the next event; this is known as the *change-over*. If the next event occurs the same or next day, these preparations must be made quickly; sometimes the operations crew may have to work through the night to complete the task on time (A. Chetta, personal communication, September 18, 1991).

```
PARKING POST EVENT REPORT

EVENT: _____ LOT SECURED @ _____ DATE:_____
EVENT START TIME: _____     EVENT ENDING TIME:_____
WEATHER: _____

LOT CLEAR:  EAST 1: _____      TIME TO CLEAR: _____
            EAST 2: _____      TIME TO CLEAR:_____
            CENTER: _____      TIME TO CLEAR: _____
            NORTH: _____       TIME TO CLEAR: _____
            WEST: _____        TIME TO CLEAR: _____
TOTAL CARS PARKED:
            EAST 1: _____  EAST 2:_____  WEST:_____
            CENTER: _____  NORTH:_____  BUSES:_____
            TOTAL: _____ LOCKOUTS_____JUMP____OTHER_____
SET-UP COMMENTS:  BARRICADES ON 303  YES _____  NO _____
_____
_____
_____

INCIDENTS OR OTHER COMMENTS:
_____
_____
_____

MAINTENANCE NEEDED:
_____
_____
```

FIGURE 19-5 - SAMPLE POST EVENT REPORT

Evaluation

After the event is concluded, all members of the facility team, chaired usually by the facility coordinator, evaluate the event. This includes the performance of all staff, such as the ticket takers, parking attendants, box office personnel, operational crew, security, engineering, marketing, and management.

All facets are examined from a performance as well as a profitability point of view. Present at this meeting are members of the facility management as well as the promoter. Out of this evaluation process emerges recommendations for future events.

Event Cancellation by the Facility

The facility reserves the right to cancel or terminate the event for whatever reason management considers to be good cause, such as the event's showing little potential of achieving its desired objectives (i.e., financial, PR, and community impact); client deposit nonpayment, or nonperformance of the lessee to the prescribed terms and conditions in the contract) (Berlonghi, 1990). This cancellation does not guarantee that the subsequent event will occur.

The facility can terminate the contract if it believes that the specified client or audiences have violated laws, caused disturbances, or taken any action resulting in injury to persons or damage to property at any performance or activity prior to the proposed event. If termination does result, it is the responsibility and liability of the client for full payment of the rental fees and all reimbursable expenses accrued to that point. The client should have to forego all claims and have no recourse of any kind against the facility, for any reason.

Event Cancellation by the Client

The client can cancel the lease of the facility, if the facility fails to live up to any portion of the contract, for example, failure to take possession or use of the facilities. The facility should be entitled to liquidated damages equal to the minimum daily-base rental, 100% of applicable ticket-handling fees on the sale of tickets up to the time of cancellation, plus any other disbursements or expenses incurred by the facility in connection with the event.

If the client cancels any performance or activity, the client is obligated, at its own expense, to inform the public of such cancellation through the normal information media. The facility will also make sure such announcements maintain a positive public image and reputation. These announcements will be at the expense of the client.

Regardless of the reason, if the event is canceled, the facility must realize its costs to stage the event accrued to that point. The facility must also maintain a positive relationship with the community, and the media, as well as with the facility client (R. Rummel, personal communication, October 22, 1991).

League Compliance

If the facility is the home of a professional team, it is mandatory that the facility manager be very familiar with the existing league rules and insure that the rules are adhered to when hosting a game. These rules include, but are not limited to, locker-room facilities, official's facilities, access to the playing surface, security of the teams, setup for the media, access to the teams after the event, and many other operational-type items. Failure of the facility to adhere to the rules and guidelines can result in league sanctions and a great deal of aggravation for the facility manager.

Summary

1. Events are the lifeblood of every sport facility; thus, they must be conducted in an organized progression.

2. Although the facility director is ultimately responsible for all events scheduled at the facility, the planning and conducting of the event is the main duty of the event coordinator. Depending on the number of events there may be 3 or 4 different event coordinators at each facility.

3. Research about the promoter and the individual event must be conducted in order to ascertain if the event is appropriate for the facility.

4. Once an event is deemed appropriate, a cost estimate is determined; if the estimate is within the acceptable range, a contract is negotiated between the facility and promoter. The rent of the facility; division of ticket, merchandise, concession, and advertising revenue; and deposit amount are all included in the negotiated contract.

5. A work order that describes the requirements for the event is designed by the event coordinator and disseminated to the responsible parties. Various meetings are held to advise the various groups as to the specific duties.

6. After the event is finished and settlement concluded, the heads of the various departments meet to conduct an evaluation of the event. Suggestions and recommendations regarding similar events are documented for future use.

7. Events may be canceled by the facility if good cause exists or by the promoter if the facility does not perform its contracted duties. Regardless of fault, the facility must be reimbursed for all incurred costs up to the point of cancellation.

8. Managers of major league facilities must be cognizant of the specific rules and regulations that govern the sport played at their facility.

Questions

1. What rights does a facility have in case of an event cancellation? What rights does the client possess?

2. Discuss, in detail, the natural progression of an event, from its booking to postevent requirements.

3. Why is it important for a sport facility manager to be very familiar with the league rules of teams competing at his or her site?

References

Berlonghi, A. (1990). *The special event risk management manual.* Dana Point,

CA: Alexander Berlonghi.

Graham, S., Goldblatt, J., & Delpy, L. (1995). *The ultimate guide to sport event management & marketing.* Chicago: Irwin Professional Publishing.

Mulrooney, A., & Farmer, P. (1995). Managing the facility. In B. Parkhouse (Ed.), *The management of sport: Its foundation and application* (2nd ed.). (pp. 223-248). St. Louis, MO: Mosby-Year Book.

APPENDICES

APPENDIX A

THE AMERICANS WITH DISABILITIES ACT

Background on the Act

On July 16, 1990, former President George Bush signed into law the Americans with Disabilities Act of 1990 (ADA). The Act requires the Attorney General to issue regulations and standards for existing buildings and new construction to ensure that they are readily accessible to and usable by individuals with disabilities. The act was initiated to help create equal opportunities for handicapped people as employees and consumers. An estimated 50 million handicapped individuals remain unemployed or underemployed because many businesses and public services lack accommodations for those with disabilities.

The passage of the ADA shifted requirements to provide accessibility from local codes to federally mandated law. If local codes are more stringent, they still must be followed. The law is divided into several titles or sections; Title III affects all public buildings including athletic complexes. Due to its' broad scope, the ADA, and specifically Title III, will have a significant impact on building owners, managers, developers, and designers.

The Act creates additional requirements for building owners and designers to address in the design of new buildings, building additions, or alterations of existing buildings. It also requires modifications to existing buildings to provide access to those with disabilities. Architects must incorporate these requirements into their building designs. The legislation states that a "failure to design" to these requirements would constitute an act of discrimination against people with disabilities, subjecting both owners and others associated with the design construction or alteration of buildings and facilities to civil liability.

1. Disabled individuals should be afforded equal access and opportunity; it is simply the correct thing to do.

2. At some point, everyone will experience the limitations of the disabled through accident, illness, or disease and certainly through aging.

The ADA prohibits discrimination against the disabled in four general areas:

Title I   Employment

Title II   Public Services (Public transportation and governmental facilities)

Title III   Public Accommodations (buildings) and Services provided by Private Entities

Title IV   Telecommunications

Title I primarily addresses employment practices and procedures; however, it also requires an employer to provide "reasonable accommodations for the disabled" (Mulrooney & Thomas, 1993, pg. 17). *Reasonable accommodation* includes making existing facilities or work areas, or both, readily accessible to, and usable by, an individual with a disability. Title I places responsibility on the employer to make the workplace accessible.

Title II applies to all state and local governments. Title II has the effect of requiring accessibility standards on projects and facilities where past federal legislation placed this requirement only on projects where federal funding was involved.

The following analysis of sport facilities primarily deals with Title III of ADA, which prohibits discrimination against the disabled in the provision of goods, services, and facilities. Title III places responsibility on the building owner to make the building handicapped accessible.

ADA Guidelines for Existing Structures

The guidelines require the removal of architectural and communication barriers that are structural in nature, from existing facilities where such removal is readily achievable. *Readily achievable* is defined as "easily accomplishable and able be carried out without much difficulty or expense" (Mulrooney & Thomas, 1993, pg. 17).

The following guidelines provide types of measures that may be taken to remove barriers and that are likely to be readily achievable. Inclusion on this list does not necessarily mean that it is readily achievable in all cases.

1. Installing ramps.

2. Making curb cuts in sidewalks and entrances.

3. Lowering shelves.

4. Rearranging tables, chairs, vending machines, display racks, and other furniture for wheelchair access.

5. Lowering telephones and installing phones for the hearing impaired.

6. Adding raised letter markings on elevator controls.

7. Installing both visible and audible alarm systems.

8. Widening doors.

9. Installing offset hinges to widen doorways.

10. Eliminating a turnstile or providing an alternative accessible entrance exit or both.

11. Installing accessible door hardware.

12. Installing grab bars in toilet stalls.

13. Rearranging toilet partitions to increase maneuvering space.

14. Insulating lavatory pipes.

15. Installing a raised toilet seat.

16. Installing a full-length bathroom mirror.

17. Lowering the paper-towel dispenser in a bathroom.

18. Creating designated accessible parking spaces.

19. Installing an accessible paper-cup dispenser at an existing inaccessible drinking fountain.

20. Removing high-pile, low-density carpeting.

21. Providing a sufficient number of accessible seats in the assembly area, in all price ranges.

The Department of Justice recognizes that removal of barriers may not necessarily be readily achievable and that it may be the combination of barriers that becomes a burden rather than each barrier independently; therefore, a list of priorities has been established. These priorities include

1. Provide access to a place of public accommodation from public sidewalks, parking, or public transportation.

2. Provide access to restroom facilities where they are used by the public on more than an incidental basis.

3. Provide access to those areas where goods and services are made available to the public.

4. Take other measures necessary to provide access to the goods, services, facilities, privileges, advantages, or accommodations of a place of public accommodation.

The guidelines state that the "obligation to engage in readily achievable barrier removal is a continuing one. Over time, barrier removal that initially was not readily achievable may later be required because of changed circumstances" (Mulrooney & Thomas, 1993, pg. 18).

ADA Guidelines for New Construction

New buildings, including additions, will be required to comply with the guidelines with very few exceptions. "Undue burden" will be difficult to prove in a new building. Many requirements architects currently use to design buildings are part of the ADA guidelines. The following is a short list of basic design items required to make a facility accessible and more usable by a disabled person:

1. Parking should be closest spaces to accessible entrances, 1 handicapped space per 25 regular spaces, or with 500+ regular spaces, 2% should be handicapped.

2. Accessible parking spaces should be a minimum of 8 feet wide with an adjacent 5-foot access aisle (shared) reserved for disabled persons' use.

   One in eight (but not less than 1) handicapped parking spaces should accommodate vans with a minimum width of eight feet and a minimum access aisle of eight feet.

3. The maximum slope of a ramp for new construction is 1:12 (1 inch rise per 12 inches) or less.

4. No steps or curbs should interrupt paths to entrance doors.

5. All stairs must have a uniform riser height and have continuous handrails on both sides.

6. Handicapped-sized elevators are required (except in buildings 3 stories or under) with less than 3,000 square feet per floor except when the facility is a shopping center, shopping mall, assembly building, or office of a health-care provider.

7. Elevators must contain 42" high controls, visible and audible signals, door sensors, raised and Braille characters, and have self-contained emergency communications.

8. Doors should have a 32" opening and be equipped with a push/pull or lever action knob.

9. Hallways should be 36" wide for one-way traffic and 60" wide for two-way traffic.

10. Water fountains should be 36" from the finished floor to the spout outlet and have front controls.

11. Auditory and visual alarm systems must be used.

12. Room signs should have raised letters or numbers, or both, and be placed 60" above the finished floor to the center line of the sign. Building directories, menus, and temporary signage are exempt.

13. Public Text telephones are required. When four public telephones are provided on site, one must be text; one per facility in places of public assembly; if public telephones are available adjacent to hospital emergency, recovery, or waiting rooms, one must be a text phone; and in any telephone bank, of three or more public pay telephones, one must comply with shelf and outlet requirements of the guidelines to accommodate portable text telephones (TDDS).

14. Sinks should have a 29" clear lap space and lever faucets.

15. Toilet facilities should be equipped with at least one wide stall (60") featuring an out-swinging door and grab bars.

16. There should be no more than a 40" reach to towels, dispensers, shelves, etc.

17. Only low-pile carpet should be used in public areas.

Issues Special to Sport Facilities

1. Places of assembly with fixed seating must provide locations for wheelchairs consistent with the following table:

Table 1

SEATING CAPACITY	# OF WHEELCHAIR LOCATIONS
4 TO 25	1
26 TO 50	2
51 TO 300	4
301 TO 500	6
OVER 500	6 plus 1 additional space for each total seating increase of 100

** Another generally used rule of thumb is to make 1% of the total seating capacity handicapped accessible.

2. Wheelchair seating should be an integral part of the seating plan.

3. Sightlines from these areas should be comparable to those from all viewing areas.

4. Level changes greater than 1/2 inch must be ramped.

5. Provide one companion fixed seat next to each wheelchair seating area.

The previous listing of ADA requirements for newly constructed facilities is by no means a complete and detailed listing. The previous lists identify the major concerns for providing ample accessibility for disabled persons in newly designed and constructed facilities, specifically assembly facilities.

The Effects of ADA on Major Sports Facilities

ADA legislation has compelled most sport facilities to upgrade their accessibility for the handicapped. To do this and comply with ADA legislation, money must be spent to modernize elevators, entrances, parking spaces, drinking

> *Effective Dates*
> Title III - Public Accommodations
>   January 26, 1992 - Existing Buildings
>   January 26, 1993 - New facilities designed and constructed for first
>   occupancy after January 26, 1993

fountains, telephones, ramps, restrooms, and wheelchair seating locations. However, none of the current major sports arenas have completely complied with ADA legislation mainly because all were designed and built before the act took effect.

Some sport facilities and arenas built in the past 5 years have anticipated ADA legislation and have incorporated more accessibility into their designs. The Delta Center (built in 1991), and America West Arena (built in 1992) made significant design changes to make their facilities more readily accessible, even though the ADA was not in effect at the time construction was completed. Gund Arena is currently the most accessible NBA arena and, it does completely comply with all of the elements within the ADA. Smaller facilities on college campuses also will need to comply and make accommodations similar to those made by the Delta Center and America West Arena.

The major issue regarding the ADA and sport facilities is the issue of wheelchair seating. Wheelchair seating must be provided throughout, in addition to providing access to all ticket prices, sightlines, and amenities offered to the general spectator. Sport facilities built before the ADA must do the best they can to provide this service to the handicapped spectator. New facilities, however, must fully comply with ADA guidelines regarding seating for the wheelchair bound.

All future sport facilities must completely comply with ADA legislation without any excuses. If an accessibility element is omitted in the design and construction of any future sports facility, the facility and its designers, architects, contractors, and owners could be sued for discrimination and be subject to a civil suit and fines, and be required to correct the elements that are not in compliance with the ADA standards.

References

Mulrooney, A., & Thomas, W. (1993, Fall/Winter). A glance at the Americans with Disabilities Act. *Future Focus, 2*, 17-20.

PLANNING AND DEVELOPING A MULTIPURPOSE SPORT FACILITY

To successfully plan and develop a multipurpose sport facility the following topical areas must be addressed:

1. Area availability

2. Size of the area

3. Appropriate historical information records and information

4. Topography of existing terrain

    (a) natural drainage of the area

    (b) amount of grading and fill necessary

    (c) soil of the area: foundation subsoil and surface top-soil

    (d) vegetation of the area: condition and value of existing turf (if appropriate)

5. Issues such as eminent domain, legal issues, transportation, parking, support facility needs (i.e., restaurants, hotels, retail stores and attractions), and location of the area: desirable aspects for players and spectators as to

    (a) accessibility

    (b) convenience

    (c) transportation

    (d) parking

    (e) safety

    (f) practicality

(g) adaptability: multipurpose consideration

6. Funds available:

    (a) initial cost of the area

    (b) cost of development

    (c) cost of maintenance

7. Orientation of playing field, with special consideration for safety of players and comfort of spectators

8. Availability of utilities

    (a) water

    (b) electricity

    (c) sewage

    (d) drainage outlets

    (e) telephone and telecommunications

9. Time allotted for development

10. Adaptability of facility for immediate plans

11. Future development possibilities

12. Organizational goals and objectives of the organization and how this intended facility will attempt to meet these defined elements

13. Interests and needs of the patrons and the community, as perceived through surveys

14. Evaluation of present level of community facilities and planned future needs;

15. Determination of potential attendance, occupancy levels based on demographic studies of local and regional population characteristics (i.e., age, sex, income, and employment level) and

16. Comparison of like or comparable national, regional, and local facilities, in the area of market share, cost-benefit analysis, and other pertinent factors.

References

United States Baseball Federation. (1987).(Vol. 3). *A baseball facility: Its construction and care.* Trenton, NJ: United States Baseball Federation.

DESIGN AND CONSTRUCTION OF A PHYSICAL EDUCATION FACILITY

The following suggestions should be kept in mind when designing and building a physical education facility.

1. Determine the number of teaching stations required should be determined.

2. The location in regard to site and balance of school or recreational facilities should be determined.

3. Dimensions of all areas such as gymnasiums (high and low ceiling), teaching stations, or service areas that include locker rooms and shower facilities, must be constructed in accordance with the nationally accepted norms.

4. All floor covering and wall materials should be appropriate and meet the necessary codes.

5. Desired acoustical treatment should be determined.

6. Lighting, heating and ventilation requirements should be determined.

7. Desired storage and office space should be planned.

8. Spectator requirements, if any, and type of seating should be determined.

9. Type of floor, wall, and ceiling fixtures or mountings to accommodate all types of apparatus should be determined.

10. Lobby size requirements should be determined.

11. Type of basketball backstops to be used (swing up, roll away, or fixed)

should be noted.

12. Type of folding partitions, if needed, should be determined.

13. Wainscot and eye bolt locations in wall should be planned.

14. Type of floor finish should be decided upon.

15. Location and type of court markings desired on floor should be determined.

16. Special electrical fixtures (PA system, television) should be determined.

17. Location of exit doors should be determined.

References

Ezersky, E. & Theibert, R. (1976). *Facilities in sports and physical education.* Saint Louis, MO: C. V. Mosby Co.

SWIMMING POOL CONSTRUCTION

Swimming pools range from small recreational pools to large Olympic-size structures with diving attachments and other enhancements. These facilities are expensive athletic propositions, but can positively influence a community sport, recreation, and fitness program.

Planning and Design Issues

The type of pool constructed depends upon its primary and secondary purpose and the programs to be conducted. A needs-assessment instrument should be utilized to ascertain these elements that guide the planning and design process. Direction and related activities may include competitive swimming and diving, recreational swimming, instructional swimming, lifesaving, swimming for people with disabilities, water polo, scuba diving, and water shows. The type of activity will determine the type of pool, pool depth, anticipated usage, income, ceiling height, construction type, intended user population, access, and special equipment needs. Other elements that should influence pool construction are the type and number of pools within the immediate area.

As with any construction project there are recommended steps to the development of a swimming-pool structure. These are the development of the planning committee, development and implementation of a needs assessment instrument, visitation to other swimming-pool structures, engagement of a swimming-pool consultant, and finally, employment of the architect and engineer experienced in swimming-pool design and construction.

Financing Swimming-Pool Structures

There are various methods of financing pool structures. These include municipal taxation, grants from state or federal governments, endowments, donations, or user fees. The finance method depends upon the community or institutional climate and existing financial policy.

Pool Types

A variety of pool types and configurations can be developed to serve the needs of the targeted group. The first is the wading or *familiarization pool*. This pool is less than two feet deep and used for nonswimming children under five years of age. The second type is the *training pool*. Ranging from 2 to 3 1/2 feet in depth, it is primarily utilized for training people to swim. The Olympic pool is 50 meters long and 25 meters wide with a depth of 4 to 6 feet. It is used for a variety of activities such as instruction, and competitive and recreational swimming. The last pool-type structure is the diving pool. It ranges from 30 to 60 feet long and 40 to 45 feet wide, with a depth of 13 to 17 feet. This facility can accommodate up to four springboards and a diving tower.

Auxiliary and Operational Pool Facilities

All pools should have a variety of auxiliary and operational facilities that provide a full-service operation. These include changing rooms, showers, toilets, saunas, lockers, sunbathing area, concessions, first-aid room, administrative office, storage facilities for cleaning and instructional equipment, relaxation or television facility, child care, and game room.

Operational Budget

The operational budget will depend upon the purpose of the pool, pool size, program type, and services offered. Budget elements should include personnel salary and benefits (full and part-time), utilities, services (publications, advertising, and engineering), supplies, maintenance, repairs, capital expenditures, debt service, insurance, and contingency.

Design and Construction Team

When determining the elements of the design and construction team, the decision makers are the architect, engineer, and general contractor. In addition to an experienced design and construction team, a qualified and experienced pool consultant should be engaged. The advantages of this individual's working in the design and development stages are that he or she can provide insight and expertise into the latest technology and aquatic trends. This bonded consultant is contracted through the architectural or engineering firm responsible for the project. Although the primary job of this consultant is in the planning and design stages, it is advisable to have this individual involved with the project from its inception through its completion.

Design and Construction Criteria

According to Ezersky and Thiebert (1976), the following are the criteria pertaining to the design and construction of an aquatic facility:

1. Pool shape determines the program function of the pool. Competitive shapes are primarily rectangular, whereas free-form shapes are usually for recreational structures.

2. Bulkheads divide the pool into various swimming-activity areas that can be used simultaneously for competitive and recreational swimming.

3. Automation systems ensure that filtration, chlorination, and temperature-control systems operate efficiently.

4. Gutter or overflow designs must also be considered. Originally the gutter was developed to remove debris and other materials from the pool to the sewage system. The original recessed gutter not only provided the pool with a method to remove unwanted material, but it also supplied the swimmer with a hand-hold and a safe place to rest and recover. Modifications of the recessed gutter were the partially recessed, roll-out, surface skimmer, and finally the rim-flow method. This innovation provided the pool with a gutter or overflow system that could be minimally maintained, achieve low wave motion, and provide ease of access to and egress from the pool. This last advantage is appropriate to people with disabilities who utilize the facility.

Construction Material

Today, pools are constructed of various materials. The pool basin is constructed of materials that include reinforced poured concrete, pneumatic concrete or dry-pack concrete, pre-cast concrete, steel, aluminum, fiberglass, and liners made of vinyl. After the base has been laid, finishes, such as tile, marble dust or plaster, neoprene rubber and hypalon, rubber-based paint, and epoxy, are used. The type of base and covering installed is as a result of the budget and recommendations from the pool consultant and design team.

Filtration Systems

Filtration is an important aspect of pool maintenance and operation. Water circulating through filtration systems maintains safe and sanitary conditions. This filtration process operates using a 6 to 8 hour flow rate pump. The types of filtration systems in use today are vacuum diatomaceous earth, pressure diatomaceous earth, and pressure granular media. The filter media utilized within these systems are granular media, diatomaceous earth, sand and gravel, anthracite, high-rate sand, and cartridge.

References

Ezersky, E., & Theibert, R. (1976). *Facilities in sports and physical education.* Saint Louis, MO: C.V. Mosby Co.

CASE STUDIES

This section of the text contains several case studies. These case studies were specifically developed to allow the students some application of the theory presented in the text. The cases cover different types of facilities from their initial planning and design through the actual planning of events that could be held at the facility.

To use these cases effectively the following points, at a minimum, should be discussed and analyzed:

1. Look for errors in planning and design.
2. Check the management structure.
3. Check the risk management plans.
4. Look at the budgets.
5. Analyze the advertising plan.
6. Check the event plan.

After reviewing these points, students should redevelop the entire case making changes to improve on what is presented in the case. This would include an in depth discussion of the changes made and evidence of why the new plans are superior. At the conclusion, a new facility with better planning and structure should be produced that has incorporated the ideas and theories presented in the text.

Case #1 - CUSHING COLISEUM

Design and Construction

The Cushing Coliseum will be built in Cushing, Oklahoma. In addition to being available for special events such as concerts, the Cushing Coliseum will be the home of the latest NBA expansion team, the Oklahoma Scissor-Tailed Fly-Catchers (or Fly-Catchers, for short) and a minor league hockey team, the Oklahoma Oglethorpes.

These teams will be state teams (such as the Colorado Rockies or Florida Marlins), drawing support from across the state (which, after the move of the National Professional Soccer League's Tulsa Ambush to St. Louis, has no major-league, professional sports at this time). For this reason, the arena will be built in Cushing, which is within a 2 hour drive and is accessible via main roads from the major Oklahoma cities of Tulsa and Oklahoma City. Although we are intending to draw our fan support from a wider base than do most arenas, the uniqueness of our product (especially the Fly-Catchers) should compensate for this.

The construction of the Cushing Coliseum will be financed through two sources. Private donations from wealthy businessmen will be solicited, and a state-wide "sin tax" will be implemented, through the support of state government. Public reaction to this tax will not be as negative as reaction has been to similar taxes, because this arena will not be replacing a previously existing one. Also the tax is a necessity to bring these two teams to the state.

Cushing Coliseum Data

19,500 seats
  17,500 permanent
  2,000 portable
  50 luxury boxes
Seating capacities:
  Concerts: 18,000
  Basketball:19,300
  Ice events:17,350 (hockey, professional ice shows, figure-skating
    competitions, etc.)
117,000 total square feet
64 ft. ceiling
Concrete floor
Portable basketball floor (owned by the arena)
Regulation (85 ft. x 200 ft.) ice rink
8,000 parking spaces within walking distance

Risk Management

Accidents
Identification: People slipping on wet spots
Assessment: Prevention
Treatment: Make sure all ushers are scanning the arena and reporting wet spots to maintenance clean-up crew.
SOP: Make sure ushers are looking out for this situation.

Personnel
Identification: Ticket takers letting people in without a ticket Assessment: Prevention Treatment: Fire guilty employees
SOP: Be careful whom you hire; check ticket takers' backgrounds

Pure Risk
Identification: Tornado Assessment: Transfer (to insurance company)
Treatment: Make sure that any damages can be covered through insurance.
SOP: Choose a good insurance company. Have an emergency procedure if a tornado occurs during an event (i.e., adequate shelters).

Contracting
Identification: People selling illegal merchandise outside the arena that is not contracted through concessions
Assessment: Avoidance
Treatment: Remove these sellers from the premises immediately
SOP: Have an undercover member of the security force to look out for these incidents.

Concessions
Identification: Selling alcohol to under-age patrons
Assessment: Prevention
Treatment: Fire any employees who sell alcohol to under-age patrons.
SOP: Train concession workers to ask for legal ID from any patron who appears younger than 30. This must be a policy, and someone needs to   go around to make sure that this is done on the day of an event.

Marketing
The purpose of this marketing plan is twofold: first, to make the public aware of our facility and its benefits to the community, and second to increase awareness of, and attendance at, events held in our facility.

Most of the efforts should be directed to an area within a one-hour driving distance of the facility and to other populated areas one to two hours from the facility.   In the latter areas efforts should be directed mostly toward groups. Because our arena will house the state's only major league professional team, however, individuals will be more likely to drive greater distances to attend our sporting events than they would be in a more professional sports-populated state.

To reach these target markets, a marketing director is needed. The director will have an assistant marketing director and a secretary to assist these efforts. Both the marketing director and the assistant marketing director will be responsible for convincing local businesses and corporations to purchase luxury boxes, season tickets, and other preferred-seating plans.

Local businesses and corporations will be approached to buy advertising space on the dasher boards, scoreboards, and other advertising signage space throughout the arena.   Included in this advertising area will be giveaway nights and other promotional nights for the teams using the facility. Further, these businesses will also advertise, using posters or pocket schedules for the events or the concerts, when applicable.

To increase visibility to the general public, advertisements in newspapers and local publications will be necessary. Further, radio and television advertisements for upcoming events should be made available. Because we will be leasing the facility to teams playing there, they will have the responsibility of establishing ticket prices and group-ticket sales.

Selected practice times will be publicized so that the public will have an opportunity to see the teams without always having to pay. This practice prioritizes public exposure of the teams, which in turn will entice the public to attend. The projected costs for the marketing plan will be as follows:

Marketing Director Salary	$35,000
Assistant Marketing Director Salary	22,500
Marketing Secretary Salary	18,000
Postage	2,000
Gas	1,000
Commercial Air-time/Print Space	5,000
Total	$83,500

The anticipated benefits of this marketing plan are as follows:

Luxury Boxes	50	at	$100,000 =	$5,000,000
Dasher Board Advertisements	25	at	5,000 =	$ 125,000
Scoreboard Advertisements	4	at	100,000 =	$ 125,000
Arena wide Advertisements	8	at	2,000 =	$ 16,000
Advertisements Above Entrance	8	at	2,000 =	$ 16,000
		Total		$5,187,000

Advertising Campaigns

The first example of our advertising campaign will be for a special one-time hard rock concert. Posters from the promoters will be distributed to area record stores, college campuses, and appropriate bars. Air-time on local radio stations would be purchased, provided no specific station is sponsoring the event. For 2 weeks leading up to the concert, in addition to advertising through local media (newspapers, radio stations, television stations), advertisements will be purchased for appropriate cable stations (such as MTV). In addition, announcements will be made during breaks in the action of hockey and basketball games for this concert, as well as any other upcoming special events. Concert information (performer, date, ticket prices, and availability) will be posted on the arena's Upcoming Events Calendars, located at the entrances. This information will also be run on the arena's message boards throughout the games.

The second advertising campaign will be for a home basketball game (of which there will be 41). This campaign is for a generic game, not a specific game (home opener, play-off game, etc.) against a specific opponent (top road attractions like the Chicago Bulls or the Boston Celtics). Because the Fly-Catchers are an NBA franchise, and the only major league team in the state of Oklahoma, developing awareness of this product is not anticipated to be any problem. In addition, despite the team's probable lack of success during its first few seasons, attendance is expected to be high because of its newness and the high quality of the overall product (an NBA game).

Upcoming games and ticket information will regularly be available to area newspapers and local publications, as well as local television and radio stations (especially sports stations). In addition, a coaches' show on a local radio station (the highest bidder) will precede each game's radio broadcast. Coaches answering questions from a local sportscaster will help generate interest for the games. Posters, calendars, and pocket schedules will be distributed to area merchants, especially sporting-goods stores, bars, and restaurants.

These advertising pieces will not change from game to game like radio spots or newspaper advertisements. They will include any specific information about the opposing team, marquee players, special significance, and any other specific promotional benefits of that game, such as giveaways. Group-ticket sales, such as youth basketball teams, civic groups or businesses, also will be encouraged. These practices will be done in conjunction with the team, because the arena will receive a set rental fee, regardless of the attendance.

Zero-Based Budget

Administrative Offices (Total = $439,000)
1) Secretaries (1 of 5)
   3 positions: $54,000
   Function: type, file, answer phones, manage office
2) Event Director (2 of 5)
   1 position: $45,000
   Function: administrate all events
3) Building Manager (3 of 5)
   1 position: $45,000
   Function: coordinate personnel, negotiate contracts, schedule events
4) Chief Operating Officer (4 of 5)
   1 position: $55,000
   Function: handle marketing, finance, and human relations
5) Board of Directors (5 of 5)
   4 positions: $240,000
   Function: administrate coliseum

Marketing and Accounting (Total = $115,500)
1) Secretary (1 of 4)
   1 position: $18,000
   Function: type, file, answer phones, manage office
2) Assistant Marketing Director (2 of 4)
   1 position: $22,500
   Function: assist marketing director
3) Marketing Director (3 of 4)
   1 position: $35,000
   Function: coordinate all marketing efforts, sponsorship, publications
4) Accountant (4 of 4)
   1 position: $40,000
   Function: handle accounts payable, accounts receivable

Housekeeping (Total = $718,000)
1) Housekeepers (1 of 3)
   40 positions: $624,000
   Function: clean arena
2) Housekeeping Supervisors (2 of 3)
   3 positions: $54,000
   Function: supervise arena cleaning
3) Special Cleaning Services (3 of 3)
   2 positions: $40,000
   Function: provide special cleaning services

Ushers (Total = $425,600)
1) Ushers (1 of 3)
        60 positions: $384,000
        Function: assist patrons to their seats
2) Usher Supervisors (2 of 3)
        4 positions: $32,000
        Function: supervise seating for one fourth of the arena
3) Head Usher (3 of 3)
        1 position: $9,600
        Function: oversee ushers, resolve problems, scheduling

Box Office (Total = $361,680)
1) Ticket Takers (1 of 4)
        20 positions: $128,000
        Function: sort, take, and count tickets
2) Ticket Sellers (2 of 4)
        12 positions: $199,680
        Function: sell tickets
3) Ticket-Taker Supervisors (3 of 4)
        2 positions: $16,000
        Function: oversee ticket takers, scheduling
4) Box Office Manager (4 of 4)
        1 position: $18,000
        Function: oversee ticket sellers, get tickets, scheduling

Parking (Total = $276,000)
1) Attendants (1 of 4)
        22 positions: $123,200
        Function: control traffic flow
2) Cashiers (2 of 4)
        8 positions: $51,200
        Function: take money, give change, count money
3) Security (3 of 4)
        10 positions: $80,000
        Function: patrol parking lots
4) Supervisors (4 of 4)
        3 positions: $21,600
        Function: oversee attendants and cashiers, scheduling

Security (Total = $529,600)
1) General Security (1 of 4)
        20 positions: $160,000
        Function: handle crowd control, event supervision, and escorting
2) Security supervisor (2 of 4)

      1 position: $9,600
      Function: oversee security operations
3) Local Police or Sheriff (3 of 4)
      10 positions: $120,000
      Function: arrest and book unruly, disruptive or intoxicated patrons
4) State Highway Patrol (4 of 4)
      20 positions: $240,000
      Function: control flow of traffic on streets

Maintenance (Total = $521,760)
1) General Maintenance (1 of 8)
      10 positions: $176,800
      Function: maintain upkeep of the facility
2) Groundskeepers (2 of 8)
      10 positions: $176,800
      Function: maintain area surrounding facility
3) Maintenance Supervisors (3 of 8)
      2 positions: $40,000
      Function: oversee and assist maintenance crew
4) Grounds Supervisor (4 of 8)
      1 position: $20,000
      Function: oversee and assist grounds crew
5) Painter (5 of 8)
      1 position: $24,960
      Function: paint where needed in the arena
6) Carpenter (6 of 8)
      1 position: $24,960
      Function: build wooden items, redesign areas
7) Engineer (7 of 8)
      1 position: $27,040
      Function: handle upkeep of all utilities
8) Electrician (8 of 8)
      1 position: $31,200
      Function: run and check electrical systems

Restaurant Staff (Total = $107,000)
1) Dishwashers and Cleanup (1 of 6)
      3 positions: $11,400
      Function: wash dishes, clean-up restaurant
2) Waiters and Waitresses (2 of 6)
      10 positions: $22,000
      Function: serve food to patrons
3) Bartenders (3 of 6)

3 positions: $14,400
Function: make drinks and serve them to patrons
4) Chefs (4 of 6)
3 positions: $36,000
Function: prepare food
5) Hostess (5 of 6)
1 position: $5,200
Function: greet and seat patrons
6) Manager (6 of 6)
1 position: $18,000
Function: scheduling, order food, manage restaurant

Specialty Positions (Total = $125,000)
1) Stagehands (1 of 4)
6 positions: $48,000
Function: handle event setup
2) Stagehand Supervisor (2 of 4)
1 position: $20,000
Function: manage and assist event setup
3) Scoreboard Operators (3 of 4)
2 positions: $12,000
Function: operate and program scoreboard
4) Changeover Crew (4 of 4)
51 positions: $45,000
Function: change floor over for events

TOTAL ZERO BASE BUDGET FOR SALARIES - $3,619,140

Traditional Budget

Wages
    Full time ....$ 1,859,260
    Part time ....$ 1,759,880
Insurance ....$ 90,000
Utilities ....$ 240,000
Phone ....$ 24,000
Marketing ....$ 83,500
Supplies
    Cleaning...$ 20,000
    Office..$ 20,000
    Security...$ 5,000
    Restaurant ....$ 100,000
    Tickets...$ 10,000
    Uniforms...$ 10,000
    TOTAL BUDGET ....$ 4,221,640

Legal Concerns

Accidents
A. Automobile accidents in the parking lot
B. People falling over rails inside arena
C. Objects flying into crowd
   1. Hockey pucks flying over the glass
   2. Basketballs flying out of bounds
D. People slipping and falling
   1. Outside, in parking lot
   2. On wet spots
E. Interaction between players and the crowd

Security
A. Stolen possessions
B. Weapons brought into events
C. Cars vandalized
D. Fighting, inside or outside arena
E. Trespassing
F. Ticket scalping
G. Evasion of admission fees

Contracts
A. Ensure validity of all event contracts.
   1. Competing teams
   2. Bands
   3. Special event entertainers
B. Ensure validity with concession and merchandise vendors.
C. Prevent invalid contracts.
   1. Illegal merchandise sales outside the arena (bootlegging)

Personnel
A. Fraud by workers
   1. Cheating on hours
   2. Letting people into events for free
   3. Stealing money

Financial
A. Bills paid on time
B. Tax returns
   1. Must be filed accurately
   2. Must be filed on time
C. Maintenance of sufficient reserve funds

Environmental
A. Ensure that local economy is suitable for arena
B. Effective marketing and advertising

Pure vs. Speculative Risk Management
A. Pure
  1. Disasters
     a. Tornado
     b. Fire
     c. Flood
B. Speculative
  1. Examples
     a. Workers' strike
     b. Failure to salt icy walks causing a fall

Traffic flow
A. Evacuation plan

Concessions
A. Alcohol
  1. Selling to minors
  2. Selling to intoxicated patrons
B. Counterfeit merchandise

Design and Construction
A. Unsafe design
  1. Proper approval for construction
  2. Building kept up to code
B. Repairs taken care of in a timely manner

Event Management

A hard rock music concert would involve the following special-event management needs:

1. Security personnel would wear distinctive uniforms to distinguish them as a security force. Neckties would not be part of this attire, because in a fight situation neckties could be used as weapons.

2. More security will be used, both inside the arena and in the parking lot (including increased state troopers for more traffic control).

3. Beer sales will be stopped early (when the main act comes on the stage).

4. Purses and bags will be checked (without security personnel actually reaching into the bags).

5. Ushers will direct patrons to their sections, rather than lead them to their seats.

Concessions

Concessions at our arena will include

- Food and souvenir stands, located throughout the arena, which will be open during events;

- A souvenir shop located at an end of the arena's main floor (so that it can be entered from outside the arena or from within), which will be open during normal business hours, in addition to during sporting events;

- Catered food for luxury-box patrons.

All concessions described would be leased to an independent contractor such as Ogden, Marriott, or ARA. This arrangement would reduce liability, both financially (if sales are poor, we would not lose money) and in terms of product liability, and eliminate the cost of purchasing and preparing our concessions. This contract will be put out for bidding to ensure the best deal, a figure of around $1,000,000 per year is anticipated.

Cushing Coliseum will also own and operate the Coliseum Club, a restaurant-bar located on the second floor, open only on event nights. With 50 tables, the Coliseum Club will comfortably seat 200 patrons. The menu will include steak, chicken, and Italian cuisine. For patrons sitting at the bar, an appetizer menu will be available. Television monitors will allow patrons to watch the game while dining in an atmosphere of quiet comfort.

Case #2 - THE VANITY HEALTH AND FITNESS CENTER

Design and Construction
Planning

This facility will offer the following:

- Weight room, including both free weights and Nautilus equipment.

- Handball and racquetball courts

- Gymnasium for basketball and exercise programs

- Running track

- Additional exercise program rooms

- Swimming pool, including whirlpool

- Men's and women's locker rooms

- Administrative offices

- Snack bar.

In order to build this facility, an architect will be hired. The architect will have previous experience in building health and fitness facilities; therefore, an additional objective opinion may be used in deciding the design of the facility. The selection of the architect will be based on a comparison of several architects from recommendations of other facility owners. The architect will be paid in a lump sum. This payment will be approximately 8 to 10% of the total budgeted construction costs. The responsibilities of the architects include predesign plans, design development, and hiring and supervision of the contractors.

Location is the most important factor in the site of the facility. The facility should be in a place perceived to be convenient for the consumer. Other factors involved in the site decision include availability of sewage and gas lines, drainage of the property, amount of parking available, and the number of accessible streets the facility has. A rule of thumb in the cost of the real estate is between 20 and 25% of the total project cost. We will follow this concept when looking at possible sites for our facility.

After finding the site and an architect to build the faculty, there are some musts for the design of our facility:

- Swimming pool and whirlpool

- Handicap-accessible areas in all parts of the facility, including entrances, bathrooms, and parking areas

- Adequate administrative office space

- Adequate storage space for additional equipment and supplies

- Potential plan for facility expansion in the future

- User friendliness, including large locker rooms, separate areas for the swimming pool and maintenance, and enough room for peak-hour use of the facility.

Development.

Five areas of concern will be handled by the architect regarding the design of the facility.

The first area, the floor plan, is the scale drawing of the entire facility. This design will look at traffic flow and crowd control for the facility, entrances and exits, city codes, storage, and ways in which space in the facility can be utilized. These plans will be looked at closely, because this is the basis from which the facility will take shape. The specific elements of this plan include actual floor plans and the basic architecture and elevation of the building itself.

Furniture and equipment arrangements are also planned during the design period. These decisions are made by the architect based on the price of the furniture and the style that we want for our facility.

Once contractors are hired, a detailed budget of estimated costs and expenses will be developed. The budget is developed after showing the plans to contractors and their subcontractors, who give estimates of their costs and expenses, called bids. These figures are the source for the final bids by both the architect and contractors. These bids are not the final budget because the expenses and costs reported by the contractors are only estimates, not final figures.

The facility will begin to take shape with the construction documents, which give the exact specifications of the building, including the precise measurements of the building, location of furniture, and the landscaping that will be done outside of the facility. They also include all electrical and mechanical systems and their wiring.

The design of the facility will take into account safety at all times. Risk management will be discussed later, but if safety features are built into the facility, they will lessen the potential for possible risks.

Hiring of contractors.

Contractors will be selected by competitive bidding for the job. After a review of each contractor's experience with building health facilities and a review of their employees, bids will be taken for the work that needs to be done. This screening process is done to eliminate inexperienced or shoddy contractors who may underbid other, more experienced and better qualified contractors. The contractor with a low bid, not necessarily the lowest, and good experience and references will be selected to build the facility.

The contractor will be paid in a lump-sum amount. This lump sum will include the cost of materials, labor, and other associated costs. This is preferable to us because we can budget the lump sum into the budget of the facility. The figure will range from 55 to 60% of the total project cost.

The site of the Vanity Health and Fitness Club.

We have chosen Kent, Ohio, for our health club facility. There are a number of reasons for this selection. Although Kent is a relatively small town, there are a larger number of markets to choose from. There is the working population of Kent, plus a great number of cities within a 10 mile radius of Kent. There is also Kent State University, comprising over 25,000 students. The college crowd is key because there are few recreation or fitness facilities on the Kent State campus for students and faculty. Another factor is that Kent has a low cost of living, which makes the construction of the facility less expensive.

Operations Management

The following are the descriptions of the operational management of the Vanity health and Fitness Club.

Executive Director
Duties
- Doubles as the president of the corporation.
- Handles financial operations of the faculty, including budgets and financial reviews.
- Oversees all parts of hiring and staff selection.
- Conducts job performance evaluations for employees.
- Follows Board of Directors' wishes when considering major projects, such as expansion of the facility.

Qualifications
- Must have significant experience in the health and fitness field as a director.
- Should have at least a master's degree in physical education or management.
- Has strong financial background to oversee financial reports and budgets.
- Salary: $45,000.

Fitness Supervisor
Duties
- Coordinates and helps develop all fitness programs.
- Hires and trains the fitness staff.
- Supervises operations of the fitness center.
- Develops exercise prescription programs for members.

Qualifications
- Must have master's degree in exercise physiology or physical education.

- Has previous experience as a fitness supervisor.
- Has background in both health and personnel management.
- Should have certification in health and fitness instruction.
- Should have lifeguard certification.
- Salary: $28,000

Dietitian

Duties
- Develops nutrition information packages and seminars for members.
- Provides nutritional guidance for members who ask for such programs.
- Designs healthy menus for members to follow if they wish.

Qualifications
- Must have college degree in nutrition or similar field.
- Should have experience dealing with people in nutrition.
- Salary: $18,000

Marketing and Sales Director

Duties
- Hires, trains, and oversees sales representatives.
- Sells personal memberships.
- Creates marketing and advertising plans for facility.
- Creates budgets for marketing and sales operations.
- Supervises operations of the facility.

Qualifications
- Must have college degree in marketing or public relations.
- Should have some experience as a sales representative in the health club market.
- Should have personnel management experience.
- Salary: $22,500

Operations Manager

Duties
- Supervises the operations of the facility.
- Hires and trains facility personnel.

- Provides membership services.

Qualifications
- Holds bachelor's degree in physical education or health fields.
- Should have experience in health club field.
- Must have personnel management experience.
- Salary: $22,500

Fitness Instructors
Duties
- Develops and teaches exercise classes.
- Creates exercise programs for members.
- Helps members with fitness questions and problems.

Qualifications
- Must hold bachelor's degree in exercise physiology or physical education.
- Should have experience as fitness instructor.
- Must be certified in CPR and first-aid.
- Should have lifeguard certification.
- Should have certified health and fitness instructor.
- Salary: $12.00/hour part-time

Sales Representative
Duties
- Sells personal memberships.
- Assists in marketing and advertising promotions.

Qualifications
- Must have bachelor's degree in communications, marketing, or sales.
- Should have experience in sales.

Executive Secretary
Duties
- Works directly with the executive director.
- Types letters of correspondence.
- Answers telephones.
- Schedules appointments for executive director.

- Trains and oversees receptionists.
- Handles miscellaneous jobs in facility offices.

Qualifications
- Must have considerable experience as secretary, preferably with a health and fitness facility.
- Must have ability to work with people.
- Salary: $13,000

Besides these main facility employees, there will be a large number of other employees who need to be hired and trained by the operations manager. These include receptionists, who will greet members at the entrance and answer any questions they may have. They will also answer telephones and perform some secretarial work for the facility supervisors. Other employees will include janitors and cleaning people, maintenance workers, and club attendants, who will assist the supervisors. They will also do the laundering of towels and other club-owned items.

Budgeting
Financial Budget.

In order to prepare a budget like the one below, each portion of facility will have its own budget. These departmental budgets will be combined to make the facility budget. Without accurate figures from the departments, the final budget becomes guesswork; thus, it is almost invalid to the facility. To help monitor the budget process, budgets will be designed each month. This process will help to determine if the projected yearly budget is on track.

Financial Budgets for Vanity Health and Fitness Club
Year 2 Income Statement
Income

Membership Dues	$ 950,000
Activity Fees	130,000
Other Income	20,000
TOTAL INCOME	$ 1,200,000

Operational Expenses

Salary and wages	$ 300,000
Utilities	80,000
Maintenance	70,000
Marketing & Advertising	50,000
Equipment & Supplies	60,000
Other	40,000
Total Operating Expense	$ 300,000

Fixed Expenses

Debt	$	140,000
Taxes		30,000
Insurance		30,000
Depreciation		90,000
Other		110,000
Total Fixed Expense	$	400,000
TOTAL EXPENSES	$	1,000,000
NET INCOME	$	200,000

Year 2 Statement of Retained Earnings

Beginning Retained Earnings	$	60,000
Net Income		200,000
Ending Retained Earnings	$	260,000

Year 2 Balance Sheet

Assets		Liabilities	
Cash	$ 200,000	Accounts Payable ...$	400,000
Accounts Receivable	140,000	Bonds Payable	575,000
Land	300,000		
Building	700,000	TOTAL LIABILITIES $	975,000
Depreciation	(105,000)	Equity	
		Retained Earnings..	$260,000
TOTAL ASSETS	$1,235,000		
		TOTAL LIABILITIES AND EQUITY	$1,235,000

Zero-Based Budget.

Zero-base budgeting looks at the programs and activities of the facility in terms of their effectiveness and efficiency instead of using the line-item requests of the traditional budget.

There are advantages to using this type of budget. The facility manager automatically knows what needs to be cut from the facility budget if adjustments are needed. The reallocation of money to different programs and services can be accomplished more easily.

There are also some disadvantages to ZBB. It takes a great deal of time and knowledge to complete a zero-based budget. Some service levels cannot be distinguished from others, whereas it is also sometimes difficult to keep track of all the different services. Usually, after a zero-based budget is completed, the management staff of the facility wants and needs a traditional budget.

The executive director will have to identify each job in the facility with a budget unit, then rank each job in that unit from least important to most important. For our facility, the jobs split up into budget units as follows:

Administration
Executive Director
Operations Manager

Fitness
Fitness Supervisor
Dietetics Supervisor
Full time Fitness Instructors
Part time Fitness Instructors

Cleaning
Full time Custodian
Part time Custodian

Sales
Marketing and Sales Director
Sales Representatives

Secretarial
Executive Secretary
Receptionists

Operational
Club Attendants
Concession Workers

Maintenance
Maintenance Workers

A sample zero-based budget for the fitness budget unit is below. The jobs are ranked from the least important to the most important. The budget includes the names of the jobs, the number of positions for each job, the amount of money spent paying for that job, and the function that the job serves.

Budget Unit - Fitness
Part-time fitness instructors (1 of 4)
    4 positions - @ $10,000
    Function: These are part-time instructors who teach exercise classes
    for the club.

Full-time fitness instructors (2 of 4)
    4 positions - @ $70,000
    Function: Full-time instructors who develop and teach exercise classes
    as well as perform fitness tests on members.

Dietetics supervisor (3 of 4)
    1 position - @ $20,000.
    Function: Registered dietitian who creates diet guidelines for
    members.

Fitness supervisor (4 of 4)
    1 position - @ $30,000.
    Function: Supervises all fitness functions of the health club.

Marketing Plan
Situational Analysis

Economic Climate.

Marketing a service or an activity-based program differs from marketing a product, and different products perform differently in changing environments. Some products or services may perform well in recessions, whereas others may excel in inflationary periods. Products or services that are not considered a necessity have a tendency to perform poorly in stagnant economic conditions. Because sport-related products are not considered a necessity to consumers, they are less than eager to spend more of their disposable income on it. Currently, our economy is in a transitional period with the effects of a recession not too far behind. It is a time when consumers are regaining their confidence to spend their income on luxury items.

Demographics.

The demographics are the characteristics that make up a population and more specifically, the characteristics of the market one wishes to target. The target market characteristics for the Vanity Health and Fitness Club are as follows:

1. 16 - 65 years of age
    a. 16 - 28 years of age   25,000 potential consumers
    b. 29 - 45 years of age   50,000 potential consumers
    c. 46 - 65 years of age   25,000 potential consumers
2. Average annual household income = $35,000
3. Multiple exercise and recreation interests
4. Single and double-parent households
5. Married and non married

The population base that we have to work with as marketers is 100,000 consumers, with an adjusted target market base of 75,000. This means that there are 75,000 potential customers in a drawing radius of our facility that can be targeted and attracted to the sport club.

Demand Trends.

The nature of the U.S. economy is governed by supply and demand forces. Any sport-related venture that explores a new product or service is taking a risk. Who can predict if the demand for a product is going to exist with 100% certainty? No one! However, the very essence of the question fosters hope and excitement when penetrating markets with a product.

In the marketing setting of our product, a health and fitness club, we feel confident that a demand will exist for our product because of the social trends that have occurred since the 1980s. The desire for healthier, stimulating exercise was compounded with the urgency to watch what one eats and take care of oneself. It did not take long for the health and fitness craze to accelerate, to spread into every phase of the U.S. society. Since the early 1980s, America has seen everything from fitness shows on television to the President's Health and Fitness program. Because of the phenomenal increase of this social trend, we feet confident that a marketing demand for our product will exist.

Marketing Objectives

The establishment of our marketing objectives should serve as a control system for our entire marketing process. A suitable control system is essential in achieving the marketing objectives set forth and for correcting any deviations from the marketing plan. In order to have a successful control system, our marketing objectives must be specific and results oriented. The marketing objectives we are going to implement to achieve success for our facility are the following:

1. The primary marketing objective of this plan is to establish a 5% customer base, or 3,750 customers, from our target market within the first year of operation (Budget = $10,000).

2. We will develop a specific promotional campaign targeted and geared toward the baby boomers segment of our target market (29-45 years of age) and establish a 4% customer base (2,000 customers) from this segment within the first year of operation (Budget = $5,000).

3. We will conduct market research analysis of our target market to determine our customer needs and wants within the first 6 months of operation (Budget = $1,000).

4. We will conduct and sustain special events and promotional activities to stimulate consumption of our product within the first year of operation (Budget = $5,000).

Marketing Strategies

In order to link an action plan with the previously stated marketing objectives, an examination of our product's strengths and weaknesses is needed. A SWOT (strengths, weaknesses, opportunities, and threats) analysis of our product, the Vanity Health and Fitness Club, includes the following:

Strengths
*   Our facility is geographically located within a two mile radius of our target market base of 75,000 consumers.
*   The construction of the facility is approximately two miles from a major thoroughfare, for easy access to and from the club.

- The location of the facility is adjacent to a popular plaza and clearly visible from the street.
- The average traffic flow in front of our facility is approximately 2,000 cars every two hours and 4,000 cars during the peak hours of 7 a.m. to 9 a.m. and 4 p.m. to 7 p.m.
- There is a traffic light located in front of the plaza, causing cars to stop every 90 seconds in front of our facility and the plaza.

Weaknesses
- There are three competitive sport clubs within two miles of our facility, including the YMCA, Racquetball South, and the 21st Point.
- Traffic has a tendency to become congested on the main thoroughfare in front of our sport club, causing some difficulty in entering and exiting.
- The proximity of the plaza to our facility can overwhelm our location. Consumers may not notice it because of the size and the commotion of the plaza.
- The cost of our property tax is high because of our proximity to the shopping plaza.

Opportunities
- We have the chance to develop a large and lasting consumer base because of the proximity of our target market.
- We can easily generate local exposure to our sport club because of the visibility of the facility.
- We can tap into the customer base of the plaza because of our proximity to those stores.
- We can initiate cost-efficient advertising because of the traffic flow and location of the sport club.
- We have the opportunity to differentiate ourselves from the competition and offer a better product.

Threats
- The existing sport clubs in the area may initiate an advertising and incentive war to thwart our customer base.
- Consumers in our target market may not see a demand for our product.
- The economy could slip back into a lull or recession and squeeze the purse strings of our target market.

The marketing strategy that we will implement to accomplish our objectives is a market-penetration strategy. In the marketing setting of our facility, we did not feel that we were introducing a new product into the market, but rather trying to penetrate an existing market with an existing product. Initially, our strategy will take on the sole dimension of attracting customers and then become more of a repeat-purchase strategy; however, we will continually give effort toward increasing our consumer base. The most difficult aspect of this marketing strategy will be to attract customers to their first visit.

In order to establish a consumer base, we will initiate a promotional campaign during the first month of operation. This campaign will be geared toward the entire target market with the incentive that if someone brings a friend, he or she can buy two, one-year memberships for the price of one. We will facilitate this promotion by launching an advertisement campaign using a large banner on the front of the Vanity Health and Fitness Club to introduce the idea and local advertising in the newspaper to broadcast it. This campaign will foster word-of-mouth and bring-a-friend types of advertising, which is very cost-efficient.

To meet the challenge of establishing a consumer base of 2,000 from the baby boomers' segment of our market, we will target them specifically with some promotions and programs. We will initiate exercise and aerobic programs geared only toward them because people enjoy exercising with people their own age. We will also promote social gatherings like holiday parties on their behalf to foster friendships.

Finally, we will periodically distribute a market research survey targeted at our customers. The aim of these surveys will be specific to their needs and wants, in order to help generate ideas and solutions to increase our consumer base and service level.

Evaluation.

The evaluation of this marketing plan will be easy. A year after our official opening day, we will check to see if we reached our goal of establishing a customer base of 3,750. At least 2,000 of our memberships should be those people ranging from 29 to 45 years of age. We will also be able to monitor the changing demographics of our consumers because of the marketing surveys and membership forms we will distribute.

Event Management

As facility managers of the Vanity Health and Fitness Club, we believe that consumers will be satisfied and motivated to return to our club once we get them inside for a visit. In order to stimulate consumption and increase customer flow for the facility, we are going to establish an annual, special event. The event will be a yearly three-on-three basketball tournament for everyone, called the Roundball Classic. This event will be targeted to members and nonmembers of the sport club. The small fee to enter this competition will pay for the additional personnel and management needed to hold the event.

The additional personnel that this event will require are the following:

· an event director

· a parking supervisor

· parking attendants

· scoreboard operator

· basketball referees

· event secretary

· director.

The event director is ultimately responsible for supervising and coordinating the entire event, with all the special-event personnel reporting directly to him or her. The event secretary is responsible for registering contestants, for checking them in before their competition, and for recording the wins and losses of each team. The marketing director will coordinate all the marketing activities for the event, obtain sponsors if needed, and provide any publications and programs. The secretary and marketing director will report directly to the event manager for any updated information. The scoreboard operator will report to the secretary announcing who won and lost, and the referees will check with the secretary to make sure the games are conducted fairly and end on time. The parking supervisor will be in charge of the parking attendants, sectioning of the parking lots, and the flow of traffic. The Roundball Classic can be a great success with the cooperation and commitment of all the special-event personnel.

Concessions

The concessions that we will incorporate into our facility consist of a juice bar. The function of our juice bar will be simply to provide our members with the opportunity to have a refreshing, healthy beverage in order to replenish their fluids after exercising. We have determined to lease the space for the concessions and receive a percentage of the sales. We will lease the property for a juice bar to relieve ourselves of any liability, or potential lawsuits, and also so we do not create any excessive overhead. We will require a 15% commission from each sale because the cost of leasing will not be significant, and the demand for a beverage at our facility will most likely be high. Our juice bar will be provided for our members so they can purchase a refreshing drink, and we can generate some additional income.

Risk Management and Legal Concerns
Risk management.

The risk management of this facility refers to five areas: personnel risk, equipment risk, probability of the risk, actual loss, and any hazardous conditions that cause possible risks. All of these areas are important because they cover the entire spectrum of the facility. We have to be sure to exercise "reasonable care" to discover dangerous situations and conditions against which patrons cannot be expected to protect themselves.

Because we deal with the public and anyone could walk through our doors, we have to hire competent employees and employees who care about the individuals they service. By going through the proper steps of hiring and training personnel, including background checks and an intensive interview, personnel risk will be limited to a minimum. The employees of a company make the company what it is, so hiring good people is a necessity.

When choosing our site, we picked an area that has little crime. This will help the facility's reputation with the public, thus cutting down on environmental risk.

The fitness equipment, including weights, that are used in the facility will be tested and proven to be safe for the members of the club. The staff will learn to use and maintain the equipment to help prevent any accidents from happening. Also, members will be given detailed personal instructions about how to use the equipment that the club provides. Instructions on the use of the equipment will be posted in conspicuous places for constant reminders to the members about their safety. These warnings should help prevent accidents from occurring.

We will provide a risk assessment for each of our members to help members understand what they should and should not be doing when working out. This will give the members advice on the type of workouts they do and also the types they should not be doing.

Any potential risks that do occur in the facility will be documented, so that they can be eliminated in the future. Documentation will also help define the greatest risks in the facility. From these reports, the facility can develop standard operating policies to keep them from happening again.

Possible risk management scenarios.

1. A person is working out on the free weight bench press, but forgets to put the collar on one end of the bar. The individual begins lifting the weights, but on the fifth bench press, one arm gives out on the side where the collar is missing, causing the weights to slide off the bar onto an unsuspecting member's foot.

   To prevent this from happening, the staff must be trained to know the procedures for lifting the free weights, including putting collars on the ends of the barbells. The staff is to remind everyone personally of this type of danger when in the weight room, so the members will not forget. Signs would also be posted, showing the proper procedure and reminding the members to act in a safe manner for everyone's sake. A spotter should also be required on the free weights to help prevent a scenario such as this.

2. A woman slips on the wet floor outside of the pool area while walking to the locker room and breaks her arm.

   A non-slip surface will be installed in the area from the pool to the locker rooms. Warning signs to walk, not run will be posted in the area for members' safety. Also, a swimmer must go to the locker room and dry off before entering the rest of the facility, which is termed a "dry area."

3. A fire begins inside one of the bathrooms at the facility, and the fire extinguisher nearest to it does not operate correctly.

    A safety inspector will make routine inspections of the facility to check the fire extinguishers and the rest of the facility for any potential hazards. This will allow the management of the facility to correct these possible dangers before they happen. It is necessary for an outsider, who does not see the facility every day, to inspect because the potential dangers are much more noticeable.

4. In one of our high-intensity aerobic fitness classes, an elderly person, not in shape, has a heart attack.

    Each member will receive a risk assessment by our fitness management team to let the member know what he or she is capable of doing. This way, each member will actually get a true exercise program that will help their overall health, instead of one that causes overexertion. In addition, each of our fitness instructors will be certified in CPR and first aid.

Legal concerns.

Some legal concerns in addition to those also mentioned in the risk management section include medical injuries to members, contractual agreements, and a safety expert.

Because of the potential stress involved in some of the exercise classes that the club would offer, we have concerns with members overexerting or seriously injuring themselves. All members of our staff will be certified in CPR and first aid. Some of the fitness staff will have sports medicine certification in order to provide some diagnosis of less serious injuries. In general, we want to make sure that our members can be well treated if injured at the facility. We do not want to become liable for serious injury or death of a member because of a lack of CPR or first-aid skills.

Contractual agreement will be administered to the members specifying the nature of the facility to be provided and the member's own obligation to safety. This agreement would be subject to a court test for validity when the occasion arises. Even though members have signed the agreement that does not mean that our employees can ignore their duties to the members of the faculty. The contract that members sign will not be valid under gross negligence of an employee. This is where personnel risk becomes a factor. We must make sure that our employees are hard working and responsible to avoid any possibility of gross negligence.

A safety expert will be helpful in that the person will frequent the facility to look for any unnecessary dangers in the building and its equipment. Having these areas checked frequently will help reduce our liability and losses if a lawsuit is filed against the facility. Such a reduction will occur because we have taken the proper precautions necessary to prevent injury to our members.

Case #3 - STATE UNIVERSITY FIELD HOUSE

The Field House is an athletic facility that was intended to be used as an alternative site for athletic team practices when constructed in 1990. There are three main categories for the priority use of the facility:

1. State University Athletic Department

2. Inter-university use (i.e., intramural, ROTC, Club Sports, etc.)

3. Outside university or community

State University athletics.

The decision as to which athletic team has priority use of the facility is left up to the discretion of the athletic director. This decision would most likely be based on which sport is in or out of season; competitions and contests; time of year etc. Athletics needs to be restricted to using the facility only during a specific time block each day, and this time block needs to be strictly followed.

Inter-university use.

Groups within the university, but outside athletics may use the facility only during times outside of the time blocks as previously designated by the athletic department. The usage will be based on a first come - first served basis. Groups included in this category include Intramurals, ROTC, Club Sports, and Other. These groups may use the facility only for its intended uses as described in the section titled "**Outside Use Statement.**"

Outside university or community.

Organizations or groups within this category may use this facility during time blocks outside of athletics and during those times not already occupied by any other university group or organization. Organizations may schedule use of the facility only if they are using the Field House for one of its intended uses as described in the section titled "**Outside Use Statement.**" Groups or organizations included in this category could be the following: Peewee Football, indoor soccer, Little League Baseball, local track teams or groups, rugby clubs, and others as long as their uses comply with the set standard usage.

Comparisons and reasoning.

The primary reason for the construction of this facility was to benefit the university and most specifically intercollegiate athletics. This purpose will help support recruiting and improvement of overall quality of all athletic teams, and improve competitiveness as a member of the NCAA's Division I category. In doing so, it seems reasonable to have athletics as its primary user. Second, to benefit the university as a whole inter-university use would therefore be second in priority of usage. Last, to benefit the surrounding community and promote State University as a whole, groups outside the university would then be permitted to use the facility whenever it is not already scheduled for use by some other group.

Events to be Held at Field House
Outside use statement.

Since the Field House opened in January 1990 there have been many requests about the availability of the facility to groups outside athletics and the university. These requests have come from a wide variety of groups and organizations. Some of these requests have been accommodated, whereas others have been denied use of the facility. The hierarchy listed below will be the standard policy used at State University to determine usage of the Athletic Department's Field House.

The majority of groups who have requested time or accommodation in the Field House may be broken down into several main groups. These groupings and a brief explanation are as follows:

1. Local: within a specified area or where there is a sphere of influence regarding the university.

2. Community: more specific than local, could be used to address groups from the surrounding area.

3. Charity: groups or organizations that either fund themselves or are nonprofit organizations.

4. Service Organizations: organizations that provide a service or program that may be of value to the university or local community.

5. Schools or Educational: may include any of the following: band practice, athletic team practice, supervised physical education or recreation program, etc. This would pertain to the local school systems.

6. Schools (College/University): mainly pertain to with athletic teams. Has been used by many different teams and schools.

7. Professional Athletic Teams: has been used by both the local baseball and football organizations.

8. Public: the broadest, least defined group. It is included to catch any groups not named previously.

The Field House, when originally designed and constructed, was intended to be solely used for intercollegiate athletics. The facility was specifically designed to accommodate the following activities:

I.   Football

II.   Soccer

III. Baseball

IV.   Softball

V.   Field Hockey

VI.   Golf

VII. Track and Field

    A. Running Events

- 55-meter hurdle
- 100-meter hurdle
- 110-meter hurdle
- 55-meter dash
- 100-meter dash
- 4 x 400 relay
- 4 x 800 relay

    B. Field Events

- triple jump
- long jump
- pole vault
- high jump
- shot put

Outside groups or organizations must be associated with these athletic events to be considered for possible use of the facility. Groups or organizations, such as Peewee Football or Little League Baseball, will be permitted to use the facility for these types of activities. Groups or organizations wishing to use the facility for other types of athletic activities will need to get prior approval from the facility manager and the athletic director, or both. If these groups want to bring in special equipment to use while they are using the facility, they will also have to get prior approval from the facility manager and the athletic director, or both.

Other groups or organizations wishing to use the facility for activities other than those listed above, such a, bingo or a craft fair, will not be permitted use of the facility. This would require special preparation of the facility, to ensure that damages would be avoided, which the Field House is not equipped to do at the present time. If a sub-floor or tarp were needed to cover the area the facility does not own such a piece of equipment. Due to budget constraints, unnecessary wear and tear of the facility is strictly forbidden. This is why the facility can be used only for its intended uses.

Policies for Facility Use by Outside Groups

1. All outside requests for the use of the facility are to be directed to the appropriate authority (athletic director or facility manager)

    A. Requests must be in written format.

    B. Need to specify

       1.   planned activity

       2.   number of participants (approximate)

       3.   projected date and time

       4.   number of spectators (approximate)

       * Maximum number of occupants is 600 at all times. *

2. Liability Release and Financial Responsibility

    A. Signed and notarized release of liability

       1.   approved by State University legal staff

       2.   signed by requesting group and Field House representative

    B. Signed and notarized financial responsibility form

       1.   Covers damage or excessive use above normal expectations

    C. Both documents filed in advance of event

3. Rules and Agenda Meetings

    A. Follow current policy for clinics and track meets as listed in the Operations Manual

4. Fee Structure will be based on the following scale:

    A. Base charge for 8 hours

    B. Base charge for 4 hours

    C. A deposit equal to two times the quoted fee will be required one month prior to use

    D. Deposit will be returned after event if

       1.   no additional charges were incurred

       2.   no damages were done to the facility

    E. If event is canceled, the deposit, less 25% scheduling fee, will be refunded if

       1.   written notification is received 7 working days prior to event

       * If inclement weather causes cancellation, a full refund will be given, if deemed appropriate by facility. *

5. Fee is for use of the building and does not include any extras

    A. Any additional setup or take-down charges will be quoted on request.

    B. Special equipment needs or requirements must be addressed in advance.

6. Charge may be waived by the President's Office or the Athletic Director.

7. Staffing charge for Field House supervision needs to be included as an

additional charge for staffing above and beyond normal hours.

8. Standard operating rules of the Field House will apply for all special events with no exceptions.

Staffing of Field House

Management

Facility Manager (one person): The overall controller of the facility. This position is directly responsible to the athletic director and has   to keep good communication with all of the coaches and leaders of the groups and organizations who will use the facility, as well as with auxiliary staff who assist with the operation of events (trainers, ticket takers, police, etc.). This position is ultimately responsible for all aspects of the Field House. The facility manager is responsible for staffing the facility, scheduling events, scheduling workers, overseeing maintenance and custodial departments in Field House, approving facility usage, approving special equipment brought into the facility, developing annual budget, and other duties as assigned by the athletic director.

Assistant Facility Manager (one person): Directly responsible to the facility manager and must have good communication with the coaching staffs and outside usage groups, has control over graduate assistant and student workers. Assistant facility manager is responsible for all aspects of the facility when facility manager is not directly or readily available. Must have good communication with auxiliary and support staffs (trainers, ticket takers, police, etc.), and other duties as assigned by the athletic director or facility manager.

Graduate assistant (one person): Available to assistant the facility managers in all aspects of the facility and its uses. Must take on responsibility of overseeing student workers and in general give support where it is needed most.

Student workers (four workers): Responsible for maintaining record of usage as patrons come into facility. Must be aware of number of people in facility, especially during outside events to ensure the capacity level is not surpassed. In general assist with the operation of the facility where needed as instructed by one of the facility managers.

Support Staff.

Maintenance (one supervisor and two workers): This department is responsible for the all-around maintenance of the facility. Responsibilities would include, but not be limited to, repairs (with in their capacity), electrical, plumbing, structural, snow removal, severe spills, equipment maintenance, and other responsibilities as assigned by facility manager.

Custodial (one supervisor and two workers): This department is responsible for the overall upkeep of the facility. The daily cleaning, restocking of supplies, cleaning up of accidents, and other "housekeeping" duties as assigned by the facility manager.

Auxiliary.
Police (campus): As needed for specific events that the facility manager deems necessary. Whenever a crowd will gather to watch and pay admission or if facility is rented out for competition, the police need to be at the event. Security need not be present for practice sessions.

Ticket Takers: Will be provided by the group holding the event. A student worker will assist to ensure that the capacity level is not exceeded. If it is an Athletic Department function, their ticket managers will be responsible for the event.

Athletic Trainers: The determination whether an athletic trainer need be present is left up to the head athletic trainer and facility manager. The level of risk of the event must be considered. The level of trainer (head, assistant, graduate assistant, or student athletic trainer) will also be determined in this manner.

Chain of Command

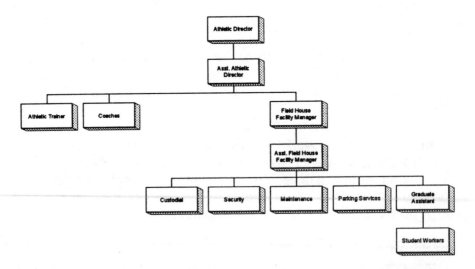

Field House Budget - (one fiscal year)

Budget Unit - Field House Staff

Facility Manager	$40,000.00
Asst. Facility manager	$25,000.00
Graduate Assistant	$10,000.00 (stipend & fee waiver)
Student Workers	$ 2,720.00
Total	$77,720.00

Budget Unit - Trainers

Full Time

Graduate Assistant	$10,000.00 (stipend & fee waiver)

Hourly (for outside events)

Head Trainer	$25.00 per hour
Assistant Trainer	$20.00 per hour
Graduate Assistant	$15.00 per hour
Student Trainer	$10.00 per hour

* For trainers at Field House, during an outside usage, a back charge of a minimum of 4 hours is charged to Athletics or event sponsor at 1.5 time **(time and a half).** *

Budget Unit - Custodial

Supervisor	$24,960.00 @ $12.00 per hour
Workers (2)	$33,280.00 @ $ 8.00 per hour x 2
Total	$58,240.00

* Overtime: A minimum of 4 hours per function is back charged to Athletics or event sponsor @ a rate of 1.5 time (time and a half). *

Budget Unit - Utilities

Electricity, water, gas, phone	$182,500.0 average $500 per day for 365 calendar days

Budget Unit - Maintenance

Supervisor	$24,960.00 @ $12.00 per hour
Workers (2)	$33,280.00 @ $8.00 per hour x 2
Total	$50,240.00

* Overtime: A minimum of 4 hours per function is back charged to Athletics or event sponsor @ a rate of 1.5 time (time and a half). *

Budget Unit - Supplies
Uniforms, Office Supplies, etc. $5,000.00

Budget Unit - Equipment Maintenance
Eagle Cybex Equipment $1,000.00

Budget Unit - Security
Police (campus)

Supervisor	$31,200.00 @ $16.00 per hour
Patrol Officers	$20,800.00 @ $10.00 per hour
Student Security	$3,060.00 @ $ 4.25 per hour

* For security at Field House a back charge of a minimum of 4 hours is charged to Athletics or event sponsor at 1.5 time (time and a half).

Grand Total   **$392,700.00**

Field House Budget- (one fiscal year)   **Plus 20% cutback**

Budget Unit - Field House Staff   (* see note 1 *)

Facility Manager	$38,250.00
Asst. Facility Manager	$23,250.00
Student Workers	$ 2,720.00
Total	$64,220.00

Budget Unit - Trainers
Hourly (for outside events)

Head Trainer	$25.00 per hour
Assistant Trainer	$20.00 per hour
Graduate Assistant	$15.00 per hour
Student Trainer	$10.00 per hour

* For trainers at Field House, during an outside usage, a back charge of a minimum of 4 hours is charged to Athletics or event sponsor at 1.5 time (time and a half). *

Budget Unit - Maintenance (* see note 2 *)

Supervisor	$23,210.00 @ $11.60 per hour
Worker	$16,640.00 @ $ 8.00 per hour
Total	$39,850.00

* Overtime: A minimum of 4 hours per function is back charged to Athletics or event sponsor @ a rate of 1.5 time (time and a half). *

Budget Unit - Custodial   (* see note 3 *)
Supervisor	$23,210.00 @ $11.60 per hour
Worker	$16,640.00 @ $8.00 per hour
Total	$39,850.00

* Overtime: A minimum of 4 hours per function is back charged to Athletics or event sponsor @ a rate of 1.5 time (time and a half). *

Budget Unit - Utilities   (* see note 4 *)
Electrical, water, gas, phone	$167,500.00 average $500 per day for 365 calendar days

Budget Unit - Supplies   (* see note 5 *)
Uniforms, Office Supplies, etc.	$1,740.00

Budget Unit - Equipment Maintenance   (* see note 6 *)
Eagle Cybex Equipment	$1,000.00

Budget Unit - Security   (* see note 7 *)
Police (campus)
Supervisor	$31,200.00 @ $16.00 per hour
Patrol Officers	$20,800.00 @ $10.00 per hour
Student Security	$ 3,060.00 @ $ 4.25 per hour

* For security at Field House a back charge of a minimum of 4 hours is charged to Athletics or event sponsor at 1.5 time (time and a half). *

   Grand Total with 20% cutback $314,160.00

Notes for Revised Field House Budget with 20% cutback
Note 1. Facility Manager's salary was cut $1,750.00 for a cut of 4.4%. The assistant Facility Manager's salary was reduced $1,750.00 for a cut of 7%. The Graduate Assistant was eliminated for a $10,000.00 savings. Total cuts for Field House Staff were $13,500.00.

Note 2. Graduate Assistant Trainer who was assigned to the Field House was eliminated for a savings of $10,000.00.

Note 3. In the maintenance department the supervisor's wages was cut by $1,750.00 or 7%. One maintenance worker was eliminated. Total savings were $18,390.00.

Note 4. The custodial department cut the supervisor's wages by $1,750.00

or 7%, and one custodial worker was eliminated for a total savings of $10,390.00.

Note 5. Utilities were reduced by $15,000.00. This was accomplished through better management and a shutdown period of 30 days (scattered throughout the year — vacations, breaks, no events scheduled, and etc.) $500.00 x 30 = $15,000.00.

Note 6. Cutback of supplies by $3,260.00 or 35%

Note 7. The maintenance money for the Eagle Cybex Equipment was not cut, because it is more cost-effective to spend the money annually, rather than to have to pay for replacement or a major repair.

TOTAL AMOUNT CUT   =   **$78,540.00**
                             (20% of original budget)

Field House Rental
Breakdown of Costs
Event: Track Meet (4 hours in length)

	Hourly cost	Total	Type
Lighting: * Note 8 *	$62.00	$248.00	Fixed
Field House staff: * Note 9 *			
Grad. Asst.	$15.00	$60.00	Variable
Student Worker	$10.00	$40.00	Variable
Athletic Trainers: * Note 10 *			
Assistant	$20.00	$80.00	Variable
Grad. Asst.	$15.00	$60.00	Variable
Maintenance: * Note 11 *			
Worker(s) x 2	$12.00	$96.00	Variable
Custodial: * Note 12 *			
Worker	$12.00	$48.00	Variable
Security: * Note 13 *			
Supervisor	$16.00	$96.00	Variable
Student(s) x 4	$ 5.00	$100.00	Variable
TOTAL	$828.00/4 hrs	$1,656.00/8 hrs	

Notes for Field House Rental

Note 8.   Lighting is charged $62.00 per hour @ 4 hours. This equals $248.00 for 4 hours.

Note 9.   The Field House will be staffed by at least a graduate assistant and a student worker. The facility manager has the right to add additional staff if the event requires them. The event will be charged for the additional staffing. One graduate assistant @ $15.00 per hour for 4 hours equals $60.00. One student worker @ $5.00 per hour for 4 hours equal $20.00. Total Field House staff cost is $80.00.

Note 10. The head athletic trainer has the right to assign trainers in relation to risk factor of the event being held. At least 1 certified trainer must be present. Assistant trainer @ $20.00 per hour for 4 hours equals $80.00. Graduate assistant trainer @ $15.00 per hour for 4 hours equals $60.00. Total cost for athletic trainers is $140.00.

Note 11. Two maintenance workers @ time and a half hourly rate equals $48.00 per worker for 4 hours, times 2 workers equals a total of $384.00 for maintenance workers.

Note 12. One custodial worker @ time and a half hourly rate equals $48.00 for 4 hours. Total for custodians is $48.00.

Note 13. Security will include 1 supervisor @ $24.00 per hour for 4 hours which equals $96.00. Four student security workers @ $5.00 per hour for 4 hours equals $80.00. Total for Security is $176.00.

Peewee Tournament
Staffing and Preparations

Staffing
Field House:

Facility Manager -watch for problem areas and rectify any major problems

Graduate Assistant - provide general supervision

Student Worker - assist ticket takers, counts number of people in facility

Trainers:

Assistant - in charge - on one side line

Graduate Assistant - on other side line

Maintenance:

2 workers - oversee and address any problems, work with setup and take-down, snow removal, etc.

Custodial:

1 worker - clean spills, maintain clean rest-rooms, etc.

Security:

1 supervisor - oversee student workers, watch entire area

4 Student Workers - watch crowd, assist where needed, crowd control

Preparations.

Slip and falls. Maintenance has the responsibility for the walkways and the lobby of the Field House. On a frequent basis, maintenance must survey those areas to see if any areas need attention. Once spills or slippery walkways are reported, maintenance must respond in a timely fashion.

Snow removal. The university has a private contractor for snow removal. The majority of the snow removal should be completed before the event. However, additional snow removal may be required during the event. If during the event the snow plow hits a car and causes damages, the contractor will be liable for the accident. Under the borrow-servant theory, the university must have direct control in order to be liable for the contractor's actions. In this case the university hires the contractor to remove the snow. The university does not tell the contractor how to remove the snow; therefore, the university cannot be held liable.

Jump starts. Jump starting stalled cars or dead batteries will be provided through the university's parking services. This is performed free of charge. This service will be provided after a waiver form is signed by both parties.

Auto accidents. These occur very infrequently, but the overall cost is very high. This could cause a problem if one person involved in the accident does not have auto insurance and sues the university for damages. The Field House should be covered through the university's liability policy.

Frost bite. Cost is low and incidence is very infrequent. This is not seen as a major threat.

Case #4 - YAHOO STADIUM, CLEVELAND, OHIO

Yahoo will be one of the few stadiums in the world specifically designed to host Major League Baseball games and National Basketball Association (NBA) games. Although the plans focus on these facts, the design of the facility has been made with provisions for future expansion. Insofar as possible, the requirements for future expansion should and have been built into the initial structural plans. The major consideration is the ability for the facility to accommodate football without making any structural changes to the building.

This plan represents the following considerations, which have been made with rightful justification for each.

Building Design
Checklist for Site Evaluation

Regional Factors
1. Demographic factors
2. General character of region (rural, industrial, and residential)
3. Distance to competitors in sports events
4. Traffic and transportation

Local Factors
1. Character of environs (urban, suburban)
2. Community acceptance
3. Accommodations for visitors
4. Character and quality of adjacent structure
5. Civic services (fire, police protection, health care)
6. Access
7. Traffic and Transportation
   - Access from major highways and local street
   - Existing traffic volumes and patterns
   - Public transportation
8. Climate

Features of the Site
1. Acreage
   - Adequate for buildings, parking, picnic area, snow removal, etc.
   - Additional acreage for expansion
2. Shape
   - Generally rectangular usually best shape
   - Acute angles or odd shapes possible wasted space
3. Topography
   - Generally level terrain desirable
   - Consider extent of earth-moving in adapting to steep slopes

4. Soil and Subsoil
5. Vegetation
6. Drainage
   • Essential that site be welldrained
   • Possible recharging basin
   • Method of disposing of runoff
   • Environmental regulations
7. Climate
   • Precipitation
   • Prevailing winds
   • Climatic extremes
8. Zoning regulations
   • Permitted use
   • Parking
   • Setbacks, buffers
   • Height limitations
   • Allowable coverage
   • Procedures
9. Access
   • From principal roads
   • From local streets
   • Traffic capacity to streets
   • To accept additional volume
   • Truck and bus access
   • Emergency access
10. Security Considerations

Site Utilities

1. Sewage
   • Capacity of municipal system
   • Location of sewage lines
   • Possible on-site plant
2. Electrical power
3. Water
   • For buildings
   • For site sprinklers
   • For fire protection
4. Storm drainage
5. Energy sources
6. Telephone
7. Solid waste disposal

Economic Factors

1. Acquisition costs

2. Taxes
3. Financing
4. Development costs

Developmental Constraints
1. Restrictive zoning
2. Easements
3. Covenants
4. Other legal constraints
5. Community resistance

Lighting, Heating, and Ventilation

Walls and ceilings will be light in color. A false ceiling with catwalks above will permit servicing and maintenance of the ceiling lights, spotlights, and ventilating system.

Efficient and quality illumination will be designed by an illuminating engineer. However, as a guideline, the Illuminating Engineering Society of North America has recommended the following foot-candles (the foot-candle is a measurement of light intensity at a given point) for each area:

· Lighting in the playing area is to be mounted to the structure up high with a brightness of 200 foot candles for television. All existing lights will be used for both basketball and baseball.

· Incandescent lighting will be used in addition to mercury-vapor lighting (bluish in color) to obtain a highly satisfactory electrical illumination system in terms of maintenance, repair, replacement, and cleaning. (An incandescent light would throw off too much heat with 200 foot-candles of light).

· Vapor-proof lighting units will be used in all damp areas (toilets, showers, dressing and locker rooms, whirlpool), as recommended. Locker-room lights are to be spaced to light the areas between lockers.

Condensation problems need to be considered for extreme temperatures and when large crowds witness events in the dome. To promote absorption of excess condensation, the building will be heated by the circulation of warm air in addition to radiant heat. Adequate means will be provided to supply and exhaust air. The walls inside and outside should be impervious to vapor pressure. Technical heating, ventilating, and lighting problems will be referred to a specialist.

All electrical service, wiring, and connections will be installed in accordance with the requirements of the National Electrical Code of the National Board of Fire Underwriters, and of Ohio and Cleveland building codes and fire regulations.

Checklist for Encapsulated Spaces
1. Provide ample space for activities desired.
2. Include adequate administrative, entertainment, and service facilities.

3. Design for future needs.
4. Provide accommodations for men and women.
5. Provide drainage around the exterior of the building.
6. Provide adequate storage space.
7. Install proper lighting.
8. Provide for maintenance of light fixtures.
9. Provide adequate wiring with provision for high-voltage current.
10. Provide windows and skylights with minimum glare intensity.
11. Install sufficient and well-placed heating vents.
12. Provide for sufficient natural ventilation.
13. Include adequate exhaust fans and vents.
14. Provide well-placed ticket-sale and ticket-taking facilities
15. Provide for telephone, television, radio, telegraph, and fax facilities.
16. Provide an adequate sound system.
17. Provide an entrance large enough for the delivery of equipment.
18. Provide waterproof insulation for the ceiling.
19. Place pipelines an adequate distance from the floor.
20. Provide sufficient shower and locker facilities.
21. Install an adequate public-address system.
22. Include adequate facilities for cleaning and maintenance.
23. Include sufficient water outlets.
24. Provide for expansion or change.
25. Provide for portable facilities.
26. Plan for accommodation of spectators in areas where needed.
27. Provide well-designed spectators' exits.
28. Include an adequate lobby and vestibule.
29. Provide a sufficient number of electrical outlets and place them for easy access.
30. Select good paint colors for the interior of the building.
31. Place windows away from baskets.
32. Provide filters in the air-circulation system.
33. Include movable and folding partitions.
34. Include wall plates located where needed and firmly attached.
35. Include hooks and rings for nets placed (and recessed in walls) according to court locations and net heights.

Planning for the Disabled

Parking
a. Is an off-street parking area available adjacent to the building?
b. Is the parking lot surface hard and smooth?
c. Are there parking spaces wide enough to allow a car door to be opened to full extension (approximately 12' wide)?

    d. Are there specifically identified parking spaces for the disabled?
    e. Are there curbs, wheel stops, or parking barriers within the parking area?
    f.   Has a curb cut, ramp, or passageway been provided to eliminate these barriers?

Building Access

    a. Are there walkways at least five feet wide with smooth hard surfaces (no sand or gravel), free of deep cracks, ruts, or sudden changes in level?
    b. Is the most accessible entrance to the building one that avoids unsafe traffic crossings from the parking area to the building entrance?
    c. Is the approach to the entrance door on ground level?
    d. Are there steps in the approach to or at the entrance door, and if so how many are there?
    e. If there are steps, is there a sturdy handrail in the center or on either side of the stairs?
    f.   If there are steps, has a ramp been provided to eliminate barrier?
    g. Are the ramps constructed in such a way that the grade does not exceed a 1:2 ratio; that is, for every foot in length it gains no more   than 1" in height?

Building Entrance

    a. Is the doorway at least 30" wide?
    b. Are thresholds and door saddles flush with floor or no higher than 1/2"?
    c. Is the door automatic?
    d. Are there steps or interior level changes?
    e. If there are steps or interior level changes, have ramps been provided to eliminate these barriers?

Visually Impaired

    a. Have Braille markers or relief graphics been used to communicate important information to the visually impaired?
    b. Has textured paint or a change in surface texture been used to alert the visually impaired to curb cuts, sudden   level changes, or other vital information important to the independent use of the area by the visually impaired?
    c. Have any other adaptations for the visually impaired been provided?

Elevator or Lift

    a. Is the building multistory?

b. Is there a passenger elevator or lift?
c. Does the elevator or lift provide access to all essential areas?
d. Are there any steps, or interior-level changes between essential areas, that are not served by an elevator?
e. Have ramps been provided to eliminate these barriers?

Public Telephones

a. Is the public phone mounted low enough to be used by children and the wheelchair bound?
b. If located in phone booth, is the opening into the booth at least 30" wide?
c. Would one have to go up or down steps to use the phone?
d. If yes, have ramps been provided to make the telephone area accessible?

Rest Rooms

a. Would one need to go up or down steps to reach the rest room?
b. If yes, have ramps been provided to make these areas accessible?
c. If there are steps, does each flight of stairs have a sturdy handrail in the center or on either side?
d. Is the width of the toilet-room entrance doorway at least 30" wide?
e. Are thresholds and door saddles flush or no higher than I/2" to the floor?
f. Is there enough space within the rest room to allow a wheelchair to turn around (approximately a 5' diameter)?
g. Is the width of the toilet-stall door opening at least 30"?
h. Are toilet stalls and urinals equipped with grab bars?
i. Does the stall door open outward?
j. Has the door been replaced with a privacy curtain to eliminate doors?
k. Are sinks and mirrors low enough for use by children or a person in a wheelchair (bottom of mirrors no higher than 40")?

Wall-Mounted Controls

a. Are vital controls (light switches, door knobs, elevator controls, etc.) located within reach of child or person in wheelchair approximately 48" from the floor?
b. Is all emergency equipment (fire alarms, instruction panels, fire extinguishers, etc.) located within the reach of children and the disabled?

Water Fountains

a. Are water fountains low enough to be used by children and

persons in wheelchairs (approximately 33" from floor)?
b. Are there any barriers, such as steps, around or leading to the water fountain?
c. If so, have ramps been provided to eliminate these barriers?

Air-Supported Structure

Description. Air-supported fabric structures are supported by a positive air pressure within a totally enclosed structure. This positive air pressure is produced by a group of large fans. In conventional structures the internal columns, walls, and foundations must support a roof weight of from 10 to 40 pounds per square foot. On the other hand, in air-supported structures, a roof weight of about one pound per square foot is transmitted directly to the ground by columns of air. This increased air pressure of about 4 or 5 pounds per square foot greater than ambient pressure is usually unnoticed by the building's occupants. Some of the instances when an air structure may be preferable to a tension structure are
• When column-free spans of greater than 150 feet are desired.

• When large, column-free spans are desired at a cost that is greatly reduced compared to the cost of conventional structures. In fact, cost-per-unit area usually decreases as the size of the span increases.

• When a low silhouette is desired.

Specifics of the air-support system. Twenty electric fans, six feet in diameter and 90 horsepower each, are available to support the 290-ton roof. Rarely are all 20 fans used except when large crowds exit the stadium. Three or four are used under normal conditions to pump in 250,000 cubic feet of air per minute.
• The interior volume is 60 million cubic feet.
• The roof rises to 148 feet above ground.
• The playing field is 47 feet below street level.

Seating

Basketball change-over
a. Total seating capacity is 23,000 to attend basketball games and 43,000 for baseball.
b. Portable seating for 7,856 people.
c. Nine (9) portable grandstands (Irwin Telescopic Platform) to form a J-shape and include Sections 1 through 11, four (4) in right field, three (3) in left field, four (4) in corner.
d. Each independent grandstand unit (96,000 lbs. each) is moved on tracks by a roller system built on channels in the concrete for quick   and easy changeovers as well as more cost and time-

efficient efforts.

e. Additional 3 rows of 11 sections of portable seating around court for 350 people (from first-base area and wrapping around to third-base area).
f. 5,000 of 7,600 retractable seats pulled back (behind right field).
g. 115 private boxes.

Additional sideline seating
a. Tables for 497 media representatives on sidelines
b. Scorers' table on one side; teams at each end.

More Seating Specifics. The width of each seating space will be not less than 18 inches. The required space per person will vary from 2.7 to 3 square feet. Sight lines will be considered in relation to the increase in elevation between successive rows. Spectators should have focal points of vision at the court and at the field boundary lines nearest the seat. Focal points more than 3 feet above those boundary lines are unsatisfactory.

When the removable bleachers are pulled out and repositioned for basketball, the first row should be at least 10 feet away from the court sidelines and end lines. The depth of closed bleachers varies from 3 feet for 10 rows to 4.5 to 7.5 feet for 23 rows.

The elevated-seating deck or platform can be used to supplement the number of seats provided at floor level. Removable bleachers for the deck should be the same as those used at floor level. By adopting this design, we are providing additional activity space on the deck and in the area under it, as well as allowing for a quicker change-over from baseball to basketball (in addition to the ease of the tracks that the bleachers will move on) when the two seasons overlap (as opposed to bringing portable bleachers in through the side of the court by the delivery area).

Flooring Surface
Basketball (68'x 128')
a. Made of 260 4' by 8' hardwood maple panels.
b. Court marked for standard 50' by 94' playing area.
c. A Douglas fir frame providing bounce.

Baseball Field (400'x 400', approximately 3 acres)
1. Artificial turf in removable strips, in order to move grandstands
    a. Cost- effective to only take up part of turf when and if necessary.
2. Pitchers' mound is 10-12 inches above turf level.
3. Bases are 2-3 inches above turf level.
4. Pitchers' mound and bases will move on a hydraulic system that lowers them on giant trays descending below the turf surface.
5. Decking will be put on top to allow for change-over.

Made of synthetic turf (grass), which is a turf carpet made from plasticized polyvinyl chloride. It will be applied on an asphalt or concrete subsurface. Installation of the combined fibers and sub-carpet base will be accomplished with rolls that are five yards wide. The turf will then be bonded to the base. Synthetic turf will be used for a number of reasons. It provides a consistently smooth and uniform surface that greatly increases the playing area under all adverse weather conditions.

The official diamond is 90 feet down the foul lines, with a dimension across the diamond of 127 3/8 feet. There should be a minimum of 60 feet from home plate to the backstop. From home plate down the foul lines to the outfield fence, the distance will be 350 feet. The shortest part of the ball park is usually down the foul lines with the fence gradually extending to its deepest point in center field. A large frame backstop with a sturdy, yet removable fence will be located 60 feet behind home plate. This backstop should be a minimum of 20 feet high to help keep the ball in the field of play and to protect fans from foul balls. Attached to each end of the backstop should be a fence at least 4 feet high extending to the outfield fence where the two fences join in foul territory at least 45 feet from the foul line. The outfield fence should be at least 8 feet high for maximum safety and to take a proactive stance in risk management. Dugouts will provide plenty of headroom and storage space at the end of each dugout.

Scoreboard

Basketball.
1. Center hung over the court: 4-sided, hexagon shaped, 6000 lbs.
2. Portable, on trailer drive, under cables and raised with hydraulics.
3. Metal protective shell mechanically closes in around the hexagon shape to fully protect the scoreboard from fly balls in baseball.
4. The scoreboard and timing devices will be centrally located for easy viewing by players and spectators, as well as easy access for maintenance purposes.

Baseball. Two scoreboards will be built into the structure, one along first base line and the other in the outfield. More specifically, JumboTron screens will be used in the scoreboard to ensure good viewing from all seats in the stadium.

Communications
1. TV camera platform behind grandstands in right field.
2. 2 JumboTron color replay systems.
3. Football press box (foreseeable future expansions) used for media darkrooms, team offices, and cheerleader warm-ups.
4. Provisions for a public-address system, with acoustical treatment of the building in mind.

Accommodations for the media (reporters, sports broadcasters, etc.). These include a media room, locker room, a food and beverage area, and a private media entrance. These rooms will be equipped with soundproof broadcasting and television booths. At basketball games, however, the press prefers to be as close to the action as possible, and space will be provided at courtside as well (as described in seating). The baseball press boxes will occupy some portion of the grandstand behind home plate.

Locker Rooms

The development of a team complex should include offices for the coaches and dressing rooms and locker, dressing, and toilet facilities for players, visiting teams, officials, and coaches. A training room, equipment-issue room, meeting room, storage facilities, and adequate ventilation system for drying clothes are other needs for these team locker areas. Locker doors should be of open construction to encourage air flow for drying. All team lockers will be 75 inches in height and 18 inches in width, to allow for the storage of football equipment if and when such storage is ever necessary.

The meeting room will be large enough to seat an entire team informally. It should include a bulletin board and chalkboard and be equipped for such audiovisual equipment as films, overhead projector, and videotape review.

A suitable storage system actually has significant economic advantages because of increased security and because of the proper care and maintenance of supplies and equipment. Adequate storage space is imperative.

Accessibility is an important aspect. The locker room should be located on the same floor as and have direct access to serve the field or court, the practice courts, as well as the doctor's office, the training room and office, the whirlpool, and other service facilities requiring dressing space. The dressing room should be immediately accessible from the corridor.

The size of the dressing or locker room is based on the number of individuals using the area. A general rule of thumb recommends a MINIMUM of 20 square feet per person. Based on that, estimating 30 square feet per person, with thirty NBA Basketball players in each basketball locker room and 30 Major League Baseball players in each baseball locker room: each locker room will be, approximately 900 square feet. One should keep in mind the possibility for the future hosting of NFL Football games and the need for larger locker rooms, more general storage areas and more (large) equipment storage areas.

Shower facilities. Shower rooms should be centrally located in relation to the dressing rooms. In general, lavatory, sink, and shower facilities should be grouped in close proximity (reduces costs of piping too).

The size of the shower room will relate directly to the number of players on the team. Approximately ten (10) shower heads are recommended for the first 30 players and an additional shower head for every additional 4 athletes.

Training Room

The training room should be accessible to all team locker and shower rooms. There should be access to the area for ambulance services too. There will be six main areas in the training room: a) general first aid and taping area, b) hydrotherapy area, c) electrotherapy area, d) rehabilitation area, e) athletic trainer's office, f) a good-sized storage area.

Traffic control is important for efficient use of these spaces. The frequently used areas should be located close to the entrance and placed as follows: first, the taping tables; second, the electrotherapy section, and third, the hydrotherapy section. The rehabilitation area will have another entrance.

Entrances and Exits

Provisions have been made for a paved access roadway and one entrance large enough to accommodate trucks for deliveries. This loading dock is located on the south side and will also serve as the field ramp.

The team entrance and the (separate) media entrances are also located in this area. Upon entering the building the media will have immediate access to their specific interview area, media working area, and media food and beverage area. The teams will have immediate access to the four locker rooms (one for each of the baseball and basketball home teams). Direct access will be available to the court and the field. In addition, officials and employees have a separate entrance in the same area. This allows the officials to enter with ease and have immediate access to the officials' room and their locker room, and the employees to the uniform room and employee locker rooms.

One exit, or stairway leading to an exit, should be within 100 feet of a doorway of every room designed for occupancy. Every floor should have at least two exits, remote from one another. Exits have been located for convenience as well as for safety. It is important to note that the number of exits and their locations have been properly planned in relation to the seating capacity and the space in the facility.

The seating capacity and the number of seats in each section determine the number of entrances and exits required. It is important that spectators be dispersed quickly. To allow this we will plan to have exit ramps leading from stepped aisles. Ramps, stairs, and passageways should be as wide as the deck aisles served. Adequate stair aisles must be provided for all bleachers of more than three rows, whether they are movable or fixed.

Entrances and exits into Yahoo will also be located with reference to parking and traffic approaches. There will be eight spectator entrances to the building, four on the first concourse level and four on the second concourse level. Gate A, Gate C, Gate E and Gate G will be located on the upper concourse level, with Gate A being on the northeast side of the building. Gate H, Gate B, Gate D and Gate F are each located on the lower concourse level in each corner of the building with Gate D being on the south corner. Each gate will have five turnstiles on the lower concourse level and four turnstiles on the upper concourse level. Each gate on the southeast side of the facility will be directly accessible from inside the two levels of the parking garage.

All doors will open outward, with the entire door swinging free of the door opening (side hinges). Double exterior doors will be provided with a removable center mullion so that each door will operate independently, with each opening being 38 inches wide (36 inches required). These outside doors will be equipped with panic hardware and protected against Cleveland weather with overhangs. Outside entrances will also be provided with a grate-covered recess six feet long and the width of the door opening for cleaning mud and dirt from the patrons' shoes. The size of the openings in the grates will take into consideration the prevention of accidents to patrons wearing high heels.

Box Offices

The main concourse will be designed for ticket selling and collecting so that the traffic will flow in a straight line from the entrances to the box office to the ticket collectors. To avoid congestion, approximately two-thirds of the lobby is planned for accommodating box offices and ticket purchasers. The remainder is reserved for ticket holders, who will have direct access to admission gates.

Ticket offices will be located at two of the eight gates, with the windows on the outside of the building. The ticket offices will be at Gate C and Gate G, with Gate C being directly accessible from the main parking lot on the southeast side of the building. An additional ticket office will be located at the Yahoo subway terminal stop for the added convenience to those spectators taking advantage of the public transportation (Rapid Transit Authority).

Stairways and Elevators

Stairways and exits are most important in preventing traffic congestion; therefore, they will be wider than Cleveland (city) requirements. Buildings comprising two or more stories should have no fewer than two stairways, located at the extremes. All stairways will be of fire-resistant construction, and all main stairways will lead directly to gate exits. Therefore, based on the size of our facility, we plan for four stairways located at each corner of the building and next to each gate (exit). Each stairway will be two lanes, with a width wider than code requirements. The stairways will be divided into runs of not more than 16 risers, which will not exceed 6 1/2 inches, and the treads will be at least 10 1/2 inches measured from riser to riser. The rounded edges of all treads and landings will have nonslip, flush surfaces. In addition, nonslip ramps of equal width to the stairs will run parallel to the stairs, to accommodate the special needs of the people with disabilities, as well as traffic overflow.

Ramps. Ramps must have a slope of at least one-foot drop for every 12 feet. Minimum landings are 5 by 5 feet and extend at least one foot beyond the swinging area of a door. The ramps should have at least a 6-foot clearance at the bottom and level platforms at 30-foot intervals on every turn. To determine exact requirements for ramps, stairs, exits, doors, corridors, and fire-alarm systems, we consulted local and state laws and the local safety and fire codes.

Services

Concession areas (42). The dome is designed to accommodate basketball, along with baseball, and four (4) auxiliary concession areas will be placed in the outfield during basketball games for better convenience for the fans. They will be equipped with electric stoves, sinks, running water, and sewer connections and will be located so that they do not interfere with the normal flow of traffic. The booths will be accessible from all seats. Approximately 100 square feet per 1,000 spectators will be allowed for permanent concession booths.

Permanent concessions areas will be located throughout the upper and lower concourses, between men's and women's rest-rooms. In the lower concourse, there will be four (4) concession areas, including commissary areas, between each gate, for a total of sixteen (16). In the upper concourse, there will be five (5) concession areas between Gates E & G; five (5) between Gates E & C, including commissary areas; six (6) concessions, between Gates G & A and six (6) between Gates A & C, including commissary, for a total of twenty-two (22).

Spectator rest-rooms (34). There will be sixteen (16) on the upper concourse and eighteen (18) on the lower concourse (21 women's, 13 men's). The concept of more women's rooms than men's rooms has been adopted by all state-of-the-art facilities being designed today. Because traffic flow runs through the men's room at a quicker pace than through the women's rooms, this ratio allows women adequate time to get in and out of the rest-rooms and get back to their seats.

The locations of the rest-rooms throughout the facility are beside each stairway between the first and the second concourse. The spacing and location of the men's and women's rest-rooms is also an important factor. With the proposed arrangement, if necessary, a patron could run directly up or down the stairs to another bathroom, rather than running to another corner of the facility.

In addition, two large rest-rooms (1 women's and 1 men's) and a storage room will be underneath the bottom quarter of seating Sections 141, 100, and 101. More specifically, these sections are to be located behind the portable concession area for basketball, where baseball's (left) outfield would be.

Rest-rooms will be designed for proper ventilation, lighting, and sanitary care, as influenced by Ohio state codes.

Storage

Storage rooms are one of the most common shortcomings when it comes to facility design. It is essential to have adequate and conveniently located storage space for complete efficiency. Adequate maintenance and control over supplies and equipment are possible only when proper storage space is available. We have made storage considerations in our planning stages simply because after a building is completed, it is impossible to add storage space unless space is taken from areas designed for other uses.

A major consideration that will dictate the placement of large storage areas is the need for a loading dock and elevator for heavy and large equipment and supplies.   Provisions of adequate entrances to storage areas have also been made.

Other space considerations.   Storage space will be needed for equipment, supplies, novelty, maintenance shops and storage, mechanical, electrical and pump rooms, concession food storage and preparation, uniform room, janitors' closet, tenant storage, officials' room, video room, weight room, training room, whirlpool, laundry, receiving area, loading room or dock, press boxes, and media area.

Offices:
- doctors
- trainers
- security
- administration
- facility manager
- coaches
- managers

Locker Room:
- officials
- men's employees
- women's employees
- home baseball team
- visiting baseball team
- home basketball team
- visiting basketball team

Parking

Parking for Yahoo consists of a four-level garage (4,000 spaces) and a lot (6,000 spaces). In the garage, 1,000 spaces are reserved for Yahoo personnel (everyone from janitors to athletes). The parking lot is divided into two sections by a barrier. The barrier is big enough to prevent cars from going from one section to another, but there will also be occasional breaks in the barrier to allow total access for people walking to the arena from the far lot. To avoid congestion in the parking lot when people are leaving, it is advisable to have only one entrance or exit. To alleviate traffic even more, there are two separate parking sections, each with a single entrance or exit. Each entrance or exit is to a different street, and both are very close to the highways. The highway ramps have been enlarged from one lane to three in order to handle the increased traffic.

The Ontario Street entrance or exit is aligned with traffic coming from downtown, while the Carnegie Road entrance/exit is aligned with traffic coming from the eastern and western suburbs. There are four booths at each entrance/exit. The rows of parking are aligned in such a way that traffic can flow easily in and out of the area. The parking lot is heated, so it does not need to be plowed. Consequently, no spaces are sacrificed during the winter for areas to hold the plowed snow. Rather than letting local garages have the traffic, Yahoo's parking will earn revenue. The convenient parking is also expected to attract more people to the arena. In addition to parking for events, parking is available for people working downtown during the workday. This is a legitimate source of revenue because people used to park on this lot of land before Yahoo was built. More revenue can thus be acquired. People are subject to fines or towing, or both, if they don't remove their cars from the lot two hours ahead of events on game days.

The entrance or exit to the parking garage is on East 8th St. The media and delivery entrance is on Huron Rd. Being on different roads from each other and from the ones on Ontario and Carnegie, these entrance or exits are positioned so as to avoid traffic as much as possible. The Rapid Transit Authority (RTA) station is another means of avoiding traffic. A tunnel leads from the station directly into Lower Level 1 of the arena. There will be a box office there to accommodate those who have not bought tickets yet, and the nearby escalators bring spectators up to the lower concourse.

Staffing

Guidelines for Supervisors.
1. Establish and follow standard operating procedures and other facility policies.
2. Be visible, accessible, and willing to deal in a prompt and professional manner with problems that come up.
3. Coordinate scheduling of personnel within their department
4. Communicate with other departments to ensure efficient operations throughout the event.
5. Note any problems or potential trouble spots.
6. All supervisors will communicate via multi-channeled radios so as to maintain contact with other personnel and the facility manager.

Job Title: Facility Manager
General Responsibilities. The facility manager is the top decision maker and supervisor of the facility.
Specific Duties:
1. Schedule and direct event, admission, and crowd control staff, including ushers, ticket takers, security guards, private duty police officers, parking attendants, and emergency service personnel.
2. Ensure that patrons understand and comply with house policies and rules and regulations.
3. Develop, implement, and monitor emergency operations and evacuation procedures.
4. Ensure compliance by all patrons with federal, state, and local

fire, building, and safety codes.

5. Develop policies for confiscation of bottles, cans, and other items that may cause injury to persons or damage to property.
6. Evaluate architectural design to ensure the health and safety of patrons, guests, and employees.
7. Establish building maintenance policies and procedures and a system to check various aspects of the facility for damage or inadequate function.
8. Establish and implement a working budget for all operations and departments of the facility.
9. Hire and terminate various employees within the facility, assign supervisors to each position, and delegate responsibilities regarding certain departments.
10. Develop standard operating procedures and communicate them to the various departments and supervisors.
11. Be visible and accessible to employees and establish open lines of communication that include a chain of command to deal quickly and efficiently with problems that may occur.
    SALARY: $50,000/year

Job Title: Marketing Director

Specific Duties:

1. Implement a communication system between the athletic team(s) and the facility regarding promotions, advertising, and the media.
2. Obtain sponsorships for the scoreboard and any other advertising to be displayed within the facility.
3. Print the facility event calendar and obtain any advertising support necessary.
4. Promote tickets for events other than basketball and baseball.
5. Develop a direct mail system for promotion of events, which will include a well-designed flyer, order form, and will require budgeting.
6. Develop fan support for all athletic events during the year. This can be accomplished in conjunction with promotion techniques for ticket sales and special day attractions.
7. Acquire corporate sponsorships, special day promotions, and public appearances.
8. Develop promotional plans for attracting season-ticket holders, package deals, and loge sales.
9. Communicate with the facility manager regarding all sponsorship packages and promotional ideas to ensure agreement and consensus prior to any signing of a contract.
    SALARY: Start $25,000/year, commensurate with experience and qualifications

Job Title: Security Supervisor

General Responsibilities. Report to the facility manager; be responsible for the safety of patrons and for the supervision of officers and employees under his or her direction.

Specific Duties:

1. Coordinate, schedule, and supervise security personnel for events
2. Follow standard operating procedures for emergencies, that is, fights, injuries, crowd-control problems, etc.
3. Act as liaison between facility manager and security personnel.
4. Maintain order and safety of patrons, personnel, and guests.
   WAGES: $14.50/hour, guaranteed 4 hours; 1 head supervisor, $15.00/hour

Job Title: Ticket-Taker Supervisor

General Responsibilities. Reports to the facility manager. This supervisor is responsible for ensuring that ticket takers perform their tasks appropriately.

Specific Duties:

1. Coordinate, schedule, and supervise ticket personnel for events.
2. Organize and implement efficient methods for taking and accounting for all event tickets.
3. Report a final count of tickets, patrons, or both to facility manager and event director.
   WAGES: $9.50/hour, guaranteed 4 hours- 1 head ticket supervisor, $10.00/hour

Job Title: Usher Supervisor

General Responsibilities. Reports to the facility manager and security supervisor. The usher supervisor must be alert for any problems or unusual difficulties encountered by any usher under his or her supervision and offer assistance and advice if needed.

Specific Duties:

1. Coordinate, schedule, and supervise usher personnel for events.
2. Assist with any problems or emergencies that arise during an event.
3. Develop system for placement of personnel throughout facility during an event.
   WAGES: $10.00/hour, guaranteed 5 hours- 1 head usher supervisor, $12.00/hour

Job Title: Parking Supervisor

General Responsibilities. Reports to the facility manager and traffic control. The parking supervisor is responsible for ensuring that the parking area is prepared for event traffic and parking needs.

Specific Duties:
1. Coordinate, schedule, and supervise parking personnel for events.
2. Establish and maintain traffic patterns in and out of parking lot before, during, and after event.
3. Be visible, accessible, and willing to deal in a prompt and professional manner with problems that arise.
4. Note any problems or potential trouble spots in lot.
   WAGES: $9.50/hour

Job Title: Maintenance Supervisor
General Responsibilities. The maintenance supervisor will report to the facility manager and be responsible for ensuring that the facility is maintained in a safe and operational manner.
Specific Duties:
1. Note any problems or potential trouble spots in facility.
2. Coordinate, schedule, and supervise maintenance personnel before, during, and after event.
3. Direct staff to make daily and emergency repairs.
   WAGES: $11.00/hour, guaranteed 4 hours for events

Job Title: Housekeeping and Janitorial Supervisor
General Responsibilities. This supervisor is responsible for maintaining a clean and orderly facility.
Specific Duties:
1. Note any problems or potential trouble spots.
2. Inform staff of tasks or needs that require attention either immediately or upon event completion.
3. Coordinate, schedule, and supervise all housekeeping and janitorial staff for event preparation, event itself, and post-event clean-up.
4. Maintain adequate inventory of supplies for facility cleanliness and appearance.
   WAGES: $9.00/hour, guaranteed 5 hours for event

Job Title: Cashier Supervisor
Specific Duties:
1. Coordinate, schedule, and supervise cashier personnel for events.
2. Receive reports from individual cashiers and compile them into an event report.
3. Collect money and deposit it properly.
4. Oversee actions of personnel and be available to offer advice and answer questions when needed.
5. Communicate all information of final totals to event or facility

manager.
6. Be accountable for all fees received.
   Wages: $8.00/hour, guaranteed 4 hours.

Job Title: Security Officer
Specific Duties:
1. Be alert at all times while on duty. Always be on the watch for activities, conditions, or hazards that could result in injury or damage to persons or property.
2. Have an attitude that reflects proper human and public relations.
3. Be courteous but firm at all times.
4. Properly obey and execute all orders given by superiors.
   WAGES: $10.00/hour, guaranteed 4 hours

Job Title: Usher
Specific Duties:
1. Be sure that each patron is properly greeted.
2. Check each ticket completely for event, date, performance time as well as section, row, and seat.
3. Offer clear direction to seating location and service accommodations.
4. Act on customer complaints and if necessary report to usher supervisor.
5. Keep aisles clear at all times.
6. Ask patrons to surrender any bottles or cans in their possession and if necessary report to usher supervisor or police or security officer.
7. Enforce facility policy, such as "No Smoking."
8. Be sensitive to the needs of impaired people such as senior citizens and the disabled.
   WAGES; $8.00/hour, guaranteed 5 hours.

Job Title: Parking Attendant
Specific Duties:
1. Be visible to incoming and outgoing traffic so as to avoid injury to person or property.
2. Direct traffic in an orderly fashion towards designated parking spaces.
3. Report any inappropriate patron behavior to security immediately.
4. Monitor vehicles as they enter spot to ensure other patron automobiles from being damaged.
5. Assist in efficiently and quickly directing autos to outgoing traffic patterns following events.
6. Act on customer complaints and if necessary report to parking

supervisor or security.
WAGES: $6.50/hour, guaranteed 4 hours.

Job Title: Maintenance Crew
Specific Duties:
1. Report any spills immediately to a supervisor.
2. Maintain facility and grounds per the supervisor's directions.
3. Assist with facility equipment setup or tear-down procedures before, during, and after events.
4. Attend to any necessary repairs or adjustments within facility immediately upon request of manager or supervisor.
    WAGES: $7.50/hour, guaranteed 4 hours on event date.

Job Title: Housekeeping and Janitorial Staff
Specific Duties:
1. Maintain cleanliness of facility including walkways, restrooms, and seating areas during event.
2. Sweep and dispose of all garbage left in seating areas following event.
3. Sanitize all restroom stalls, basins, and floors following event.
4. Empty all waste receptacles throughout facility including offices, restrooms, and concourse.
5. Attend to any special needs as a result of spills, accidents, etc., following event.
    WAGES: $7.50/hour, guaranteed 4 hours

Job Title: Cashier
Specific Duties:
1. Be sure that each patron is properly greeted.
2. Act on customer complaints and if necessary report to cashier supervisor, facility director, or security.
3. Take fees applicable for parking and deny further entrance without payment of said fees.
4. Have an attitude that reflects proper public relations.
5. Be able to account for all money received from event patrons.
6. Complete final report for day's intake of fees and deliver to cashier supervisor.
    WAGES: $7.50/hour, guaranteed 4 hours.

Other Positions
1. Nurses: $20.00/hour, guaranteed 4 hours for events
2. Electricians: 3 full-time, salaried electricians at $23,000/year
3. Carpenters: 2 full-time, salaried carpenters at $21, 000/year
4. Event Crew: $1,200/event for breakdown and setup

5. Wardrobe: $7.50/hour, guaranteed 4 hours
6. Local police, sheriffs, and fire marshals: $13.00, 5 hours guaranteed
7. Highway Patrol: : $12.00/hour

Total Staff (part-time and full-time): 2,115 employees

Staffing for Yahoo Events
Total Number of Employees for Average-Sized Event:
- Parking attendants: 40 attendants, 3 supervisors
- Cashiers: 20 cashiers, 1 supervisor
- Ticket Takers: 28 ticket takers, 1 supervisor, 1 head supervisor
- Ushers: 77 ushers, 7 supervisors, 1 head supervisor
- Security: 63 officers, 1 supervisor, 1 head supervisor
- Event Crew: 8 members
- Nurses: 2 nurses
- Wardrobe: 1 wardrobe person
- Maintenance: 4 crew, 1 supervisor
- Housekeeping: 6 crew, 1 supervisor
- Sheriff: 1 deputy in charge, 15 deputies
- Highway Patrol: 10 highway patrol
- Fire Marshal: 2 fire marshals
- Local Police: 7 officers

Total expenditure on wages = $11,740   **[$3,064,140 per year]**

Employees for Average Attendance Basketball Game
- Parking attendants: 30 attendants, 3 supervisors
- Cashiers: 20 cashiers, 1 supervisor
- Ticket Takers: 20 ticket takers, 1 supervisor, 1 head supervisor
- Ushers: 70 ushers, 6 supervisors, 1 head supervisor
- Security: 60 officers, 1 supervisor, 1 head supervisor
- Event Crew: 6 members
- Nurses: 2 nurses
- Wardrobe: 1 wardrobe person
- Maintenance: 4 crew, 1 supervisor
- Housekeeping: 5 crew, 1 supervisor
- Sheriff: 1 deputy in charge, 10 deputies
- Highway Patrol: 10 highway patrol
- Fire Marshal: 2 fire marshals
- Local Police: 5 officers

Total expenditure on wages: $10,446   **[$428,286 per year]**

Employees for Average Attendance Baseball Game
- Parking attendants: 50 attendants, 4 supervisors

- Cashiers: 20 cashiers, 1 supervisor
- Ticket Takers: 38 ticket takers, 1 supervisor, 1 head supervisor
- Ushers: 100 ushers, 8 supervisors, 1 head supervisor
- Security: 60 officers, 1 supervisor, 1 head supervisor
- Event Crew: 4 members
- Nurses: 2 nurses
- Wardrobe: 1 wardrobe person
- Maintenance: 4 crew, 1 supervisor
- Housekeeping: 8 crew, 1 supervisor
- Sheriff: 1 deputy in charge, 10 deputies
- Highway Patrol: 10 highway patrol
- Fire Marshal: 2 fire marshals
- Local Police: 5 officers

Total expenditures on wages: $12,710   **[$1,016,800 per year]**

Minimum Number of Employees to Administer an Event
- Security: 55 officers, 1 supervisor, 1 head supervisor
- Ticket Takers: 20 ticket takers, 1 head supervisor
- Ushers: 70 ushers, 5 supervisors, 1 head supervisor
- Sheriff: 1 deputy in charge, 12 deputies
- Local Police: 4 officers
- Highway Patrol: 6 highway patrol
- Fire Marshal: 1 fire marshal
- Event Crew: 6 members
- Nurses: 2 nurses
- Cashiers: 10 cashiers, 1 supervisor
- Maintenance: 2 crew, 1 supervisor
- Housekeeping: 3 crew, 1 supervisor
- Wardrobe: 1 wardrobe person
- Parking attendants: 25 attendants, 1 supervisors

Total expenditure on wages: $9,402   **[$2,453,922 per year]**

Wages for Personnel for 216 Events
Basketball	$ 428,286
Baseball	$1,016,800
Other events	$1,562,120
	$3,007,206

Total Expenditures Per Year on Wages and Salary
Facility Manager	$50,000
Marketing Director	$25,000
Electricians (3) @ $23,000	$69,000
Carpenters (2) @ $21,000	$42,000
	$186,000
Total	$3,193,206

Budget
Yahoo Stadium

Assumptions Regarding Arena Costs:

The arena will already be completed and furnished. All offices will also be furnished and ready to open. This budget will not include costs for these two areas; however, estimates of total costs are as follows:

Yahoo	$353.2 million
Underground Service Garage	$35.7 million
Retractable Roof	$20.2 million

Team Expenses

Both the Pythons and the Walleyes will be responsible for covering the following expenses:

1. Salaries and wages for all personnel directly associated with the team, such as players, coaches, management, trainers, doctors, statisticians, publicity, lawyers, office personnel, and equipment manager.
2. All equipment and uniforms for the players and the games and practices.
3. All costs for the leasing and maintenance of the basketball floor and the baseball field. This will also include the scoreboard and sound systems for each team.
4. The equipping and maintenance of all areas directly used by the
5. teams: training room, team locker rooms, weight room, media room, offices, practice court, laundry room.
6. All publicity, advertisement, and promotions for the team and events there related.

Concessions. Concessionaires will be responsible for all equipment and maintenance in their rented space. They will be responsible for all costs related to running their business, including wages for workers, cost of supplies, insurance, advertising uniforms, etc. A more detailed lease agreement has already been submitted.

Other events. Any events leasing space in the stadium will be responsible for their own publicity, equipment, scenery, costumes, personnel, and setup. Any event crews used in setup, as well as the staff electricians and carpenters, will be paid by the outside event promoter. Any damages resulting from said event will also be charged to the organizer, and Yahoo reserves the right to withhold some money for damages if the situation presents itself. Deposits required for events are nonrefundable in event of cancellation.

Parking. Because Yahoo will have parking space available in a prime area, we will take advantage by renting out space during the work week (Monday through

Friday) from 6:00 a.m. to 6:00 PM. Adjustments will be made for events.

We will be installing the cash-control system currently employed by Tower City at a cost of $450, 000. The parking garage will house 1,000 spots for employee parking whereas the remaining 3,000 will be rented out on a monthly basis at $170 a month. Access will be controlled through a key card that can be programmed or deprogrammed by computer at any time by the parking cashiers. All employees will have a free card, but must pay $25 to replace lost cards. Cards can be canceled by making an entry into the computer.

The 6,000 spaces in the lot will be sold on an hourly basis of $2 an hour, or $5 for the day. An analysis of the costs and projected income shows this area to be easily cost-effective.

Projected Income

Major sources of income will be the gate and loges, which will be shared with the Pythons and the Walleyes. All projections are on 65% occupancy of the facilities. All profits from parking will go to Yahoo, as will the rental fees. We will take 30% of the gross profits from concessions as well. The indicated ticket prices are based on an average-priced ticket.

Operating Expenses

Very little adjustment can be made in utilities costs, but room is available in the category of wages and salary. The following is a projected 20% zero-based budget. The categories show what could be projected at the lowest possible limits for Yahoo Stadium to remain operational. Benefits, insurance, and workers' comp are determined to be 10% of wages.

Basic Income Statement

1. Income ($47,543,299)

   a. Loges

(115 @ $50,000) = 5,750,000 (50%)	$2,875,000

   b. Ticket Sales

41 Python games (23,000 seats @ $22)	20,746,000
80 Walleyes games (43,000 @ $10)	34,400,000
140 other events (23,000 seats @ $16)	51,520,000
	106,666,000
261 events at 65 % occupancy factor	69,332,900
Will take 25% of ticket sales	$17,333,225

   c. Parking

Event parking	7,634,250
($5 @ 9,000 spaces 261 events at 65% occupancy)	
Monthly parking	3,978,000
($170 @ 12 for 3,000 spaces at 65% occupancy)	

	Hourly Parking	<u>3,295,500</u>
	($3.25 for 6, 000 spaces for 260 days at 65% occupancy)	
		$14,907,750

d. Concessions
    30% of gross profit $2,048,521

e. Events and Rentals Income

	Pythons	$2,500,000
	Walleyes	$3,500,000
	Other events ($30, 000 @ 140 events)	$4,200,800
	Concessions ($25, 000 @ 38)	<u>950,000</u>
		$10,298,000

Total Projected Income $47,463,299

2. Operating Expenses
    a. Utilities

	HVAC-$2/sq. ft. @ 375,000 sq. ft.	$ 750,000
	Electric- .10/sq. ft./month	$ 450,000
	Water and Sewer	$ 210,000
	Garbage	$ 90,000
	Phone	<u>$ 60,000</u>
		$1,560,000

    b. Wages and Salaries

	Salaries	$ 206,800
	Wages	$4,710,537
	Benefits, Insurance, Workers' Comp	<u>$ 491,734</u>
		$5,409,071

    c. Insurance $ 256,000
    d. Building and Field Maintenance

Arena		$ 902,000
	Field	$ 100,000
	Repairs and Replacement	$ 700,000
	Landscaping	<u>$ 60,000</u>
		$1,762,000

e.	Equipment Purchase and Rentals	$ 850,000
f.	Legal, Accounting, and Marketing	$ 220,000
g.	Supplies and Office Expenses	$ 350,000
h.	Uniforms	
	Purchase (2000 @ $60)	$ 120,000
	Cleaning	<u>$ 60,000</u>
		$ 180,000

i. Parking Garage/ Lot(Off-Hours)

Wages/Salaries/Benefits	$ 231,088
Cash Control System	$ 450,000
Parking Cards (4,000 @ $20)	$ 80,000
	$ 761,088

Total Projected Operating Costs:	$11,348,159

Zero-Based Budget Cut
Operating Expenses
1. Utilities

a. HVAC- $2/sq. ft. x 375,000 sq. ft.	$ 750,000
b. Electric- .10/sq. ft./month	$ 450,000
c. Water and Sewer	$ 210,000
d. Garbage	$ 90,000
e. Phone	$ 40,000
	$1,540,000

2. Wages and Salaries

a. Salaries and Wages	$3,933,870
b. Benefits, Insurance, Workers' Comp.	$ 393,387
	$4,327,257

3. Insurance	$ 107,000
4. Building and Field Maintenance	
a. Field (covered by Walleyes)	0
b. Landscaping (Barter)	0
c. Arena	$ 732,000
d. Repairs and Replacement	$ 502,000
	$1,234,000

5. Equipment Purchase and Rentals	$ 600,000
6. Legal, Accounting, and Marketing	$ 115,000
7. Supplies and Office Expenses	$ 235,000
8. Uniforms	
a. Purchase (2,000 @ $60)	$ 90,000
b. Cleaning	$ 45,000
	$ 135,000

9. Parking Garage/ Lot(Off-Hours)

a. Wages, Salaries, and Benefits	$ 231,088
b. Cash Control System	$ 450,000

    c. Parking Cards (4,000 @ $20)   <u>$ 80,000</u>
                                                $ 761,088

Total Projected Operating Costs $9,054,345

Opening Day Emergency Snowstorm Problem
Risk Management Techniques
Staffing Adjustments
- 5 additional parking attendants - jump starts, etc.
- 5 additional ushers
- 1 additional cashier
- 1 additional ticket takers
- 2 additional nurses/first-aid personnel
- Contact City of Cleveland to notify that event will continue as scheduled in order to guarantee city snowplowing and the presence of additional patrol car units
- make preparations for emergency shelter:
  - blankets
  - coffee, tea, etc.
  - 2 additional staff members to remain in facility through duration of night
  - 1 nurse to remain in facility through duration of night

Assessment
- Falls in parking lot; infrequent occurrence, very high loss (note heated lot and walkway surfaces)
- Jump-starting cars; moderate occurrence, very low loss
- Car accidents on premises; very infrequent occurrence, medium to high loss
- Staff calling off; infrequent occurrence, low loss
- Frostbite; very infrequent occurrence, very low loss
- Shelter; very infrequent occurrence, very low loss

Treatment or Remedy Phase
A majority of the risk assessments fall into the "Keep the Event and Decrease the Risk" category of the grid. Therefore, the event will continue. Extra staff will be called in for two reasons: a) eliminate vacancies caused by others being unable to come in because of the weather, and b) to provide extra assistance in areas if needed due to poor weather conditions. We have also brought in two additional first-aid personnel and provided additional crew members for jump-starting cars following the event. The city will be notified that the event is going to be held as scheduled so as to provide an opportunity for the surrounding roads to be plowed and salted. We have also requested that additional Cleveland City Police units be

dispersed in the area in the event of accidents occurring as the fans depart.

The heated parking lot and sidewalks will have been engaged long enough that slips and falls will be very infrequent. The problems regarding plowing and car accidents in the lot will be a minimal factor.

Because the categories of risk mostly fall into the "Keep the Event and Decrease the Risk" category with only two falling in the shift category, we feel that the event can successfully be held with no extreme financial losses to the facility.

CASE #5 DESERT DOWNS

Needs Assessment

It is important that before any facility is constructed, the planning group perform an assessment on who their proposed market will be. It would not be feasible to build any form of entertainment complex if there were no available market for the products being built. Therefore, before construction of Desert Downs, the planning group has done a thorough research analysis of the market and demographics of who would be most likely to attend a racetrack as well as the demographic makeup of the city of Phoenix. By using this information, the planning group will be more equipped with information on how to attract potential consumers as well as how to combine this information with a comprehensive strategic marketing plan that will entice consumers who ordinarily would not attend thoroughbred racing.

The first question that needs to be asked is "who is the typical racing consumer?" By doing a thorough research analysis using the Simmons Market Research Bureau, the planning group has come up with the following distinct characteristics of a horse racing consumer:

- Sixty-one percent of consumers are males whereas 39 % are females.
- Thirty percent of consumers are above age 50
- Approximately 52% live in a metro suburban area
- Sixty-six percent have incomes of over $30,000
- Seventy percent own their own homes.
- Twenty-eight percent of all horse racing enthusiasts come from the West Coast and 24% are from the South.
- Seventy-one percent have no children in their household.
- Sixteen percent read Sports Illustrated.
- Sixty percent have cable TV.
- Twenty-six percent watch "ESPN" whereas 13 percent watch "The Nashville Network."
- Thirteen percent list country music as their favorite type of music.

Now that we know what the average horse-racing consumer is about, it is important that the planning group design and place the facility in an area consistent with the characteristics of the typical racing consumer. The planning group has decided to locate this facility in a suburb of Phoenix, Arizona. Some distinct characteristics of citizens of Phoenix are

- Twenty-four percent of the population is retired.

- The median age is 45.2 years whereas the age of the head of household is between 35 and 44 years.

- Of families 27.7 % have at least one child, however, over 50 % of these children are over age 18.

- Fourteen percent of all married couples are between the ages of 45 and 64.

- The median income is $31,946.

- Approximately 39 % listed "watching sports on TV as their favorite leisure activity.

The planning group feels that Phoenix is an ideal area for the construction of a horse racing facility. Because 28 % of all horse racing consumers come from the West Coast and 24 % come from the South, it is feasible to design a racetrack in the southwest portion of the U.S. Furthermore, Phoenix is the home of many older and retired citizens. The planning committee believes that these people are prime consumers for this type of entertainment. With 24 % of the population retired and the median age over 45 years, this is an ideal situation for the attraction of a new type of sport entertainment. One characteristic that was not discussed but can be used to influence this consumer base is gambling. Over 17 % of the Phoenix population engage in casino gambling. Even though casino gambling and gambling on horses are two separate entities, the planning committee sees a possible niche in the gambling market. Consumers who enjoy gambling as well as sporting events would be the prime targets for the horse-racing industry. Moreover, locating the racetrack in Phoenix would in all likeliness increase visitor travel to the area, especially from Nevada, where gambling is the number one source of entertainment. The planning committee sees a real opportunity to increase the number of visitors to the area while spending money gambling at the racetrack.

The Arizona Department of Racing collects pari-mutuel commission fees and license fees, which are deposited into eight separate funds. Revenues received from fines are deposited directly into the State General Fund. More than 98% of state revenues are generated from the pari-mutuel commissions, the share of racetrack handle paid the state according to statute.

In Fiscal Year (FY) 1994, state revenues increased to $8,685,065. Overall, five of the state's eight commercial tracks showed gains in total handle during the year with a great deal of the increase a result of the commercial explosive growth associated with off-track betting. Teletrack handle at Turf Paradise gained 20% from the previous year, whereas Phoenix Greyhound Park showed a 37% increase in off track wagering. Both Turf Paradise and Phoenix Greyhound Park reported increases in total handle of more than 12%. In the case of Phoenix Greyhound, this figure is more remarkable since on-track handle actually declined. Phoenix Greyhound Park now handles more money off-track than on-track.

Although some tracks generated solid handle figures, Apache Greyhound Park and Tucson Greyhound Park experienced significant declines, whereas Yuma

Greyhound did not offer live racing during the 1993-94 year. Handle at Apache Greyhound nearly reached fiscal year 1992-93 levels, but only because of handle generated by extensive simulcasting, which brought in more than 860 programs to the track. Tucson's Greyhound Park's business was affected by the opening of two tribal casinos in its market.

With all of the above information concentrating on Arizona's current horse and greyhound tracks, it is the job of the planning committee to come up with an estimate of revenues for the state's newest thoroughbred park, Desert Downs. In order to come up with a fair estimate of revenues, the committee must look at revenues from previous years from the other facilities. Projections developed by the department of racing to estimate future handle are based on historical levels, industry trends, and the continued operations of each of Arizona's seven current commercial tracks.

With the passage of S.B. 1373, significant changes in racing law will become effective July 17, 1994. Among the consequences of changes resulting from this new law will be a reduction in state pari-mutuel revenues beginning in FY 1996. These revenue projections are contingent on continued operations of the seven tracks and based on handles similar to those attained in FY 94. If a track were to cease operations, it would affect revenue estimates. Furthermore, the situation of Phoenix Greyhound Park is very sensitive for purposes of determining State revenues. Because more than 65% of State pari-mutuel revenues is generated by Phoenix Greyhound Park, any decline (or increase) in business will have a significant impact on resulting revenues. Because Desert Downs will be an exclusive thoroughbred racetrack, revenues stated will be from horse tracks only.

It is easy to see the planning committee for Desert Downs faces many tough tasks ahead of them to make this new facility a reality. The committee, however, has done its research and feels it has come up with the proper information that will be needed in order to create this racetrack. Although there is still much more to be done, and this will be discussed in more detail further in the proposal, the assessment of needs for possible consumers has been well detailed. In the following pages, the rest of this state-of-the-art facility will be discussed.

Planning and Design of Desert Downs

Desert Downs is a 5,600-seat racetrack located in Phoenix, Arizona. The site is located near Interstate 10. The cost of the site was $6.5 million. The grandstand and the other buildings along the grounds of Desert Downs were designed with an old southern theme. All the buildings were constructed of steel and concrete with a foundation consisting of coarse-grained, noncohesive soil made with sand and gravel.

The roof is A-shaped and made of galvanized steel with a perimeter drainage system that will carry any runoff into the two ponds located in the infield of the track. The exterior of all the buildings are covered with white vinyl siding. The front of the grandstand has 16 large windows each with 16 panes of glass. This allows for sunlight into the facility, which assists with lighting. The second level of the grandstand will have 32 circle-shaped windows for sunlight. The use of these windows will cut down on electrical costs. Foam insulation will be used throughout the buildings to protect against the heat during the day and cold during the Arizona nights.

The cost to design the facility totaled $10 million, with the architectural firm of Ewing, Cole and Krause receiving the contract to design the facility. The construction totaled $123 million with the ACME Construction Company winning the bid for the building Desert Downs. The cost of furnishing and decorating the facility totaled $12 million. The total cost for the facility was $151.5 million.

The design of the facility is broken down into the grandstand, a paddock, barns, administration areas, the track, and outlying grounds (parking).

The Grandstand

Admissions lobby. The admissions lobby is a glass-enclosed lobby and includes gates and turnstiles for admission to the facility for the general public. There are four doors; one is equipped for patrons in wheelchair. Space is provided to accommodate large crowds waiting for admission into the facility. Special gates are provided for individuals with disabilities, to allow for accessibility. The area is provided with park benches around the perimeter for seating. This area is staffed by security personnel and ticket takers.

Main lobby. The main lobby, which is accessible to the general public, is broken down into sub areas: programs and racing forms, teletheater, study tables, mutuals, newcomers' corner, food-court concession areas, self-betting areas, and restrooms. Each area is lighted by chandeliers. In addition to interior lighting, windows throughout the main lobby provide an external source of lighting for the facility.

Programs and racing forms. The programs and racing forms area consists of the racing program for the facility and the racing forms for off-track racing. In addition to these programs, other publications on horse racing are available. This area is staffed by vendors.

Teletheater. The teletheater is a 212-seat area with a large 10 foot video monitor. This area's primary use includes simulcast off-track racing at other facilities and telecast of the racing card at Desert Downs. Other uses include telecasts of other special events such as concerts, championship boxing, football games or other sporting events. Space is provided for patrons in wheelchairs. The screen is equipped for the hearing impaired, the teletheater is staffed by courtesy staff member(s).

Study table. The study-table area consists of eight long tables, which seat up to

81 patrons. This serves as an area where betters can analyze the past performances of the horses and prepare for the races that will be wagered. A large video screen is available to provide updated odds and information on races. The tables are high enough to accommodate wheelchair seating. This area is staffed by courtesy staff person(s).

Mutual betting. Five mutual betting areas are located throughout the main lobby. Nine windows are located at the newcomers' corner. Twenty-four windows are located adjacent to the study table area. Twenty windows are provided next to the teletheater, and two areas with eight windows each are provided at the entrance to the bench seating area. All the mutual betting areas are equipped for off-track racing wagering. This area is staffed by security personnel and clerks who work the windows. One window is low enough to accommodate patrons in wheelchairs. The windows are enclosed by bullet-proof glass with openings for cash exchange.

Newcomers' corner. A newcomers' corner is a 42-seat area with a large video monitor that provides first-time patrons with information about the facility. The video also provides information on how to wager and the various difficult types of wagering. This areas has staff member(s) from the mutual department providing assistance at various times during the day. This area can be utilized on nonrace days for special events or can be rented to organizations for private parties.

Food court. A food court with a seating capacity of 232 is adjacent to the concession stands. This area is available for all patrons. Two concession areas provide patrons with snacks or meals. Each concession area and the food court are staffed by food services personnel.

Auto betting. Fifteen auto-betting machines will give the wagerer the convenience to place quick bets. The machines also save the facility money by cutting down on the staff needed for betting transactions. Auto betting is staffed by a member from mutuals and security personnel.

Restrooms. There are 4 large restrooms throughout the first floor, two men's and two women's facilities with a utility closet for maintenance and supplies. The restrooms have change stations and accommodate customers with disabilities, due to the large wheelchair stalls and urinals. The sinks also accommodate patrons in wheelchairs. The women's restrooms have 10 stalls while the men's restrooms have 4 stalls and 6 urinals. The upkeep of the restrooms is the responsibility of the janitors in the maintenance department.

Replay monitors. Twenty replay monitors are located throughout the first floor providing the patrons with replays of previous races, and any judgment rulings that may occur. Electricians are in charge of any malfunctions of the monitors.

Game room. A game room for young people is located in the main lobby. This room has numerous coin games for children and teenagers. Opportunities to win prizes are available through winnings in skeet ball and other boardwalk games. This area is staffed by courtesy personnel.

Information office. The facility has a glass-enclosed information office that is easily accessible and seen at the entrance of the admissions lobby. The information office provides all patrons with any needed information and services while at the facility. Also, any information of accommodations for those with disabilities can be secured at the information office. The information office has courtesy personnel available to answer any questions the patrons have.

Administrative Office. The administrative offices on the first floor consist of a sales department, personnel department, switchboard, marketing department and public relations. It houses the sales director, the vice president for group sales, the marketer, the personnel director, the administrative assistants, and the public relations director.

Maintenance offices. There is a building maintenance office next to the mechanical and electric equipment room. The mechanical and electric equipment room consists of all pumps and generators required to power the facility. It is staffed by engineers and maintenance personnel.

Security offices. The security offices include a special holding room for any patrons who are not controllable. The room is also equipped with video monitors to regulate crowd control. It is staffed by security personnel.

First aid. A first aid room is provided for any emergencies in need of medical treatment. The first-aid room is staffed by a registered nurse and paramedics.

Mutual department. The mutual department is the control room for all wagering. The room consists of computers to record all wagering and calculates all of the winnings. The department has an on-line hook-up for off-track wagering. It is staffed by representatives from the mutual department.

Commissary. A commissary is provided for all personnel of the facility. The room provides a place for employees to relax and eat during their breaks and lunches. This is staffed by food services personnel.

Paddock Cafe. The Paddock Cafe is a 131-seat glass-enclosed restaurant overlooking the paddock area . In this cafe patrons can enjoy snacks and drinks while viewing their favorite horses as they parade in the walking ring. This area is staffed by the concession personnel.

Gift shop. A gift shop is located by the admissions lobby. The shop is equipped with merchandise and souvenirs from the race track. This is staffed by retailers employed by the facility.

Bench seating. The largest area of the first floor in the grandstand is the glass-enclosed bench seating grandstand. This area can accommodate 1,080 patrons (15 spaces accommodate patrons in wheelchairs) who can view the races at the facility as they happen. Two wheelchair ramps are provided for handicapped individuals at each end of the seating area. The ramps are sloped one inch for every 12 feet and have continuous handrails. Fifteen mutual windows and three concession areas are provided for the patrons of this area. The grandstand bench is staffed by courtesy staff and security personnel, and at the mutuals there are clerks and a security personnel.

Second floor access. The second floor of the grandstand can be accessed by stairs or by the elevators. Stairs have uniform height and have handrails with a diameter of one and a quarter inches mounted and one and one half inches from the wall. The elevators are accessible to the disabled patrons. The buttons are low for the patrons in wheelchairs, and the buttons are in Braille for the visually impaired. The elevators accommodate up to 4,000 pounds.

The first floor and second floor have a total of eight public telephones; one has a shelf and is low enough for patrons in wheelchairs and one is equipped with a portable text telephone. Also a total of eight drinking fountains 36 inches from the floor to the spout outlet that can also accommodate patrons in wheelchairs is available to the public. All signage is placed 60 inches from the floor.

The facility has audio and visual alarm systems in case of emergencies. All doors are two inches thick with clear openings to allow for wheelchair access. This allows for quick exit from the facility if an emergency arises. Two ramps on the second floor provide exit in addition to three sets of stairs. The ramps are sloped at 1:12 and have continuous handrails to allow for access of patrons in wheelchairs.

Second floor. The second floor to the grandstand consists mainly of a restaurant, food court, box seating, lounges, and sports bar.

Box seats. Air conditioned, glass-enclosed box seats with a capacity of 360 overlook the race track. The box seats are equipped for six patrons in wheelchairs. Patrons can use the box seats with an extra fee. Each box is equipped with a television monitor and cushion back seating. Each patron using the box seats have full service from waiters and waitresses and can order food and drink from a special menu. This area is staffed by waiters and waitresses, courtesy personnel, and security personnel. In addition to service from waiters, the patrons are able to summon courtesy personnel to place bets on races. Adjacent to the box seats are six mutual windows for wagering staffed by clerks and security personnel.

Restaurant. A 252-seat restaurant overlooking the race track is utilized by patrons with reservations. The restaurant is filled with paintings of horses and with carpeting resembling late-19th-century southern design. Throughout the restaurant, televisions will be available for replays and race coverage. Servers and courtesy staff will be available to serve the patrons and to make wagers for the patrons.

Food court. A food court equipped for 300 patrons (144 inside and 156 outside) is available for all paying patrons. Inside, the patrons can eat in the comfort of air conditioning while viewing the races on a large video monitor. If the patrons choose to eat on the covered terrace, they can enjoy the open-air atmosphere while overlooking the paddock and the walking ring. This area and concessions are staffed by food-service staff. The doors to the outside are automatic with push-action level knobs.

Kitchen. A fully equipped kitchen with all the necessary appliances for the restaurants is designed to be easily accessed by the restaurants and sports bar. The area is staffed by chefs with assistants and bus persons.

Teletheater. A large teletheater seating 168 patrons is used for televising off-track racing and for special events. The teletheater is equipped for the hearing impaired and has wheelchair seating. It is staffed by a courtesy staff member.

Sports bar. A sports bar and lounge with seating capacity of 64 is available, where patrons can enjoy drinks and watch various sporting events. The bar is circular in design. This area is staffed by concessions and security personnel.

Just like the first floor, the second floor is equipped with a study area where patrons can analyze the races. This area is equipped to handle 39 patrons with a video screen displaying updated odds and race information. It is staffed by a courtesy personnel.

Television lounge. A television lounge is available for use during the race card and during off-track racing hours. This area is equipped with couches and chairs to provide a comfortable atmosphere. It is staffed by a courtesy personnel.

Viewing terrace. A viewing terrace overlooks the paddock and walking ring. Wagerers have an opportunity to view the horses from this area just before race time. The doors are automatic and wheelchair accessible with a push-lever action knob. A security personnel supervises this area.

Special rooms. There are two special rooms available for groups of 40 or more. One room is an open room whereas the other is glass enclosed. These rooms are available for special parties and can seat up to 45. This area is staffed by concession personnel and courtesy service members.

Mutuals. There are four different mutual stations available (total 36 windows). Also, seven self-betting machines are available on the second floor. One large and one small concession area are available for patrons. Like the first floor the second floor has four restrooms - two for men and two for women. The mutuals are staffed by clerks and security members.

The third floor of the grandstand is utilized by personnel only. It consists of a press room, announcer's booth, stewards' booth, judges' booth, a room for photo finishes, a storage room, a television room, and restrooms. This area is supervised by maintenance crews.

Press room. The press room can hold 10 media personnel. The room is equipped with outlets and tables that can accommodate any printed or electronic media. Also, television monitors are available to aid the media. A waiter is available to serve the media when needed. The room is in the jurisdiction of maintenance personnel.

Announcers booth. An announcers booth for public address is equipped with all the required sound equipment. Furthermore, a room is available to hold spotters so they are able to assist in the announcing of the races. Maintenance personnel also assist if needed.

Judges room. A judge's room for officials in the case of making any rulings on the races is available. This room is equipped with replay monitors and a "hot line" direct to the mutuals room.

Photo finish. The photo-finish room is adjacent to the finish line. This room is equipped with special cameras that record the finishes if there are any close races.

Television Room. The television room has television cameras for broadcasting the races. The room is equipped to hold two television cameras plus technicians.

Storage Room. There are 3 storage areas on this level. A storage room for the TV equipment and audio equipment is available near the television room. The other two storage areas can be used for the facility in general.

The Paddock Area

Paddock. The paddock area is utilized for the race day card. It consists of the jockeys' quarters, the saddling paddock, the walking ring, the harness paddock, postrace stalls, mounted police stables, and the public viewing area. A paddock steward is staffed in this building.

Jockeys' quarters. The jockeys' quarters is a place where the jockeys can prepare for the races. The first floor of this building has male and female locker rooms each with toilet facilities, saunas, showers, steam rooms, masseur room, weighing room, laundry facilities, lounge, bunk area for resting and area for drug testing. The paddock office and storage facilities are also located on the first floor. A supervisor oversees this area.

The second floor of the jockeys' quarters consists of three offices, a reception area, a conference room for interview and press conferences, a television studio, which is the control center for the television coverage of the races and an equipment room. The jockeys' quarters is staffed by maintenance and housekeeping crews.

Saddling paddock. The saddling paddock consists of 16 stalls. This is the area where the racers saddle their horses in preparation for the race. This area is staffed by race personnel and maintenance personnel and a steward.

Walking ring. The walking ring can be viewed by the general public. This area is where the trainers can walk the horses to warm them up for the races, and it provides an opportunity for the patrons to view their favorite horses just before the races. The public can view the horses from the viewing terraces, the paddock cafe, or the food court.

Harness paddock. The harness paddock is equipped with stalls for at least six races, judges' room, equipment room, room for the harnesses, and a room for the numbers that the horses will be wearing. Additionally, the harness paddock will have restrooms, an electrical room, a plumbing room, storage rooms, a janitors' room, and a room for the blacksmith. This area is where the horses report and are put into their race category. These areas are staffed by maintenance, race personnel, and a steward.

Post race stalls. The postrace stalls are where the horses report after the races. This building is equipped with stalls and wash stations. Also, a veterinarian's office is located here to examine and treat any injuries the horse may incur. This facility is equipped to test the horses for illegal substances that could enhance their performance. It is staffed by the track's veterinarian and the paddock steward.

The Barn Area

Barns. There are 25 barns for housing the horses with 48 stalls to each barn. Each barn will have six washing stations for the horses, a utility room, and restrooms. Four bins for the storage of hay are located in the barn. There are four rooms for feed storage for the horses and four storage rooms for the harnesses and equipment. The facility stalls are rented by the horses' owners. The owners are responsible for providing employees for the upkeep of the barns. These employees are under the barn steward.

Stakes barn. There is a stakes barn. This special barn is only utilized during special events to house horses in large-purse races. There are 16 stalls in this barn,

4 washing stations, 2 equipment rooms, 2 feed-storage rooms, 2 hay bins and a utility closet. In addition to these rooms, there is an office and a press room. The press room is used for the media covering the race. It is staffed by a steward.

Dormitories. Two dormitories for jockeys and trainers are at the facility. These dormitories are two stories tall and contain 26 bedrooms on each floor. They are equipped with a laundry room, storage room, utility room, men's and women's showers and restrooms on each floor. The dormitories will be staffed by housekeeping personnel in each dorm.

Isolation and treatment barn. The facility has an isolation and treatment barn for the horses, staffed by a veterinarian. The building has 10 stalls, a feed room, a bin for hay, a utility room, a storage room, an equipment room, a veterinarian's office, an X-ray room, and a treatment area for injured horses. The X-ray machine is a nuclear centigraphy version.

Blacksmith shops. There are two blacksmith shops, each with four stalls to fit the horses with horseshoes. These shops are staffed by a facility track blacksmith and can be used by any owner's blacksmiths.

Maintenance building. There is a large maintenance building for repair and groundskeeping. The building houses all the equipment necessary for upkeep of the track and grounds. In addition to this area there is a repair shop and office located in this building. It will have six garages for access for equipment and vehicles. This building is the main office for all maintenance personnel.

Postmortem building. A postmortem building consists of a place where horses injured beyond repair are destroyed and where autopsies are performed. This building is staffed by the track veterinarian, maintenance personnel, and landscape workers.

The Administrative Area
Dining hall. The dining hall is a facility for all administrators, jockeys, and trainers. It is a one-floor building with two dining rooms. It has an area for a buffet-type setting. There is an office for the manager and a staff office. It has washroom facilities for men and women, a pantry for food storage, a freezer room, a receiving room, and an area for trash. The kitchen and dining hall are staffed by food management personnel.

Recreation hall. A recreation hall for the jockeys, trainers and facility administrators contains a game room, a television and card room, and a kitchen or snack bar with a dining area. The facility includes restrooms for both sexes. It is staffed by housekeeping personnel.

Administration building. The administration building that houses the racing commission, the steward department, the security department,   facility management, and operations management has an office for each high-ranking administrator and professional staff person.   In addition, the administration building has a lobby for the public, a staff lobby, restrooms, and a horsemen's lounge.

Parking Areas

Parking is ample at the race track. There are to be 4 lots for general parking, which are able to accommodate 3,300 cars. Space is provided for 500 cars for valet parking, 50 spaces for VIP parking, 250 spaces for horsemen's and officials' parking, 350 spaces for employee parking, and 50 spaces for handicapped parking. For buses, 24 spaces are available. Three hundred parking spaces, 15 of which are for handicapped parking, are located at the administration building. RV. parking is available behind barns for camping. Parking services is in control of parking. Valets, parking attendants and security personnel in vehicles are in charge of directing parking patrons, with attendants taking money for parking.

Track

Track layout. There are two tracks at Desert Downs, a one and one-eighth mile dirt track with a 6.5% grade and 100 feet distance between the inner router rails . The second track has a seven-eighth mile turf track with a 6.0% grade and 80 feet distance between the inner router rail. The infield is a grass area landscaped with various plants and two lakes. The drainage system consists of gravel under the surface with drain pipes going into the lakes. Water pumped in from the lakes to a sprinkler system is used for upkeep of the various plants and shrubs. There are two 58-foot television towers and a judge's stand at each of the four turns on the track. The landscape workers along with track maintenance will be in charge of the track.

Tote board. The tote board is located in the infield at the finish line facing the grandstand. The tote board displays odds and results along with special messages. The track is lighted with four stands of mercury track lighting at each turn of the race track with mounted lighting on the grandstand along the homestretch finish line. Lighting is under the control of the electricians.

Event Staffing at Desert Downs

Desert Downs contracted services for concessions, printing of programs, janitorial services, architecture, and for maintenance and landscaping services. Contracting these services reduced the overhead and liability of the facility. Contracting cuts costs, reduces operational expenses, and allows for provision of specialties that the management of Desert Downs cannot provide. In addition, contracting these services reduced the liability of the facility. Although employees of the contractors do not fall under the control of Desert Downs management, they are listed for purposes of event staffing.

Event Staff: 432 total

Parking Services: 25-30 total
  -Flag persons -10-15
  -Valets - 5
  -Cashiers - 5
Security: 30 total
  -Parking - 3
  -Admission Lobby - 1
  -Main Lobby - 3
  -Second Floor Area - 3
  -Betting Window - 4
  -Security Room - 3
  -Grandstand Bench Seating - 5
  -Box Seating - 3
  -Paddock Area - 1
  -Barn Area - 3
  -Infield and track - 1
Tickets and Box Office: 11 total
  -Ticket Takers - 6
  -Cashiers - 3
  -Box Office - 2
Vendors: 6 total
  -Racing Forms - 4
  -Gift Shop - 2
Mutuals: 137 total
  -Window Clerks - 127
  -Mutual Department - 10
Janitors: 14 total
  -Level 1 of Grandstand - 4
  -Level 2 of Grandstand - 4
  -Paddock - 1
  -Maintenance Building - 5
Miscellaneous
  -Stewards - 8
  -Stable hands - 15
  -Judges - 8
  -Engineers - 3
  -Electricians - 3
  -Plumbers - 3
  -HVAC - 2
  -Public Address Announcer - 1
  -Registered Nurse - 1
  -Paramedics - 2

Courtesy Staff: 63 total
  -Teletheaters - 2
  -Study Tables - 2
  -TV. Lounge - 1
  -Special Rooms - 4
  -Game Room - 2
  -Box Seating - 20
  -Bench Seating - 20
  -Ushers for Box Seating - 10
  -Information - 2
Food Services: 88 total
  -Concession Stands - 28
  -Cashiers - 8
  -Food Courts - 6
  -Bartenders - 2
  -Paddock Cafe - 8
  -Commissary - 2
  -Dining Hall - 5
    -Restaurant - 17
  -Waiters or Waitresses - 12
  -Host or Hostess -
  -Bus persons - 11
  -Cooks- 5

-Veterinarian - 1
-Blacksmiths - 2
-Housekeeping - 10
-Television Camera Person - 8
-Television Announcer - 1
-Spotters - 2
-Landscapers - 3
-Track Grounds Crew - 4

Policies

Parking services (Event management). The parking services falls under the event management of Desert Downs. The director of parking services reports to the events director. He or she is responsible for all parking lots, coordination of event parking, staffing and planning of traffic control in conjunction with the local police. The staff parking services consist of flag persons, valets and cashiers. The flag persons are responsible for routing the patrons to and from the parking lot. Also, the flag persons are responsible for reporting any unusual or suspicious behaviors to security. Valets are responsible for parking the cars of the patrons who choose not to park their cars in the general parking lots. The cashiers are responsible for collecting the money for parking.

Security (Event management). Security at Desert Downs will be in-house with extensive training for all security personnel. Security is part of event management. The director of security reports to the events director and operations director. Security personnel are on the premises of Desert Down 24 hours a day. Security personnel are responsible for crowd control and maintaining the safety of the patrons at Desert Downs. In addition, the security personnel are responsible for providing a safe environment in the parking lot, the barn area, and the grandstand. They provide the safe transfer of money throughout the facility and assist the police department when needed.

Box office (Event management). The staff of the box office are under the supervision of the events director. The staff include ticket takers, cashiers and box office personnel. Their responsibilities comprise coordinating ticket distribution, receiving any reservations for advance box seats, and taking tickets for attendance purposes. The ticket takers are also responsible for reporting any disturbances that they may observe or encounter to security personnel.

Vendors (Event management). The vendors are responsible for selling merchandise and programs either at the gift shop or at the racing program stands. They are part of event management with the supervisor reporting to the events director.

Courtesy staff (Event management). The courtesy staff are responsible for providing patrons with an enjoyable environment at Desert Downs. The courtesy staff will assist patrons with questions or supply any information they need while at the racetrack. They assist security in providing a safe environment for patrons. The courtesy staff stationed in the box seats and in the restaurant are available to place bets for the patrons so they can enjoy their meals and the race. The ushers' responsibilities will be to show patrons to their proper seats and assist security in reporting any incidents that may occur. The director of the courtesy staff reports directly to the events director.

Mutual Department (Event management). The mutuals department falls under the jurisdiction of the Arizona Race Commission along with Desert Downs race track. Staffing includes clerks who are responsible for transactions between the wagerer and the race track. The officials in the mutual office record all money exchanges and program the odds into the computers.

Race-Day staff (Event management). The following race-day staff fall under the supervision of the events director: race judges, stewards, public-address announcer, medical staff, veterinarian, blacksmiths, television technicians, and TV announcer.

Maintenance staff (Operations management). The maintenance staff persons are mainly responsible for the upkeep of the facility. Maintenance personnel for the track include the engineers, electricians, plumbers, HVAC, housekeeping, janitors, stable hands, landscapers, and grounds crew. The maintenance staff is under the authority of the operations director.

The engineers are responsible for the maintenance of all mechanical devices such as pumps, generators, computers, and the computer-enhanced tote board. The electricians are responsible for any electrical problems that may occur. The electricians are also responsible for any wiring that is needed in the facility. The plumbers are responsible for the maintenance of waterlines, sewage lines and general plumbing problems. HVAC technicians are responsible for the heating and most importantly, the air conditioning and ventilation of the facility. Housekeeping is responsible for cleaning the dormitory and offices. The janitors are in charge of general maintenance during the races and are responsible for the upkeep of the barns and grandstand areas. Stable hands make sure there are adequate supplies available for the horses such as the hay and feed in all barn areas. The landscapers are responsible for the maintenance of the surrounding grounds. They cut the grass, trim trees, plant shrubs, etc. The grounds crew are responsible for the care of the race track such as dragging and preparing the track in case of inclement weather.

Marketing

Developing a marketing plan for Desert Downs was a unique process. We needed to find out whom to attract, how to get them to attend the facility, and how to satisfy them when they do attend. To begin, we needed to establish our mission statement. We needed to make it short and sweet, so as to let all employees know the direction they need to take to reach the goals. We would also like to make the mission easy for everyone to remember. We wanted to establish the direction we were going and realize exactly what our business should be. Finally our mission statement was developed: "To provide the highest quality entertainment for all patrons in a clean, safe, and friendly environment for all to enjoy time and time again." Our business is to entertain and we want all people to feel good about coming to Desert Downs and want to come back again and again. This mission statement encompasses this and allows for employees to work as a team and know what we are all striving for.

Objectives and Strategies

Developing strategies for any sporting facility is unique in its own right. For Desert Downs, our main products are the horse races. These races cannot be touched or affected by the spectator. Therefore, the overall experience that the spectator has at the facility is what we must focus on. The ways to focus on providing the best entertainment for the patrons are through market penetration, market development, product development, and product diversification.

When using market penetration, we must improve the position of the facility's present services with our present customer base. Because we are a new facility we researched our possible customer base and looked at other facilities to see how we could make ours better. We decided to put television monitors at each table in the indoor box-seat area as well as larger televisions in various locations throughout the facility. These monitors allow patrons to watch the race on the track or races at other tracks throughout the country. Next, in the box-seat area, we will have waiters and waitresses going table to table taking orders and delivering food. This will allow the customer to stay put and not have to get up to get refreshments and risk missing a race. For those who do wish to walk around, we will have concession stands located conveniently throughout the facility. At each table we will also provide crackers and other complimentary snacks for the patrons. Finally, a souvenir and gift shop will be established selling various items from T-shirts to books and photographs.

Market development is trying to seek out new customers. To achieve this we are offering early races on Wednesday mornings called "early-bird specials." We are trying to attract the older generation, or those who are retired. They can come out early to the racetrack and receive discount prices on admission. Also, with our later races, we can attract families, couples, and single men and women. The Phoenix area is also an up-and-coming business area with more people moving in.

Product development simply looks to find new products to entice our current or expected customer base. We decided to add one new and exciting product to our facility. In what is becoming extremely popular around the country, we will provide the opportunity for off-track betting. This allows patrons to watch and wager on races that are occurring all around the country. This will occur at different times of the day because many of the races occur on the East Coast and

Midwest. While races are going on in the evening out east, it will be late afternoon in Phoenix, and races will not begin until evening in Phoenix because of the heat. Therefore, people can come earlier to Desert Downs. Another added feature is our Tour Days. Every Wednesday morning and Thursday evening we will have guided tours of the facility. This includes the track and paddock areas where patrons might get a chance to see their favorite thoroughbred horses or meet the jockeys.

Finally, in product diversification, we are looking to add features to attract new customers. With our game room, which features various arcade games, the children can enjoy themselves while the parents can go elsewhere. Next, we provide a sports bar and restaurant for all patrons. Some of its features include a fully stocked bar, a full menu, and televisions featuring horse races, as well as many other sporting events that happen to be occurring on that day. We feel that these features will bring in a new crowd and hope for repeat attendance.

Situational Analysis

In conducting a situational analysis, we were trying to find market opportunities and constraints and looking at possible environmental factors that would influence our operations. The first environmental factor we researched was the competitive environment. We needed to see what other forms of entertainment were vying for the customers' entertainment dollar. These included theater, movies, Phoenix Suns basketball, Phoenix Cardinals football, area college athletics, and most of all casinos. Because gambling is legal in the state of Arizona, we were worried that the casinos would take away a large portion of our possible customer base. We believe that casino gamblers and racing gamblers are entirely different people. Casino gambling is mostly chance, whereas betting on horse racing takes some thought as one can see which is a good horse and which is not as good.

Next, the economic environment showed us that Phoenix is a growing area with a lot of money coming in. From our demographic report earlier, we could see that there is a good mix of all age groups and many people seemed to have expendable incomes. This also related to the social environment surrounding us.

Finally, the legal and political environments that we encounter deal with views on legalized gambling. We needed to know how the political figures feel about this issue and if they plan on trying to get rid of legalized gambling. Also, how would the public feel about a racetrack coming into the area. All of these environments helped us conclude that there is a quality market to be reached in Phoenix where we can be successful.

Market Research

Market research plays an important part of any facility. We first researched other facilities that were similar to what we were planning. Various questionnaires and surveys were given to patrons to see what improvements they would like to see and what they did like about the facility they were in. Next, we wanted to research the Phoenix area, see what type of market we were looking at, and estimate the number of people who would be coming to our facility. This information played a major role in determining the size of our facility, the type of products we would provide, and the costs. We will continue to conduct market research to identify any changes in the market and then change things according to the market.

The Marketing Plan

There were eight key elements that needed to be considered when developing the marketing plan for Desert Downs. These elements include people, profit, personnel, product, price, promotion, place, and period. For the people element, as explained before, our target market is essentially all people in the Phoenix and nearby areas with an emphasis on retired people and young (25 to 34 year-old) people. Phoenix is one of the fastest growing cities in the nation, both in terms of economics and population. This trend will seem to continue as more people are moving out west to either begin their careers or retire peacefully.

The profit margin that we hope to attain is 40%. With this margin, which is an optimistic yet reachable goal, we can finance more projects and be able to attract the best races in Arizona. With this margin we will also be able to make the necessary improvements, when needed, to our facility and events. Here at Desert Downs, we have very lofty goals and feel that they can all be reached. However, we feel that bringing in an outside firm to implement the marketing plan is necessary. A firm that is experienced in marketing a racetrack and one that is familiar with the Phoenix area is preferred. Also, an outside firm will not have the bias that we have and will be able to determine what we can and cannot accomplish more precisely.

The products we offer are the races themselves, plus all the added benefits of the facility. These benefits include off-track betting, sports bar and restaurant, game room, souvenir shop, various concessions, and overall atmosphere of Desert Downs. Also, we feel that we have one of the best press accommodations in the Phoenix area. The media are an important customer also, and we must always remember to keep good relations with the media. The prices will be fair, yet the customers should know that they will be receiving a superior product.

The expected price of a ticket for admission to Desert Downs will be $3.00. Early-bird special prices on Tuesdays will be $1.50. Also, there will be special price days and promotions throughout the year. Concession prices will be determined by the firm that we hire to do concessions. Restaurant and souvenir shop prices will be comparable to prices in other similar facilities.

We will attempt to get information to our target market in various ways. We would like to get out to the public and offer free passes to companies, schools, and retirement homes. We hope to gain sponsorship from local and national companies in helping to pay for advertising and promotion as well as gain a good public image. Finally, local papers are a great way to get our name out. By advertising in the sports page as well as the entertainment sections, numerous exposures will be generated. It is hoped that we will receive positive media coverage that will not cost us anything, yet be the best form of publicity we could ask for. One promotion we would like to try is our "Two for Tuesdays." Every Tuesday, expecting a slow day, we will allow two people in for the price of one ($3). It is hoped that, this will generate more business.

Desert Downs will be open every day of the year except for Christmas Eve, Christmas Day, and Easter. Races will occur on Monday, Tuesday, Thursday, Friday, Saturday, and Sunday evenings as well as Wednesday, Friday, and Saturday mornings. With heat being a problem, races in the afternoon would be inconceivable. At these times the off-track betting will be run. When racing is not taking place, the facility will be open for the sports bar and restaurant, gift shop, and game room. There will be no charge to enter on these days. We expect to run this marketing plan for one year and evaluate it at that time with consultation from the marketing firm we hire. Any necessary changes will be made at this time.

On the following page is a SWOT analysis that helped us in developing our strategies and objectives for Desert Downs. We feel that it may take a little time to develop a strong customer base, but we are optimistic that our product will become popular. We have a lot to offer to many different groups of people in one of the fastest growing areas in the United States.

SWOT Analysis

1. STRENGTHS
   - Phoenix has a growing population.
   - Much income flows into the area.
   - Desert Downs will be only race track of this kind in the immediate area

2. WEAKNESSES
   - Brand-new product in area may cause a slow start in bringing in business.

3. OPPORTUNITIES
   - Off-track betting may bring in even more business.
   - There is a chance to provide much more than horse-racing at our facility for all market segments to enjoy.

4. THREATS
   - Possible political involvement involving animal rights and gambling on horses could present problems.
   - Casinos may still attract much of our market.
   - An assortment of activities in Phoenix is vying for the entertainment dollar of the public.

Advertising

When looking into advertising, our main goal was to find a way to create messages that can be easily understood and that created a favorable impression to our market. To do this we decided to have our advertising in-house. We will know our target market, and in the beginning, it will be more economical to stay in-house rather than spend a lot of money for an outside advertising agency.

There are two types of advertising, that of facility advertising and event advertising. Three possible types of advertising we looked at were bought advertising, bartered advertising, and earned advertising. There were many different options in buying advertising. However, we looked at buying billboard space at a couple of locations in Phoenix. Also, we looked to buy space on the local busses in the Phoenix area. We researched and found that this type of advertising will allow for a lot of exposures to the broad range of people we are trying to attract.

Next, we searched for the opportunity to barter for advertising. We contacted the local papers and offered them to our VIP night of races we are planning the night before opening day. Also, we asked for our ads to be pictured in the paper in return for the VIP night as well as free passes to all employees of the newspaper for the first month of business. The paper agreed, and our ads will appear every other day until opening day. After opening day, we will reevaluate when our ads should run. The ads will appear in the sports sections, which will attract the sports fan, and the entertainment section, which will attract those who are looking for something to do in Phoenix.

Through this exchange we will hope to attract a reporter or two who will want to do a story on Desert Downs. This earned advertising would be the best type of advertising we could ask for. First of all, it is free: and second, it will, we hope, be a positive story that the public will be more likely to believe than an advertisement made by us. We continue to look at new options for advertising. We feel that bartered advertising is something that needs to be looked into more as it can be very beneficial to us in the long run. Television and radio ads will become more important as we near opening day as well as after. Also, through our market research, we know who our main customers will be. Therefore we need to get the word out on Desert Downs to them. Ways we can do this are through brochures and direct mail. Although this is an expensive proposition, our target market is too important and must be subject to our advertisements. We always want to continue to have good relations with the media because they can make or break us.

Our promotions will play an important role in our facility. As mentioned before, we plan to offer early-bird special prices on Wednesdays. Also, we will offer family discounts (children under 12 are admitted free), as well as discounts for senior passes. One can attain a season pass for $200. So once an individual comes to the track 67 times out of a possible 360 days, the rest of the days they come are free. We will also offer group discounts (groups of more than 15). Finally, we will have promotions, such as giving T-shirts to the first 200 people to enter our facility. We will continue to look for new promotions, such as working with corporate sponsors in supporting a special event at Desert Downs. We will also evaluate our current promotional efforts every 6 months.

Our budget is not large to begin, but we hope our advertising efforts we generate excess income. We decided to plan ahead for three of our biggest events for next year. We consulted with local media and got their thoughts to see if these events could be successful. After many brainstorming sessions, the three events, which are featured on the next few pages, are our Opening Day Celebration, where we hope to get some celebrities to attend; our New Year's Eve Extravaganza; and the Battle of the 3-Year-Olds, which features Arizona's top 3-year-old thoroughbred horses.

INITIAL ADVERTISING PLAN FOR OPENING NIGHT and EVENT PLANS FOR 3 EVENTS AT DESERT DOWNS

EVENT #1

EVENT:	OPENING DAY AT DESERT DOWNS
FACILITY:	Desert Downs Thoroughbred Race Track
TIME:	Friday, May 19, 1995, 5:00 p.m. - midnight
TICKET PRICES:	$3 at the door
DISCOUNTS:	Advanced ticket prices of $1
SALE DATE:	Tickets go on sale beginning April 30, 1995
TOTAL ADVERTISING BUDGET:	$30,000
TARGET MARKET:	Young business people, senior citizens, families, horse lovers

GOALS

PROJECTED GROSS:	$120,000
PROJECTED TICKET SALES:	$12,500

PROPOSED ADVERTISING BUDGET

PRINT:	$4,000
RADIO:	$8,000
TV:	$15,000
OUTDOOR or TRANSIT	$3,000
TOTAL:	$30,000

DATE OF FIRST PRINT AD:	March 17, 1995
TV BEGINS:	April 20, 1995
RADIO BEGINS:	April 20, 1995

PROMOTIONS
1. The first 1,000 people that come to the facility will receive a Desert Downs T-shirt, sponsored by KPHX.
2. All children under 12, accompanied by adult will receive free admission as well as 4 tokens that can be used in the game room.
3. VIP night: all sponsors, media, and political officials will be invited

on May 18, 1996 to attend a special evening that will include a tour as well as charity races.

MEDIA DEALS
- Advertising that will be bought includes television ads, radio ads, print ads, and signage.
- Advertising that will be traded includes certain ads in print with the *Phoenix Daily News.*
- Advertising that will be earned includes press releasesand stories in the *Daily News.* Also, KPHX and KSUN will air feature stories on Desert Downs.

EVENT #2

EVENT:	DESERT DOWNS NEW YEAR'S EVE EXTRAVAGANZA
FACILITY:	Desert Downs Thoroughbred Race Track
TIME:	December 31, 1995, 5:00 p.m. to 2:00 a.m.
TICKET PRICES:	$10 at the door, $15 per couple
DISCOUNTS:	Children under 12 accompanied by adult are admitted free.
SALE DATE:	October 31, 1995
TOTAL ADVERTISING BUDGET:	$40,000
TARGET MARKET:	Couples, young business men and women

GOALS

PROJECTED GROSS SALES	$250,000
PROJECTED TICKET SALES	$30,000

PROPOSED ADVERTISING BUDGET

PRINT:	$5,000
RADIO:	$14,000
TV:	$20,000
OUTDOOR or TRANSIT	$1,000
TOTAL:	$40,000

DATE OF FIRST PRINT AD:	October 15, 1995
TV BEGINS:	October 25, 1995
RADIO BEGINS:	October 25, 1995

PROMOTIONS
1. All those attending will receive a commemorative program highlighting the evening's activities.

SCHEDULE FOR EVENT

5:00 p.m.	Doors open where everyone will receive their program.
6:00 p.m.	Dinner will be served.
7:00 p.m.	A schedule of eight races will begin.
11:30 p.m.	Complimentary glasses of champagne will be served.
11:59 p.m.	Countdown to the New Year occurs as party continues until 2:00 a.m.

EVENT #3

EVENT:	ARIZONA'S BATTLE OF THE 3 YEAR-OLDS
FACILITY:	Desert Downs Thoroughbred Race Track
TIME:	March 12, 1996, 5:00 p.m. - 11:00 p.m.
TICKET PRICES:	$3 at the door
DISCOUNTS:	$1.50 advanced ticket purchase
	$2.00 for seniors (over 65)
	Children under 12, accompanied by adult are admitted for free.
SALE DATE:	January 31, 1996
TOTAL ADVERTISING BUDGET:	$45,000
TARGET MARKET:	Senior citizens, singles, and the serious gamblers in the entire state of Arizona.

GOALS

PROJECTED GROSS:	$200,000
PROJECTED TICKET SALES	$14,000

PROPOSED ADVERTISING BUDGET

PRINT:	$8,000
RADIO:	$14,000
TV:	$20,000
OUTDOOR or TRANSIT:	$3,000
DATE OF FIRST PRINT AD:	January 15, 1996
TV BEGINS:	January 22, 1996
RADIO BEGINS:	January 22, 1996

SCHEDULE FOR EVENT

5:00 p.m.	Doors open and all those attending will receive their choice of a T-shirt commemorating this event or a framed photograph of Desert Downs. Both items were sponsored by KPHX, which also broadcast the main race.
6:00 p.m.	A buffet table will be set up serving sandwiches and

	beverages, courtesy of the Desert Downs staff.
7:00 p.m.	Six preliminary races begin.
9:00 p.m.	Main race begins.
10:00 p.m.	Simulcast races begin and run until 11:00 p.m.

Risk Management

When looking at risk management, we obviously want to reduce the chances for dangerous conditions at Desert Downs, as well as reduce the risk of being sued. There is a four-step process in risk management planning that consists of identification, assessment, treatment, and development of policies and procedures. After completing these stages, we will then make an insurance assessment regarding where we need coverage and how much we will need.

In the identification stage, we identified possible accidents at Desert Downs as being those of slip and falls, security problems, and faulty equipment. It is hoped that we will have a competent staff who will recognize any dangerous conditions and act upon them immediately and correctly. Next, in the assessment stage, as you see in the table provided on the next page, we felt, that slip and falls would be a frequent occurrence, but should be a low loss on average. Any accidents involving faulty equipment, we felt would be very infrequent occurrences, but would involve a high monetary loss. Finally, any problems with security should be an infrequent occurrence due to the fact that our crowds should not be of a concert type. These accidents should be of low loss from past data on facility lawsuits. This then led us to the next stage of treatment.

In the treatment stage, we investigated the types of accidents and decided which ones we would avoid, for ones we would we would retain the risk, and for ones we would transfer the risk to an insurance company. Accidents involving our security staff are those that we will accept the risk for. These occurrences should not happen and we will try to eliminate any chance of their happening by hiring a competent staff. Faulty-equipment and slip-and-fall accidents were the type of accidents that we would transfer to an insurance company. However, we still hope to keep these accidents to a minimum by developing policies and procedures for all employees to follow. We need to keep these types of accidents at a minimum to keep our premiums from rising.

The following is an outline of our policies and procedures in trying to avoid slip and fall accidents:

1. Maintenance, security, and courtesy staff personnel will be required to make continuous rounds looking for any possible dangerous situations.
2. All staff will be required to carry radio communication to contact maintenance or the required personnel needed for the problem.
3. Any spill will be required to be cleaned up within 4 minutes.
4. The time and nature of all spills will be documented, and the public is to be made aware of it.
5. Time of completion is also to be documented.
6. If a fall does occur, the person is not to be moved until the paramedics

arrive, if they are needed.

These policies and procedures should help in trying to make slip-and-fall accidents less frequent. The next section deals with our insurance assessment. Figures were based on similar facility lawsuit data.

Conclusion

As you can see, the planning crew for Desert Downs Racetrack has done a thorough research process into the building and staffing of this facility along with other notables. We feel that this facility, with the right amount of time and equipment, will become one of the best racetracks in the country. We hope to have the project implemented sometime within the next year.

INDEX

A

Advertising 62
    Budget 104
    Definition 99
    Event 100
    Facility 99
    Target 101

Advertising agencies 101-103

Alcohol
    Criteria for control 145
    Legislation 142-143
    Reasons for selling 143-144
    Training programs
        TIPS, TEAM 144-145

Americans With Disabilities Act (ADA)
    Background 221-222
    Effects on sport facilities 225-226
    Guidelines for existing
    structures 222-223
    Guidelines for new construction
223-225
    Seating 29

Architect
    Selection 41-42

Area of Dominant Influence (ADI) 12

Auxiliary Service 111

B

Boiler-plate contract 159

Booking 156,207

Bootlegging 199

Box office
    Dimensions 183-184
    Equipment 185
    Event summary 188

    Personnel 184-185
    Records 188

Box seats 189

Budgets
    Operating 16-17
    Overview 16

Business operations 165
    Bad debts and collections 173-175
    Budgets 166-168
    Budget problem solving 169-170
    Mission statement 165

C

Capacity 27

Centre Management 62

Characteristics of Sport 94

Concessions 32
    Advertising 194-195
    Hawkers and vendors 196
    Maintenance 195-196
    Operational costs 197-198
    Stocking 193
    Trends 196-197
    Types of operations 191-193

Construction manager 45-46

Construction process 46-47
    Evaluation process 48
    Fast track design option 46

Contracts 65, 207

Convenience Foods 194

Crisis media management 118

Crowd management

Components of a plan 138-141

D

Design
    Common errors 26-27
    Elements 43
    Process 44-45
    Team 42

Design build 46

E

Economic Impact 13
    Multiplier effect 14

Elected officials 118
Elevators and escalators 50-51

Event coordination 131-132
    Event coordinator 131, 206-207
    Event settlement 171-172, 212
    Work order 131-132, 208-209

Event planning
    Cancellation 215
    Hold date 205
    Negotiations 206
    Organizational structure 205
    Personnel 210
    Progression 204-205
    Set-up 20-210
    Settlement 212

F

Facility accounting 170

Facility depreciation 170

Facility environment 109-111

Facility management
    Economic success 55-56
    Responsibilities 56

Facility manager

Duties 141-142

Facility operations
    Area 127-128
    Definition 127
    Emergencies 133-135
        Action plan 133
        Manuals 134
        Response procedures 134-135
    Manager 130-131
    Security 132-133

Facility ownership
    Community and state 56
    Private facilities 57-58
    Universities 57

Facility reputation
    The media 116-117
    The public 116

Facility types
    Arena 21
    Auditorium 22
    Convention Center 23
    Exhibition Hall 23
    Stadium 21
    Theater 21

Feasibility studies 12-13

Financing
    General obligation bonds 16
    Joint ventures 16
    Revenue bonds 16
    Seat preference bonds 15-16

Food safety and sanitation 197

Food service 193

Foreseeable risks 144

Foundations 49

Framing 50

G

Governance (operation)
    Not for profit 58
    Owner 58
    Private management 58-60
        Contract terms 62
        Selection process 61
        Service contracts 60
        Trends 62

H

Hippodrome 4

Housekeeping and maintenance
    Establishing guidelines 150
    Staff 150

I

Insurance
    Personal injury liability 85-86
    Product liability 200
    Terms 84-85
    Workers compensation 88

L

Leisure Management International 62

Load out 214

Lump sum contract 45

M

Management teams 127

Marketing 62-63, 207
    Definition 93
    Event marketing plan 121-123
    Marketing mix 96-97
    Marketing plan 119-120
    Market research 96, 207-208

Media facilities 34-36

Media personnel 103
    Primary classifications 107

Media relations
    Media attention 111-112
    Press conferences 112-113
    Unsolicited media attention 113-114

Merchandise
    Sales personnel 199-200
    Splits and deals 199

Mission statement 94
    Facility mission 128
    Objectives and strategies 95
    Situational analysis 95-96

Multipurpose sport facility, planning 227-228

N

Needs assessment 11-12

O

Ogden Allied 62

Olympics 4

Operations
    Evaluation 129
    Procedures 129

P

Parking 27

Payroll 172-173

Physical education facility
    Construction 229-230

Planning
    Brief 23-24
    Checklist 25-26
    Committee 25
    Concerns 24

Initial concerns 23
Process 24-25

Publicity, earned media 108

Public relations 62-63
Definition 107

Publics 108-109

R

Renovation vs. Construction 24

Request for proposal
Private management selection process 61
Service contracts 67-69
Proposal contract 71-72
Proposal instructions 69-70
Work statement 70-71

Revenue sources 175-177
Additional sources 177-179

Risk management 51
Assessment, severity and frequency
Matrix 78-79
Definition of risk 77
Identification stage 77-78
Process 83
Treatment of risks
Avoidance 80
Retention 81
Standard operating procedures 81
Transfer 80-81

S

Sales promotions 104

Scalping 186

Scoreboard 36

Scheduling
Conflicts 161-162
Contracting 158-159
Priority policies 159-161

Reservation process 156-157, 163
Techniques 157-158

Seating
Club level 29-30

Service contracts 60,62,73
Equipment 66
Needs 67-69
Sample contract 73
Selection of contractor 72-73
Services 66
Supplies 66

Signage 32-33

Site selection 17-18

Sources of income 17

Spectacor Management Group 62

Sport and fitness facilities
Consultant 42-43
History
China 3-4
Egypt 3
Greece 4-5
Rome 5

Structural materials 48-49

Swimming pool construction
Filtration system 233
Financing 231-232
Material 233
Planning and design 231
Types 232

SWOT analysis 121

T

Team facilities 34

Theater
Ancient Greece 4
Ticket sales 105,184,208

Refunds and exchanges 185
Sales strategy 187
Variables 186-187

Toilets 30-32

Trade-outs 103

Traffic
External 27-28
Internal 28-29

U

Unions 47

W

Will call 186

Z

Zero-based budgets (ZBB) 166-168